Queer Religion

Volume I
Homosexuality in Modern Religious History

Volume II
LGBT Movements and Queering Religion

QUEER RELIGION

LGBT Movements and Queering Religion
Volume II

Donald L. Boisvert and
Jay Emerson Johnson, Editors

 PRAEGER

AN IMPRINT OF ABC-CLIO, LLC.
Santa Barbara, California • Denver, Colorado • Oxford, England

Library of Congress Cataloging-in-Publication Data

Queer religion : homosexuality in modern religious history / Donald L. Boisvert and Jay Emerson Johnson, editors.
     p. cm.
  Includes bibliographical references and index.
  ISBN 978-0-313-35358-1 (hard back : alk. paper) — ISBN 978-0-313-35359-8 (ebook)
  1. Homosexuality—Religious aspects—History. 2. Gays—Religious life—History. I. Boisvert, Donald L., 1951– II. Johnson, Jay Emerson.
  BL65.H64Q38 2012
  200.86′64—dc23

                            2011043406

ISBN: 978-0-313-35358-1
EISBN: 978-0-313-35359-8

16 15 14 13 12   1 2 3 4 5

This book is also available on the World Wide Web as an eBook.
Visit www.abc-clio.com for details.

Praeger
An Imprint of ABC-CLIO, LLC

ABC-CLIO, LLC
130 Cremona Drive, P.O. Box 1911
Santa Barbara, California 93116-1911

This book is printed on acid-free paper ∞
Manufactured in the United States of America

Contents

VOLUME II
LGBT MOVEMENTS AND QUEERING RELIGION

Introduction to Volume II

Jay Emerson Johnson

When I came out as a gay man in the 1980s, I quickly realized that I was coming out into a rather large cultural and religious space and not just into my own personal reality that I had just made more visible and public. It appeared as if a whole community of gay men waited in the wings to receive me into their fellowship. Even more, I realized that "gay" did not describe adequately the supposed "community" with which I was, in that act of coming out, identifying. There were also lesbians, potentially some bisexuals, and (though this was not at all clear on the horizon then) transgender people. Before long, I was living in a world marked by a ubiquitous acronym: GLBT.

Many now prefer a slightly rearranged version—LGBT—to indicate at least some awareness of the historical dominance of gay men at the expense of lesbian women. To foreground the centrality of gender (and its multifaceted complexities) in most if not all constructions of human sexuality, I often rearrange those letters still further in the classes I teach on queer Christian theology and put transgender sensibilities first—TBLG. Still others wish to expand the ever-widening circle of gender and sexual diversity to include those who are questioning their identities, intersex phenomena,[1] and people committed to full sexual and gender inclusion as allies. This widening circle will sometimes be evoked with GLBTQIA (among a number of other versions).

Recognizing a much broader range of human diversity has been galvanizing for social activism and fruitful for religious scholarship. Even so, since the 1990s the entire enterprise of creating acronyms, and especially the identity mechanisms on which it relies, has come under critical scrutiny. Acronyms are useful for shortening otherwise unwieldy lists of nouns and adjectival qualifiers, and many academic institutions and other organizations employ acronyms for precisely that purpose of simplifying speech. Yet for sexual and gender minorities, the LGBT acronym poses some particularly vexing questions. To be sure, the act of naming ourselves as "lesbian, gay, bisexual, or transgender," and creating a communal identity based on those labels, framed a critical strategy for resisting civic injustice and religious oppression. Other marginalized communities have relied on similar strategies for decades, which came to broader public awareness in the identity politics of the 1980s. Since then, activists and scholars alike have found those strategies a bit troubling. Simply put, how do "we" talk about "us" when "we" are so clearly comprised of many different types of individuals with varying sensibilities, diverse forms of relationships, and distinct modes of navigating cultural space?

The inclusion of bisexual and transgender sensibilities among lesbian and gay people broadened the scope of study and activism but frequently failed to account for the mechanisms of racism perpetuated by predominantly white strategists. This racial divide was only made more severe by taking into account non-Western cultural sensibilities, which tended to call into question the whole paradigm of sexual and gender identity (not to mention highlighting the legacy of Western imperialism). The intolerable choice many felt compelled to make among competing movements of solidarity raised critical questions about the notion of identity itself, which seemed clearly to operate in multiple and even conflicting ways all at the same time. Who exactly are "we"?

The proactive and provocative emergence of "queer" in both academic and activist circles in the 1990s began to address this critical question of "we," not least by destabilizing static identities. Queer theory offers ways of analyzing both civic and religious discourse (mostly within the realms of Western culture) well beyond the questions raised by "homosexuality" while still resisting normalized standards of sexual behaviour and gender performance. As Lee Edelman has aptly described it, queerness carves out a "zone of possibilities" in an otherwise static or closed system.[2]

The zone Edelman evokes raises a host of questions for religious traditions and texts, as well as the adoption of various spiritual practices within cultural spheres. In academic circles, those questions are often referenced to the work of Michel Foucault and Judith Butler. Both of these pioneers questioned the standard modes of Western cultural analysis regarding sexuality and gender, and even what any of us mean by "knowledge." In activist circles, "queer" provoked (and still does) a persistent interrogation of social liberation movements and whether such movements too quickly acquiesce to the postures of propriety and assimilation. For some, queer theorizing prompts a critical retrieval of traditional religious discourse as a culturally destabilizing force. For others, "queer" sparks innovation and radically new forms of cultural engagement and spiritual practice. In any case, the latter third of the twentieth century witnessed the emergence of a profound shift in both attitude and posture, in the goals for social activism as well as the purview of scholarly approaches to religion, and especially lived religion, or how people actually put religious traditions into practice. All of this brought uncharted terrain into view and some intrepid explorers began to map that terrain in the early years of the twenty-first century. These explorations still rely on the path-breaking work that came before, but they lead toward vistas previously unimagined.

This second volume of *Queer Religion* offers some signposts on that queer terrain and in ways that both deepen and reimagine the scope of religious discourse concerning sexuality and gender. This volume begins, appropriately enough, by engaging and assessing the work of Michel Foucault and Judith Butler—two of the quasi-canonized pioneers of queer theory. It then moves backward (but also and thereby forward) into previously unexamined modes of interrogating eroticism through a Christian lens, or perhaps better, inquiring into Christian attitudes through the lens of the erotic.

While still aiming toward uncharted terrain, some insist on retaining critical insights from the past as indispensable markers and sources for the work before us. Lesbian feminism offers a robust example of that posture, and an important reminder that destabilizing identities in theory does not thereby erase the social and religious conditions that made such identity markers necessary in the first place. In a globalized world, however, this fruitful alchemy of past and future-oriented sensibilities mixes in some powerful ways with the critically constructive and creative projects emerging from postcolonial theorists. These are the ones who wish passionately for an engagement with how all of us might reconceive questions of sexuality and gender apart from the dominating lens of Western cultural categories. The variety of projects such passion generates is illustrated here in several respects: how an indisputably Western tradition like Roman Catholicism morphs and flexes in Hong Kong; how the same tradition inflects Filipino cultural spaces; and how categorical classification schemes dissolve in hybrid forms of cultural, religious, and national identity. Engaging in postcolonial discourse is not, one should note, a leisurely activity. All of us, regardless of social location, need to do some heavy lifting in that regard, and the scholarship in this area in recent years illustrates what that kind of lifting will demand of us. Of course, the complexities involved in theorizing those postcolonial spaces are no more demanding than actually living in those spaces.

In the spirit of forward-looking retrieval, this volume also returns to questions of biblical interpretation. While the range of texts that some might consider sacred continues to expand, the Bible still provokes a host of questions and proposes new avenues for exploration. The time has come, however, to set aside anxieties over the handful of biblical texts that purportedly condemn homosexuality. There's so much more that demands attention from these sacred texts. How much, for example, of human sexual practice—let alone fantasy—can co-exist with or even enhance the interpretation of biblical texts, or more broadly, the way in which religion itself is understood? Some respond to that question with insights from leatherfolk, or those engaged in, broadly speaking, sadomasochistic sexual practice. That kind of practice, residing on the edges even of otherwise LGBT-identified communities, also poses serious questions concerning whether such a response qualifies as queer or just more generally scandalous. Leaving that question open in one hand with the Bible in the other proffers a genuinely queer position indeed; it also prompts renewed attention to other sacred institutions besides texts, such as marriage. To that issue this volume turns as well, and in ways that pose enough questions to keep both scholars and activists debating for quite some time.

The twin modes of retrieval and innovation that I would suggest are inherent to queer theorizing further highlight what mid-twentieth-century debates over homosexuality so frequently overlooked: race and gender. Generally, liberal or progressive approaches to social policy and religion have typically treated questions of sexuality, gender, race, and economics as discrete matters of concern, yet all of these intertwine in mutually constitutive ways. Recognizing those deep interconnections poses fresh—if disorienting—questions for religion and spiritual practice. That is certainly the case for transgender sensibilities as well, which encompass an astonishing array of nonconformist strategies, lives, bodies, and realities. These alone deserve a volume unto themselves. Here, we catch a least a glimpse of the personal journey of one person who traveled across that landscape, and the theological implications of doing so.

Sorting through the many markers on this vast terrain continues to pose the very question that urged the development of this two-volume anthology—how is it that "queer" in any way relates to "religion"? This volume concludes by circling back to that original question in two ways: first, by noting the queerly religious aspects of Western popular culture—a source often overlooked in religious and theological work; and second, with a sociological approach to religion and the many unexplored quandaries queer theory might provoke for those engaged in religious studies. No one can predict with any precision where those quandaries might lead in academic circles even as queer spiritual practices and queer appropriations of religious traditions continue to proliferate in some remarkable ways.

Much more than a matter of scholarly contestation, the queerness of religious and spiritual practice can contribute to ongoing movements for social justice and, at times, even save lives. The political and social oppression of sexual and gender nonconformists—often fueled by religious discourse—persists in many parts of the world today, including in North Atlantic societies. As a Christian theologian and an ordained priest in the Episcopal Church, I am particularly distressed by how often Christian rhetoric contributes to the despair and, in some cases, suicidal tendencies of LGBT-identified youth. If these essays can help reshape that harmful rhetoric and open up new spaces to engage life-giving practice for human thriving, that alone would justify the time and energy of the contributors to this anthology. Working toward that end will mean more than just refuting "bad religion"; it will entail adopting a proactive and constructive approach to religion and spiritual practice with the many and often surprising and unpredictable modes and strategies represented in these essays.

I have certainly lived and learned from such unpredictability in my own life. I'm often astonished when I consider the distance I've traveled from coming out as a gay man in an Evangelical Christian college in the American Midwest to living in the San Francisco Bay area and co-editing a two-volume anthology called *Queer Religion*. I take hope from looking back on that distance and on that journey; I trust that others will do likewise with these essays as a guide.

To be sure, "queer" usually disrupts and disturbs before it generates anything like good news. Yet this seems to be the very point that first-century Gospel writers wished to make: Jesus offered good news, not in spite of but precisely because of his scandalous practice, and most often in the way he shared meals with those on the margins of social and religious life. In that spirit, I recommend the diverse perspectives collected here, laid out in this volume like a feast to which all are welcome. I do so recalling that Jesus offered his scandalous hospitality, not for the sake of scandal alone, but for faith, for hope, and especially for love.

Notes

1. "Intersex" is itself a shorthand moniker that refers to a variety of conditions that make it difficult to determine, from standard modes of categorizing, whether a given person is "male" or "female." The website of the Intersex Society of North America is a good place to begin researching these conditions (http://www .isna.org/faq/what_is_intersex; accessed November 2010).
2. Quoted in Annamarie Jagose, *Queer Theory: An Introduction* (Washington Square, NY: New York University Press, 1996), 2.

Chapter 1

Becoming Undone and Becoming Human

Sexual and Religious Selves in the Thought of Michel Foucault and Judith Butler

John Blevins

Any serious study of Western society will reveal a great deal of tension between many of the predominant religions of that society and any form of sexual expression outside of heterosexual marriage. This essay provides some historical background for this tension for Western culture by drawing on the ideas of a French cultural historian named Michel Foucault and of a scholar in gender studies named Judith Butler, who has worked to develop Foucault's ideas since his death. Foucault believed that sexuality is a very powerful form of thought for Western culture because it claims to tell us important things about who we are as human beings. Foucault was critical of the importance given to sexuality because he believed that as soon as ideas about sexuality tell us who we are, then ideas about sexuality will also be used to tell us who we should be or what we should do in order to be the right kinds of people. In short, he argued that as long as sexuality has a power to tell us who we are, it also has a power to establish norms that can be used against some people whose lives do not meet those norms. As he developed his argument, Foucault believed that Christianity played an important role in linking sexuality to normative claims about who we are as human beings.

Exploring the importance of Foucault's ideas for queer theory and queer theology, this essay consists of four sections: first, it lays out Foucault's understanding of Christianity's relationship to the power given to sexuality in Western culture; second, it summarizes Foucault's description of the ways to resist this kind of power, a kind of resistance that Foucault described as a key practice for ethical living; third, it turns to Judith Butler's reflections on

Foucault's ideas to describe the contributions that queer religion can make in efforts to risk relating to other people who are different from us; and fourth, it offers examples of queer folk who use religious practices to strive for the kind of resistance toward which Foucault and Butler call us.

"The Seismograph of Our Subjectivity"[1]: Foucault's Perspectives on Sexuality

> What we have to understand is why it is that sexuality became, in Christian cultures, the seismograph of our subjectivity. It is a fact, a mysterious fact, that in this indefinite spiral of truth and reality in the self, sexuality has been of major importance since the first centuries of our era. It has become more and more important. Why is there such a fundamental connection between sexuality, subjectivity, and truth obligation?[2]

How do human beings know what it means to be human? Scholars from various fields of knowledge in the West—psychologists, theologians, or anthropologists, for example—have tried to answer this question in various ways. Michel Foucault's writing upsets any effort by these scholars to claim that they finally answered this question once and for all. In fact, he demonstrated the limitations of any answer by showing how each of these fields relied upon certain kinds of assumptions that limited the ways in which such a question could even be explored. From Foucault's point of view, these fields of knowledge claimed to tell us "the truth" about who we are when, in fact, they were really trying to claim that their version of "the truth" was better than anyone else's version.

The questions worth asking for Foucault were found not in some search for a universal truth about human beings and human existence but in uncovering the ways in which various cultures answered such questions in radically different ways in different historical periods. Following the development of this project over the course of his writing, one sees Foucault turn his critical gaze to a number of systems of thought: medicine, psychology and psychiatry, the human sciences, criminology, human sexuality, and, finally, pastoral practices in the church. Here I summarize Foucault's critiques of the fields of human sexuality, criminology, and pastoral practices.

The study of sexuality occupied the last part of Foucault's academic life. We will never know the full breadth of Foucault's ideas in this area because he died of AIDS in 1984 in the midst of working on a multivolume series on the history of sexuality in Western culture. We do know, however, that this history of sexuality was quite complex for Foucault because he reconceived of the project on more than one occasion and the three volumes that were published spanned almost a decade of his scholarly career. Foucault published the first volume, the introduction, in 1976. Volumes 2 and 3, a history of Greek and Roman cultural perspectives on sexuality, did not appear for another eight years. Foucault died on June 25, 1984, within weeks of their publication. The fourth volume was to be a history of Christianity and sexuality. However, Foucault did not want any of his unfinished work to be published after his death and so the full contents of the fourth volume are unknown, despite the fact that it was largely complete when he died.

We do not know all of the ideas in the fourth volume, but we do know from his public lectures and shorter essays regarding this project that Foucault was comparing Christian pastoral practices and Greek and Roman practices concerning the process of regulating sexual acts (the subject matter of the second and third volumes). Those pastoral practices, which included confession not only of the sexual acts we did with our bodies but also of the desires contained within our thoughts, were designed to mold sinful Christians into the creatures God intended them to be. At this point, having linked sexuality and Christian confession, Foucault takes his argument in a surprising direction.

Though Foucault did not expressly confess any belief in God, he was not dismissive of religion as many influential thinkers in the secular West have been. On the one hand, Foucault was critical of some forms of pastoral power, particularly as that power led to practices to regulate sexuality. On the other hand, he found an impressive capacity in Christian thought and practice to establish alternatives to that kind of power, as the following discussion shows:

> **Foucault:** I think the church is wonderful. . . . Historically what exists is the church. Faith, what is that? Religion is a political force.

> **[Thierry] Voeltzel:** It is a political force and that is why it has to be fought. In Latin America, in Spain for example, where it is completely at the service of the right. The church is cash, it is power. But it can be an instrument in struggles through the trends of the left which are developing in certain parts of the church.

> **Foucault:** Absolutely, it is a superb instrument of power for itself. Entirely woven through with elements that are imaginary, erotic, effective, corporal, sensual, and so on, it is superb!

> **Voeltzel:** Oh yes, it's superb! I've seen what happens in church schools, this continual hypocrisy, those daily lies, this malice that you find in most people of the church. It is detestable, it is something I hate. . . . When you look at the French [church] . . . well that is pitiable.

> **Foucault:** Intellectually, I believe that it has become extraordinarily weak. When you hear them talk now. Whereas they were all the same, the big

apparatus of knowledge in the West for centuries, particularly from the eigh-teenth century. It is admirable all the same! And I've seen what it is like in Bra-zil when the Jewish journalist [Vladimir Herzog] was killed by the police. . . . And the Jewish community didn't dare hold a funeral service. It was the Arch-bishop of São Paulo, Dom Evariste, who organized the ceremony, and he came forward at the end of the ceremony, in front of the faithful, and he greeted them shouting: "Shalom, shalom." And there was all around the square armed police and there were plain clothes policemen in the church. The police pulled back; there was nothing the police could do against that. I have to say, that had a grandeur of strength, there was a gigantic historical weight there.

Voeltzel: It has got to be said that, religion, is something that interests me at the level of a glance. . . . In any case I don't believe there are many people who take an interest in all that.

Foucault: No, no doubtless not. There is only me left.[3]

Like Voeltzel, many of Foucault's peers had dismissed the church, partic-ularly in its statements on sex. They argued that Christianity's unique and highly problematic influence on human sexuality was to make us believe it was something we had to feel ashamed of, not talk about, and for which we should seek forgiveness. According to these critics, sex is the secret that we cannot discuss. We confine sexuality, never talking about it, and demanding decency in behavior and language. Sex is taboo. These modernists, freed from the fet-ters of prudish Victorian moral codes and oppressive church teachings, have finally begun to throw off the heavy chains of this prudish oppression in order to talk frankly and celebrate our sexual selves.[4]

Foucault disagrees with this argument and wonders why it is that sexual-ity plays such a central role in our self-understanding. From his point of view, we are obsessed by sex and cannot stop talking about it and that has been the case throughout modernity. Rather than a pervasive silence about sex, we are part of a cultural history that chatters about it endlessly, multiplying our language and speech about sex in theories, and testimonies, and marital litur-gies, and the pages of entertainment magazines, and case studies, and senti-mental greeting cards, and television shows, and mass trade paperbacks, and late-night conversations with best friends, and beauty pageants, and locker-room jokes, and R-rated movies, and commercials, and marriage enrichment retreats, and the swimsuit issues of sports magazines, and music videos, and self-help books, and "chick flicks," and advice columns, and doctor's offices, and the pages of magazines such as *Maxim* or *Vogue* or *GQ* or *Cosmopoli-tan* or *Out*, and expert witnesses, and awkward high school prom dates, and water cooler gossip, and comedians' monologues, and print advertising, and gay pride parades, and the little blue pills of prescription medicine, and pre-marital workshops, and counseling rooms, and singles bars, and bridal maga-zines, and reality TV shows, and . . . on and on.

All of this talk about sex is very powerful. And we can see that power when we think about the ways in which this talk claims to tell us important things about the kind of people we are, the kinds of relationships that will make us happy, the kinds of things we need to buy to be attractive, the kinds of bodies we need to feel sexy or make others feel sexy, and the kinds of things we need to do in order to feel good. In short, sex has a capacity for us in the West to tell us important "truths" about who we are as human beings.

According to Foucault, the critics of religion in secular, Western culture are wrong about Christianity's role in the ways we think about and talk about sex. And they are wrong in two ways. First, Christianity did not keep us from talking about sex because we talk about it constantly. Second, Christianity did not place any new restrictions on us about what kinds of sex were or were not acceptable; those restrictions had originated in earlier Greek and Roman (particularly Roman) culture.[5] However, Foucault did argue that Christianity did make an original contribution to Western ideas about sex and he argued that this contribution was very problematic.

What was that contribution? Christianity told us how we might redeem ourselves in relation to our failings in the realm of sexual morality. When Foucault described the kinds of things we would need to do to be redeemed, he used the term "pastoral power." Religious leaders—pastors, priests, and bishops—exercised this pastoral power to regulate the practices necessary for the redemption of the Christian faithful: an endless policing of actions and also an endless searching of desires, thoughts, and wishes. These pastoral practices required that we always be on guard against the dangerous mor-tal sins that sex encouraged through our own watchful worrying, and also through the confessional and its requirement that we recite both sinful sexual actions and sinful sexual thoughts. Foucault argued that this uneasy preoc-cupation with sex is still present in the West not only for Christians but also for everyone. But this fascination is complicated. After all, we're supposed to think about whether we've thought about sex (or done it) so that if we have thought about sex (or done it) we might figure out how we can stop thinking about sex (or having it). Now, that's complicated.

Having demonstrated that pastoral power affects all of us in Western modernity, Foucault further argues that its effects are not limited to our in-dividual thoughts. There are all kinds of specialists and institutions that help keep our thoughts under control. There are therapists who ask us to reveal our deepest secrets in private. There are judges and prosecutors and police officers who make sure we are following the law in relation to sexual matters. There are counselors who tell us how to have happier marriages. There are social scientists who tell us what "normal" sexual practices look like and satisfy our curiosity about what kinds of practices are not quite so "normal." No longer are the pastoral practices that Christianity introduced limited to the confessional booth. They are everywhere. While it is true that many citizens of Western societies are not searching for salvation through the Christian church, in our contemporary culture, we do rely on other sites for a certain kind of salvation—a salvation that assures us that we are normal, well-adjusted, law-abiding citizens—as we bear witness against ourselves in order to help us become the kind of persons who work hard and play by the rules. Christianity may no longer function as the state religion, but for Foucault this does not mean that pastoral power has disappeared. Instead, this Christian exercise of power has permeated the entire culture and its secular institutions. As such, Foucault claims: "Now we must ask what happened in the sixteenth century. The period which is characterized not by the beginning of a dechristianization but by the beginning of a christianization-in-depth."[6]

Where does this deep desire—this obsession—to endlessly examine ourselves and our actions come from? Foucault sees it not only in Christian pastoral practice but also in a whole host of other contexts. He first describes it at length in a book on the history of modern prisons called *Discipline and Punish.* The book is key for understanding Foucault's ideas about a certain kind of disciplinary power that affects us all in Western culture.

Discipline and Punish opens with an extended account of a public execution in 1757, using eyewitness accounts to paint a gruesome picture of the physical pain and violence enacted upon the person convicted of a crime.[7] Foucault starts with this account to demonstrate just how much has changed within the short span of eighty years as he recounts the rules, regulations, and regimens of a prison in Paris in which physical punishment is absent and an extensive program of rehabilitation has been enacted.[8] The conditions that allowed for such a tremendous change in the punishment of the condemned within the space of eighty years were a source of fascination for Foucault. Under the rule of a king, criminals' bodies were the sites of punishment, but under the programs of humanitarian reform ushered in during the nineteenth century, the criminal's soul became the site of rehabilitation. Western thought had moved from physical punishment to moral rehabilitation and this change required new techniques and experts: "As a result of this new restraint, a whole army of technicians took over from the executioner, the immediate anatomist of pain: warders, doctors, chaplains, psychiatrists, psychologists, educationalists; by their very presence near the prisoner, they sing the praises that the law needs:

they reassure it that the body and pain are not the ultimate objects of its punitive action."[9]

This change from exacting a payment from the body of the condemned to encouraging the moral development of the reprobate seems to be a clear example of the progress of Western culture and enlightenment. The humane treatment of incarceration and rehabilitation would undoubtedly be preferable to the gruesome spectacle of torture, mutilation, and execution. Foucault does not disagree with this claim but argues a different point: namely, that this system of moral development affected not only the daily lives of prisoners but also every facet of modern human life in the West, and with unintended consequences.

In *Discipline and Punish*, Foucault shows how programs initially designed to save the soul of the criminal eventually established entire systems and mechanisms that contain all of us. As he builds his case, Foucault eventually turns around the famous quote by Socrates that "the body is the prison of the soul"[10] to claim that the soul becomes the prison of the body.[11] I take that to mean that once the practices intended to rehabilitate the soul of the criminal became practices we all felt constrained to practice, then these efforts to "save our souls" ended up trapping our bodies by creating norms that told us what kinds of things we could do and what kind of persons we had to be. People who did not meet those norms paid a steep price.

But what was the purpose of this kind of power? Why would most of us willingly accept such demands and allow those who do not (or cannot) to pay the price? In order to answer that question, Foucault reformulated the concept of power. For him, power is not a problem when it represses and excludes but when it produces and creates. To be sure, repressive power is bad and must be resisted. But the thing is, we can spot repressive power. No one thinks the tyrant is a hero. Productive power is much more dangerous because we cannot see it very easily: "We must show that punitive measures are not simply 'negative' mechanisms that make it possible to repress, to prevent, to exclude, to eliminate; but that they are linked to a whole series of positive and useful effects which it is their task to support."[12] All sorts of systems and institutions endlessly tell us who we should be and how we should govern ourselves and offer us incentives if we follow the rules laid out before us.

This is the disciplinary power of Western modernity, and this is the power that Christianity introduced into Western culture in its efforts to police sex. Though it tempts us to accept its demands, Foucault asks us to resist, because the price paid by those labeled as "abnormal" or "deviant" or "queer" is too high. For those of us who receive the benefits of this kind of power because we are, in some way or other, in a position in which we have agreed to play by the rules, then Foucault's call to resist is aimed at us. This resistance, he says, is the key to ethics, an ethics that helps us imagine a way out of this kind of power.

A Different Image of Ethics: Care of the Self

This ethical problem of the definition of practices of freedom, it seems to me, is much more important than the rather repetitive affirmation that sexuality or desire must be liberated.[13]

The power that Foucault is asking us to resist is dangerous in three ways already described in this essay:

1) The costs of the benefits given to those who agree to play by the rules demanded by this kind power are paid by those who do not or who cannot play by the rules because they are deemed to be dangerous or abnormal or foreign.
2) Many of us are easily caught up in this web of power because we enjoy the benefits it bestows on us. Because we are caught up in this type of power, we are less able to see its effects, to develop a critique, or to mount a resistance.
3) This power is tied not only to material benefits that we might enjoy by playing by the rules but also to our very sense of ourselves. We are a good son, an upstanding citizen, a faithful Christian if we accept this power. We are a pervert, a deviant, a sinner, a criminal, or a psychotic if we do not.

How is it that this kind of power is able to shape our self-understanding? How is it that sexuality and pastoral power have become so linked to the very core of who we understand ourselves to be? These are the questions that Foucault explored in comparing Christianity (the subject of his unpublished fourth volume on *The History of Sexuality*) to earlier Greek and Roman ethical perspectives on sex (the subject of volumes 2 and 3).

As Foucault studied Christian thought, he came to see that the key difference between Christianity and Greek and Roman beliefs centered on the notion of "the self." In Christianity, the believer undertook a number of specific actions of prayer, contemplation, and confession because those actions gave us a second chance—they allowed us to renounce our fallen, sinful nature in order to be saved. In earlier Greek and Roman culture, the citizen lived under certain moral demands (which Christian culture had largely adopted by the first centuries of the common era) in order to fashion an ethical life. The difference is that the earlier Greek and Roman ethical goal was to *create* or fashion an ethical self, whereas the Christian ethical goal was to *renounce* the self that was already known and real and corrupt, in order to achieve salvation. Classical culture did not have a normative picture of the human being but, rather, strived to understand the ethical tasks one could undertake in order to live a good life, marked by ethical relations to the city, the community, and the family. These tasks led to the creation of the right kind of person, the right kind of Greek or Roman citizen, the right kind of self. Christianity, on the other hand, had a normative picture of the self in place from the beginning: we are all sinners mired in sin and separated from God.

The modern critics of Victorian sexual repression, whom Foucault described in the introduction of his *History of Sexuality*, were eager to move beyond the demands of Christian morality because they had come to see those demands as oppressive. The solution, these critics said, was to encourage "the authentic self" to emerge from beneath the superstition of a religion that these critics saw as irrevocably irrational and oppressive. The problem with such campaigns, however, was that Christianity had not introduced the moral demands that these secular reformers found so troubling, but that it had invented "the authentic self." The reformers misunderstood the source of the problem of Christianity's unique contribution to Western culture. That contribution was not related to moral demands (which had already existed in other cultures) but to the modern experience of the self as a given, certain entity. Modern reformers sought to change the codes by which we understood the moral value or cost of our actions, but the "givenness" of our subjectivity was never questioned. In fact, these reformers believed that they were freeing the modern individual to experience her or his "authentic self" by overthrowing the oppressive codes.

This led to an obsession with uncovering the true self, an obsession marked in our present day by our fascination with psychology and psychotherapy. These efforts were a distraction, according to Foucault, a proverbial rabbit-hole, because they promised an answer to all of our problems while doing nothing to unsettle the real problem—the idea that we could fully understand who we are as human beings. As an alternative, Foucault was interested in exploring the historical ethical ideal of care of the self that had been so central in Greek and Roman culture; this ethical aspiration was different from the modern concept of coming to know one's authentic self:

> **MF:** We have hardly any remnant of the idea in our society that the principal work of art which one must take care of, the main area to which one must apply aesthetic values, is oneself, one's life, one's existence.
>
> **Q:** But isn't the Greek concern with the self just an early version of our self-absorption, which many consider a central problem in our society?
>
> **MF:** You have a certain number of themes—and I don't say that you have to reutilize them in this way—which indicate to you that in a culture to which we owe a certain number of our most important constant moral elements, there was a practice of the self, a conception of the self, very different from our

present culture of the self. In the Californian cult of the self, one is supposed to discover one's true self, to separate it from that which might obscure or alienate it, to decipher its truth thanks to psychological or psychoanalytic science, which is supposed to be able to tell you what your true self is. Therefore, not only do I not identify this ancient culture of the self with what you might call the Californian cult of the self, I think they are diametrically opposed. What happened in between is precisely an overturning of the classical culture of the self. This took place when Christianity substituted the idea of a self that one had to renounce, because clinging to the self was opposed to God's will, for the idea of a self that had to be created as a work of art.[14]

Our contemporary obsession with this idea of the true self reveals itself on the shelves of the "self-help" section at our local bookstores; within the pages of magazines filled with advice columns and articles designed to tell us the truth about human beings through the media of hair-care products, diet regimens, sex therapists, or relationship experts; or in the topics of afternoon talk shows such as Oprah or Dr. Phil in which the studio and viewing audience are encouraged to uncover the secret potential that is locked in their inner being in order to be truly happy. These are the twenty-first-century manifestations of the "Californian cult of the self" that Foucault described in 1984. In direct opposition to this self-obsession, Foucault was interested in a different, present-day, experience of self-formation. Though he refused to lay out a clear, certain model of what this ethical imperative should look like, Foucault, nonetheless, did make clear that he believed that this historical understanding of ethics, one of practicing care for the self, did contain important possibilities for us.

This question was important not only in a historical analysis but in our time because Foucault believed that modern culture had lost its capacity to think about ethics:

What strikes me is that in Greek ethics people were concerned with their moral conduct, their ethics, their relations to themselves and to others much more than with religious problems. . . . Well, I wonder if our problem nowadays is not, in a way, similar to this one, since most of us no longer believe that ethics is founded in religion, nor do we want a legal system to intervene in our moral, personal, private life. Recent liberation movements suffer from the fact that they cannot find any principle on which to base the elaboration of a new ethics. They need an ethics, but they cannot find any other ethics than an ethics founded on so-called scientific knowledge of what the self is, what desire is, what the unconscious is, and so on.[15]

Foucault believed there was value in thinking about the care of the self as this was practiced by the Greeks and Romans not in a desire to return to a golden pre-modern, pre-Christian age but in order for us to imagine another concept of ethical living, of human subjectivity, of a relationship to oneself, and thereby, to others.

For Foucault, this practice of fashioning one's life according to this ethics of care allows for a different relationship to the pervasive power that infuses modern life. In an interview granted only five months before his death, Foucault was asked, "Can this care of the self, which possesses a positive ethical meaning, be understood as a sort of conversion of power?" He replied: "A conversion, yes. In fact it is a way of limiting and controlling power. . . . In the abuse of power, one exceeds the legitimate exercise of one's power and imposes one's fantasies, appetites, and desires on others. . . . It is the power over oneself that thus regulates one's power over others."[16]

In this interview, Foucault not only hints that this way of understanding ethical reflection and ethical living allows one to exercise some freedom over and against modern power (by virtue of the aesthetic task of creating one's life), but also claims that this way of ethical living allows for ethical relationships with others. For Foucault, care of the self is not an exercise in selfish self-absorption but is the kind of practice necessary for us to relate ethically to other people around us:

> **Q**: Doesn't care of the self, when separated from care for others, run the risk of becoming an absolute? And couldn't this "absolutization" of the care of the self become a way of exercising power over others, in the sense of dominating others?

> **MF**: No, because the risk of dominating others and exercising a tyrannical power over them arises precisely only when one has not taken care of the self and has become a slave of one's desires. But if you take proper care of yourself, that is, if you know ontologically what you are, if you know what you are capable of, if you know what it means to be a citizen of a city, to be the master of a household . . . if you know what things you should and should not fear, if you know what you can reasonably hope for and, on the other hand, what things should not matter to you, if you know, finally that you should not be afraid of death—if you know all this, you cannot abuse your power over others. Thus, there is no danger. That idea will appear much later, when love of self becomes suspect and comes to be perceived as one of the roots of various moral offenses.[17]

Care of the self was a key ethical practice of Greek and Roman culture. In his final scholarly work, Foucault was working to re-create this practice for us today. As he described it, Foucault believed that such practice provided us some ways to resist the various forms of disciplinary power that are part of our contemporary lives. That power is very tempting because it provides us with benefits if we become the person that such power asks us to be—normal, upright, acceptable. But it is dangerous because it secures those benefits for those of us who accept them by naming others around us as sick or abnormal or undesirable or sinful. Foucault was clear that this was the wager of modern power: accept its requirements and receive its benefits only if you are willing for others named as deviant to pay the price. He worked in his scholarly, social, and political life to refuse such a wager but Foucault was no starry-eyed optimist. He recognized that he couldn't simply refuse the wager because this power is found everywhere and it is operating all the time. There is no way to refuse this kind of power; we're all implicated. But Foucault did believe that there were ways to resist. And that resistance began by refusing to accept the benefits of disciplinary power: refusing to merely be the person—the self— that such power demands you be.

In sum, the siren song of the secular critics of religion tells us that the task of modern life is to discover the "authentic self" and free it from the restriction placed on it by superstitious religion. Foucault recognized the dangers of this call and worked to develop another possibility both in his thinking and in his life: self-formation. He believed the better task, the ethical one, was to work on one's self, to create it, and fashion it. This involved making choices about how to engage with power, resisting it and working to see the real humanity of those who paid the price in the system: the abnormal, the deviant, the sinner, the homosexual, the psychotic, the Other.

In the decades since his death in 1984, various scholars have worked to develop his half-formed ideas in an effort to understand their implications. I turn now to one of those scholars, Judith Butler, whose work has been enormously influential in the emergence of queer theory. It is brilliant, dense, courageous, and groundbreaking. Throughout much of her writing, Butler uses Foucault's work. Sometimes she uses his ideas to support her own, and at other times, she raises a critique of his ideas and argues for another point of view. Regardless, Foucault's scholarship is a key source for Butler and her own work. One of her more recent books, *Giving an Account of Oneself* (2005), is a sustained reflection on the challenges and the possibilities of Foucault's ethical call.

"Our Willingness to Become Undone in Relation to Others Constitutes Our Chance of Becoming Human":[18] Foucault's Ethics after Foucault

Giving an Account of Oneself develops the idea that an experience of the self that is unsettled and ambiguous is a necessary precursor to an ethical life:

A theory of subject formation that acknowledges the limits of self-knowledge can serve as a conception of ethics and, indeed, responsibility. If the subject is opaque to itself, not fully translucent and knowable to itself, it is not thereby licensed to do what it wants to ignore its obligations to others. The contrary is surely true. The opacity of the subject may be a consequence of its being conceived as a relational being, one whose early and primary relations are not always available to conscious knowledge. . . . Indeed, if it is precisely by virtue of one's relations to others that one is opaque to oneself, and if those relations to others are the venues for one's ethical responsibility, then it may well follow that it is precisely by virtue of one's opacity to itself that it incurs and sustains some of its most ethical bonds.[19]

For Butler, the task of finding a way to maneuver around the limiting norms of secular pastoral power is risky; we put our "self" at risk in questioning the "truthfulness" of that power since the socially approved self—the upstanding citizen, the all-American hometown hero, the attentive wife, the successful business person, the beloved pastor—is the payoff for agreeing to abide by that so-called truth. If we refuse to follow the rules of this kind of power, we will pay a price. Like Foucault, Butler urges us to pay this price, recognizing that countless others—those labeled as suspect, queer, sinful, and deviant—have paid it in the past when we were reaping the benefits. The decision as to whether to pay it (or not) becomes an ethical question—an ethical risk—in the encounter with some other who is different. Will we allow that encounter, that other, to unsettle us and our sense that this is "the way things are"? Will we risk being changed and becoming undone? Will we accept that risk recognizing that we might very well lose social power? Butler does not sugarcoat the risk involved in such a decision:

If I question the regime of truth, I question, too, the regime through which being, and my own ontological status, is allocated. . . . It turns out that self-questioning of this sort involves putting oneself at risk, imperiling the very possibility of being recognized by others, since to question the norms of recognition that govern what I might be, to ask what they leave out, what they might be compelled to accommodate is, in relation to the present regime, to risk unrecognizability as a subject or at least to become an occasion for posing the questions of who one is (or can be) and whether or not one is recognizable.[20]

There are, to be sure, costs involved that are not merely personal. We will risk not only giving up our self-understanding but also risk giving up the kind of person other people assume us to be. We will be unrecognizable. Not physically—we will still look the same—but socially. People whom we know, people agreeing to be the kind of person we had earlier agreed to be, will not understand. "I don't know who you are anymore. Who are you?" Indeed, that is the crux of what is at stake. If we start trying to see and relate to others who are not like us on their terms and not on ours, our world might change.[21] We might change. And the people around us, the people who have known us, may not like it.

So why risk it? Why risk becoming unknowable, not only to myself but to others? Why risk giving up power, particularly if I have enjoyed the benefits of that power? There are numerous reasons, actually. The first answer may also be the most difficult: because we do not participate in just social systems if we continue to allow others to bear the cost of the things we enjoy, and we should strive, as much as possible, for just social systems. But there are reasons beyond this one as well. As Butler closes her book, she moves from analysis of twentieth-century philosophers and social theorists into an almost meditative framework and writes that our willingness to risk may be the source of forgiveness and of both loss and revelation:

> Perhaps most importantly, we must recognize that ethics requires us to risk ourselves precisely at moments of unknowingness, when what forms us diverges from what lies before us, when our willingness to become undone in relation to others constitutes our chance of becoming human. To be undone by another is a primary necessity, an anguish, to be sure, but also a chance—to be addressed, claimed, bound to what is not me, but also to be moved, to be prompted to act, to address myself elsewhere, and so to vacate the self-sufficient "I" as a kind of possession. If we speak and try to give an account from this place, we will not be irresponsible, or, if we are, we will surely be forgiven.[22]

Writing at this point in time in Western culture—in the opening decades of the twenty-first century—all those considered queer because of sexuality or gender have a particularly personal understanding both of the cost and of the revelatory possibilities of refusing the demands of modern power. We have this understanding because we have had to negotiate and maneuver around this power and the identities it continually attempts to pin on us from within the context of our sexuality, a context that is contested and charged as Foucault showed us. Up to this point, this essay has been very theoretical, trying to lay out complicated philosophical arguments in just a few pages. But both Foucault and Butler have taken their ideas outside the theoretical in their own lives and have used those ideas to speak and think and act in social and political contexts. In other words, they have tried to ground the theoretical in practice. This essay closes, then, with a similar impulse: to take the ideas presented thus far and to describe briefly their implications for Christian thought and practice by offering an example of Christian practice that does not reinforce pastoral power but instead resists.

"It Wasn't Like the Way They Said It Would Happen": Queer Testimonies of God at Work

Hey, John. It's Mick. I just wanted to, um—today was the day we met— and I wanted to um, state a little more concise something I was trying to say. Um, all these years, I've watched these Christians around me and these people who say they're people of God and I've never really felt, I didn't recognize—I didn't see it—I felt like they really weren't. And so, I began on my own to feel something that felt like God but it wasn't like the way they said it would happen. But I didn't find him where they said or how they said. Anyway, I'm beginning to find him on my own and it's just different from what I thought or what they led me to believe. Anyway, I'll talk to you later. Bye.

When I was a student working on a doctor of theology degree in pastoral counseling, I met weekly with a gay man named Mick.[23] Mick left the message above on my office voicemail one day, letting me know that he was indeed finding God at work in his life but not in the places he had been told by others where God would be. Mick's testimony—and countless others such as his—is testimony of a queer Christian who is surprised where he finds God. This experience gets to the heart of the ways in which Michel Foucault and Judith Butler have tried to speak about ethics: efforts to resist dominant systems that claim to tell us the truth in order to free ourselves enough to hear something new and different. From religious perspectives, these experiences are testimonies, they bear witness to how God is at work to help us resist the kind of pastoral power that Foucault described.

E. Patrick Johnson is a professor at Northwestern University in Evanston, Illinois. He also identifies as an African American queer man. His scholarship bridges both of those worlds in revelatory ways. In his essay "Feeling the Spirit in the Dark: Expanding Notions of the Sacred in the African American Gay Community," Johnson describes the Spirit breaking into what might be assumed to be an unlikely site: a gay dance club during Black Gay Pride in Atlanta:

Around 5 AM the mood of the club shifts, and there is a feeling of anticipation in the air. The music shifts to—No, it couldn't be!—what sounds like the "shout" music in my church back home. . . . [I]ntermittently dispersed throughout the music are sound bites from gospel singer Shirley Caesar's song "Hold My Mule"; "It's just like fire!"; "Somebody say yes (yes), say yes (yes), yes

(yes)"; "If you don't stop dancing!"; "You come to tell me I dance too much!";
"I'm gonna shout right here!"

While this musical interlude continues, the DJ begins to testify:" Thank
Him! For how He kept you safe over the dangerous highways and byways.
Thank Him, because you closed in your right mind!"

Somebody say yes (yes), say yes (yes), yes (yes)."

"Look around you. Somebody that was here last year ain't here tonight!
Look around you! Somebody that was dancing right next to you ain't here tonight! Look around you! Somebody's lover has passed on! Look around you!
Somebody's brother, somebody's sister, somebody's cousin, somebody's uncle
done gone to the Maker. Sister Mary has passed on tonight! Brother Joe has
gone to his resting place! But Grace woke you up this morning! Grace started
you on your way! Grace put food on your table! How many of you know what
I'm talking about?!"

"It's just like fire! It's just like fire! It's just like fire! Shut up in my bones."

"If He's been good to you, let me see you wave your hands."

"Somebody say yes (yes), say yes (yes), yes (yes)."

Kevin and I, along with others, dance to the beat of the music, waving our
hands, crying, kissing, and shouting "Yes!" A drag queen appears from nowhere and begins to walk around the side of the dance floor beating a tambou-
rine to the beat of the rhythm. The house music swells as the DJ sermonizes in
the manner of an African American folk preacher, embodying the chant-like
cadence and rhythm of the preacher's voice.[24]

In "Hold My Mule," the song that played in the background of the call-
and-response dialogue between the DJ and the people gathered on the dance
floor that morning, Shirley Caesar describes the story of Shoutin' John. The
deacons of his church come to visit Shoutin' John and they find the eighty-
six-year-old man working his land with his mule. The deacons are disturbed
because John had been dancing and shouting in church so they have come to
chastise him. But he will have none of it: "Look at me. I'm 86 years old. I'm
still able to walk down behind that old mule. I'm still able to harvest my own
crop. But you don't want me to dance in your church, hold my mule, I'm gonna
shout right here! Say Yes! Say Yes! Say Yes! Oh Lord! Hold my mule. Hold my
mule. Hold my mule."[25] And so, as four dour deacons stand in the middle of
a field holding the reins of an old mule, Shoutin' John dances and shouts and
testifies about God at work in his life. He refuses to play by their rules.

This rag-tag congregation of DJ, gay men, drag queens, and their friends
also refuse to play by the rules. And in that refusal, the Spirit breaks into
out-of-bounds lives: in a field with dour deacons, a mule, and a dancing
farmer—and in a gay nightclub with hundreds of black gay men, drag queens,
and a sermonizing DJ dancing fiercely in tears, ecstasy, and joy. Queer people

regardless of race have experienced church leaders wanting to stop their shouting and dancing. E. Patrick Johnson reminds us how important it is to refuse to stop.

I used to teach in a seminary, an odd place for an openly queer man to be. One day in conversation with an openly gay, African American seminarian, I mentioned Johnson's essay and asked the student if he had read it. He had. He replied that it helped him see how God was present in all kinds of contexts, but it also made him sad that this kind of experience of God had to happen in a dance club and not in a church. Sad, yes, but also true. Out-of-bounds lives, queer lives, have often found that they encounter God more often outside of the church's walls than inside of them.

The church has been unfaithful to its own call, refusing to take seriously the ethical demands that Foucault first described and Butler laid out in greater detail. It has refused to allow queer Others to speak out of their own experience. In that refusal, the church cannot hear our queer testimonies of the surprising revelation of God's creative work in the process of our self-formation. In the end, it is sad that queer folk may find God outside the church and not within it. The sadder reality, however, is that the church itself misses out on God by refusing to risk what it (thinks it) knows in order to build relationships with queer folks. In the end, queer folk who keep dancing and shouting and refuse to stay in the church in silence choose to listen to God before listening to the church. This choice, an ethical choice, involves the risk of stepping outside of disciplinary pastoral power practiced by the church and to trust in something else. It's a gamble, which is simply another way of saying that it is a leap of faith.

Notes

1. Michel Foucault, "Sexuality and Solitude," in *Essential Works of Foucault 1954–1984*, vol. 1, *Ethics: Subjectivity and Truth*, ed. Paul Rabinow (New York: New Press, 1997), 179.
2. Ibid.
3. Michel Foucault, "On Religion," in *Religion and Culture: Michel Foucault*, ed. Jeremy Carette (New York: Routledge, 1999), 106–9. Originally published as "La religion," a section from Thierry Voetzel's *Ving ans et aprés* (Paris: Grasset, 1978). This book is a collection of transcripts from a number of taped conversations between Foucault and Voeltzel. Foucault's appreciation for religion's complex function was not limited to Christianity. He was impressed at the power of Islam to overthrow an entire government in the student revolution in Iran in 1978. See Michel Foucault, "Is It Useless to Revolt?" in *Religion and Culture*, 131–34.

4. For a fuller description of the authors of the theory of sexual repression, see Michel Foucault, *The History of Sexuality, Volume I: An Introduction* (New York: Vintage, 1990), chap. 1.

5. Foucault's full argument that Christianity did not present any new moral codes in relation to sex can be found in a paper he initially gave at the University of Tokyo in 1978. See Michel Foucault, "Sexuality and Power," in *Religion and Culture*, 115–30. In addition, see Michel Foucault, *The History of Sexuality, Volume II: The Use of Pleasure* (New York: Vintage, 1990), for Foucault's survey of Greek ethical perspectives and practices on sexuality; see Michel Foucault, *The History of Sexuality, Volume III: Care of the Self* (New York: Vintage, 1988), for Foucault's perspective on Roman culture.

6. James Bernauer, S.J., *Michel Foucault's Force of Flight: Toward an Ethics of Thought* (Amherst, NY: Prometheus Books, 1990), 161. Here, Bernauer is quoting Foucault.

7. Michel Foucault, *Discipline and Punish: The Birth of the Prison*, trans. Alan Sheridan (New York: Vintage, 1995), 3–6. The book was originally published in France in 1975 under the title *Surveiller et Punir: Naissance de la Prison*. The book was first published in the United States in 1978.

8. Ibid., 6–7.

9. Ibid., 11.

10. The saying, attributed to Socrates, can be found in Plato's *Phaedo*. See Plato, *Phaedo*, trans. David Gallop (New York: Oxford University Press, 2009 edition), 35.

11. Foucault, *Discipline and Punish*, 30.

12. Ibid., 24.

13. "The Ethics of the Concern for Self as a Practice of Freedom," in *Essential Works of Foucault 1954–1984*, vol. 1, 283. This text is the transcript of an interview conducted by H. Becker, R. Fornet-Betancourt, and A. Gomez-Müller on January 20, 1984.

14. "On the Genealogy of Ethics," in *Essential Works of Foucault 1954–1984*, vol. 1, 271. This text is the transcript of an interview between Foucault, Paul Rabinow, and Hubert Dreyfus.

15. Ibid., 255–56.

16. Foucault, "Ethics," 288.

17. Ibid.

18. Judith Butler, *Giving an Account of Oneself* (New York: Fordham University Press, 2005), 136.

19. Ibid., 19–20.

20. Ibid., 23.

21. According to the French philosopher Jacques Derrida, the attempt to try to meet an "other" on their terms and not ours is the necessary precursor for hospitality. Derrida writes, "I'm not sure there is pure hospitality. But if we want to understand what hospitality means, we have to think of unconditional hospitality, that is, openness to whomever, to any newcomer. And of course, if I want to know in

advance who is the good one, who is the bad one—in advance!—if I want to have an available criterion to distinguish between the good immigrant and the bad immigrant, then I would have no relation to the other [as wholly other]. So to welcome the other as such, you have to suspend the use of criteria" (from Richard Kearney, "Desire of God," in *God, the Gift, and Postmodernism*, ed. John Caputo and Michael J. Scanlon [Bloomington: Indiana University Press, 1999], 133). For a discussion of the implications of Derrida's concept of hospitality for Christian theology and practice, see John Caputo, *What Would Jesus Deconstruct?* (Grand Rapids, MI: Baker Academic, 2007). See also John Blevins, "Hospitality Is a Queer Thing," *Journal of Pastoral Theology* 19:2 (2009): 104–18.

22. Butler, *Giving an Account*, 136.

23. Mick is not the actual name of the man I worked with.

24. E. Patrick Johnson, "Feeling the Spirit in the Dark: Expanding Notions of the Sacred in the African American Gay Community," in *The Greatest Taboo: Homosexuality in Black Communities*, ed. Delroy Constantine-Simms (Los Angeles: Alyson, 2001), 99–100.

25. Ibid., 103–4.

Chapter 2

Erotic Conversion

Coming Out of Christian Erotophobia

Paul J. Gorrell

The history of Christianity includes a pervasive bias against sexual pleasure and a subordination of the body to the soul. This is evidenced through official documents and praxis of the Catholic Church, prescriptive teaching of Protestant denominations, and the work of theologians who write on the topics of sexuality and marriage. This negative view of sexuality creates individual experiences of shame in the lives of Christian believers and societal efforts to oppress the body and sublimate pleasure. Christian believers would benefit from Erotic Conversion, a practical, therapeutic, and ethical response to the Christian brand of erotophobia. Similar to the experience of individuals who courageously embrace their same-sex desires in a homophobic society, Erotic Conversion is a coming out process that empowers Christian believers to be faithful and proudly erotic at the same time.

Erotophobia as an Instrument of Oppression

Erotophobia is understood as the fear of sexual desire, erotic pleasure, and the positive energies of the human body. It endorses the control and abdication of the wonder of sexual feelings, of the pleasure of erotic experiences, and of the beauty of sexual differences. Within Christian tradition, Eros is perceived as a power to be controlled, and bodily pleasure has the potential to lead the believer down the path toward damnation.[1] This consistent conclusion about sexuality led the churches to construct multiple systems of polity, forms of praxis, and theo-ethical approaches to sexuality that unabashedly linked sex to sin, focused on saving disciples from an innate tendency to sin through sexual acts, and approximated people's identities in light of their sexual activity or lack thereof. This view contributes to the belief that women need to be controlled and gays and lesbians threaten society and its children.

In the tradition, we can find both a hysterical concern that Eros leads to death and a denial that sexual pleasure is an essential aspect of human experience. It is often evidenced that believers who fail to control their sexual desires threaten their physical life and damage the chance for an eternal life in heaven, the ultimate destiny of the Christian believer.[2] To the other extreme, Christian views of sexuality downplay the place and power of Eros in the maturing life of the Christian disciple.[3] Sex is not even essential to the happiness and unity of a married couple.[4] Instead, it's identified as an appetite that should be properly controlled.[5]

Both of these erotophobic views are largely based on the dualism in the Christian tradition that downplays the body and highlights the soul (or mind) and results in the reification of the body: it becomes a machine, a cage for the soul, a thing. In downplaying the importance of Eros in the life of a person or threatening death, the tradition alienates the person from sexual desire while also alienating him or her from the body. In this dynamic, Eros has no place to empower the individual or partnered couple, is impotent in driving self-confidence, and threatens happiness and survival.

These views do not contribute to positive and healthy integration of sexuality in the life of the person. In fact, erotophobia has often been an instrument of oppression within the Christian tradition. Feminist scholars have demonstrated how women have been particularly affected by the repression of sexuality. As the Roman Catholic Church has exclusively placed sex within the context of marriage and procreation, women have been taught that their bodies are to be used as vessels that fulfill the proper end of sexual intercourse. This understanding of sexuality flows from a patriarchal dualism and contributes to the subordination of women in their married relationships.[6] Sexual parameters are strictly defined for women and a view of their bodies as procreative is core to that definition. The results of this situation include a repression of erotic pleasure in the lives of women.[7]

Sexual behavior that is tied to status inequalities ends up controlling the ways in which gender is defined.[8] In essence, women become identified with the body and sex, and with the fear of both those realities. Just as erotophobia is based on a dualistic view of the human person, misogyny follows a dualistic path where goodness is associate with male and evil is associated with female. Women, like Eros, represent the reality that leads to evil and, thus, must be controlled so that they do not threaten the life and power of the male. Like the body is to be possessed by the soul; women are to be possessed by men.

In light of the socially constructed notions of gender within patriarchal definitions of sex, women have often been understood as a temptation to men: women lead men to eternal damnation through sin by simply being desirous. The anger that is displayed in violence to women is often caught up in sexual stereotypes and the threat that women may present to men who struggle with the guilt of their sexual attractions.[9] This violence serves as a form of capital punishment: women deserve to die since they lead men to eternal damnation.[10] Ironically, due to the patriarchal definitions of the female body, women represent the desire that leads to death, while at the same time, they are essentially linked to the only allowable sexual practice, procreative sex, which includes the creation of new life.

The focus on procreative sex as the norm for all sexual behavior has been a way to control sexuality, define the role of women in society, and marginalize the sexually different. Procreationism is "the assumption that sex is naturally oriented toward creation of human life."[11] An enduring teaching throughout the Christian churches, procreationism is a structural and insidious system of repression based on the erotophobic discourse of patriarchy that acts as an obstacle toward healthy affirmation of human sexuality. The implications of the view include the following: the only real sex between persons is penile-vaginal intercourse, same-sex relations are necessarily "less than the norm" and to be opposed, sex is proper within a heterosexual marriage alone, and contraception should be banned since it encourages irresponsible parenthood.

The shame experienced by believers has the potential to do serious damage. People who experience shame are predisposed to various kinds of psychological maladjustments such as depression, low self-esteem, lack of empathy, hostility, unconstructive anger, and anxiety. While guilt can also lead to some affective disorders, such as paranoia and obsessive compulsive behavior, shame is more widely connected to psychological maladjustment.[12] Studies have shown that sex-negative training in early development increases levels of shame and damages healthy acceptance of sexuality later in life.[13]

By using sexual shame as a tactic, the churches forcefully control desire and indoctrinate the praxis of erotophobia. Within Catholicism, the practice of the Middle Ages was to encourage public confession and harsh penance for sexual sin including the wearing of sack cloth and ashes.[14] Here, sexual shame for the believer is tied up with a loss of identity as a disciple of Christ who is on the path to heaven. This proposes that the Christian identity is by its nature in opposition to non-procreative sexual behavior: the person cannot be Christian and erotic at the same time. By working at the level of identity, the tradition places significant emphasis on suppressing and dominating erotic feelings and insights in ways that can cause ongoing harm to the individual.

The Development of a Sex-Affirming Christian Ethics

With the backdrop of sex-negative history within the Christian tradition, there have been efforts over the past four decades in building a sex-positive theo-ethics that confronts Christian dualism. Many of these approaches are dependent upon liberation theologies that were birthed within the Latin American context and embraced by many groups that experience oppression within a society based on white male supremacy (i.e., African Americans, Latina women, LGBTQ).[15] Operating with a preferential option for the poor, liberation theology includes the experience of the poor as a core source for theological reflection. This is different from traditional European theologies that simply include Scripture, doctrine, and trained theologians as sources for insight and wisdom.

Sexual liberation theology also attempts to break free from the male bias of traditional Catholic and Protestant sexual ethics. We should remember that only ordained celibate men have written the official teaching of the Catholic Church and very few female voices were considered authoritative on the topic of sexuality over the course of Christian tradition.

To liberate the sexual dimension of people from the chains of the Christian teaching, sex-affirming theology takes the vantage point of those who embrace sexuality more fully, those who have suffered because of the religious limitations of sexuality, and those who are different from the mainstream when it comes to sexual preference (gays, lesbians, bisexuals, transsexuals, etc.). Sexual theologies also privilege the voices of women who, beyond religious oppression related to sexuality, experience gender oppression within society and the churches.[16]

Working within the tradition of liberation theology, Marcella Althaus-Reid notes that sex itself is oppressed within the Christian tradition, and consequently, she incorporates sex into the stories of faith, symbols of sacramental life, and the traditions of the church.[17] Believing that sexuality is too often linked to social codes of conduct and silenced within the stories of faith, Althaus-Reid places sex at the heart of the Christian story. By claiming that theology is always sexual, she critiques the dialectics of indecency and decency by bringing to surface the sexual message of the Christian faith and its major symbols.[18] At the same time, she takes the vantage point of the poor and marginalized on sexuality, critiquing the sexually neutral presentation of the poor. This is a direct challenge to the exclusion of the poor's desires when doing theology. The body, pleasure, and sexual desire are not left to the bedroom or to a discussion of ethics. They are considered in light of what it means to be poor and within the challenges to patriarchal norms.

Sex-affirming theologies offered a "preferential option for the body," arguing that the body has been oppressed within the dualistic system of the Christian tradition. Thus, they have emphasized embodiment, wholeness, and sexual pleasure as good. James Nelson has been a key voice in the promotion of a more effective understanding of the importance of fighting dualism and promoting the body as fundamentally one with the soul.[19] His prolific development of a sexual theology attempts to liberate the sexual dimension of people from the oppression it has received in society, religion, ethics, and the like and aims at constructing a healthy understanding of the whole person as a moral agent. For Nelson, sexuality is a way of being in the world: the celebration and acceptance of the wholeness of the person, in which all the aspects of ourselves are seen as integral, assists in shaping a spirit of sharing, caring, nurturing, sensitivity, responsiveness, and mutuality.

Ultimately, sex-affirming theologians and ethicists are arguing for the end of a hierarchy between agapic and erotic loves and the understanding of sexuality as a gift of God's grace. Sexuality should be seen as an aspect of God's saving grace where the love of God and the experience of lovemaking are fundamentally connected.

Sexuality is not only a source of pleasure; it is a source of relational mystery and yearning between, among, and within us. As sacred power, Eros moves from and toward a deep, shared sense of unknownness that we will never move beyond or comprehend completely. We cannot fully "know who we are" sexually because we cannot know fully the power of God. This is why terms such as "sexual orientation," "sexual preference," and even "sexuality" are vapid proximations of the real thing—the experience of touching one physically, emotionally, and spiritually in such a way that we come together.[20]

Sex-affirming theologies have had a vastly positive influence on the LGBTQ community and its own growing body of theological work. Gays and lesbians are hearing more inclusive messages regarding how they can appropriate theological concepts in light of same-sex experience. The emergence of gay and lesbian theologies provides valuable assistance in accepting homosexual orientation since they confront the negative attacks of Christianity against gay people while building an affirming theology that utilizes gay experience as a source for understanding. These theologies have provided critiques regarding the way traditional theologies and ethics have contributed to the oppression of gay people while providing fodder for the rehearsal of an erotic theology that attempts to liberate the problem of sexual oppression in traditional Christian ethics.

Elizabeth Stuart has effectively organized the history of the LGBTQ movement, classifying its major thinkers within four categories: (1) Gay Theology, which promotes the goodness of being gay as a response to the perspective of traditional Christian ethics; (2) Gay Exodus Theology, a gay form of liberation theology, which builds on the experience of gay and lesbian people as it incorporates and addresses Christian theological themes; (3) Erotic Theology, almost exclusively crafted by lesbians, which identifies the divine with Eros; and (4) Queer Theology, which attempts to create a transgressive Christian voice in order to retrieve in transformative ways traditional theology and thereby challenge Christianity's overall stance against Eros.[21]

The voices of sex-affirming theologians create the possibilities for transformation within the lives of those who experience erotophobia and its effects. These thinkers lay the groundwork for an experience of Erotic Conversion.

The Path to Erotic Conversion

For an individual to turn away from the bias of erotophobia to an embrace of himself or herself as an embodied subject is a radical challenge that requires entering into a process involving examination, insight, reasoning, and sound judgment. For this, I borrow an epistemology from Catholic theologian Bernard Lonergan, who redefines the term "conversion" as a transformational process that enables the person to grow toward authenticity and integration while shifting his or her horizons.[22] The human person can approach the world differently by experiencing intellectual and moral conversions that fundamentally challenge current perspectives. Converted, the individual can confront the biases that occur within culture and society that negatively shape his or her worldview and understand the self, culture, and world via a new dynamic relationship.

With Erotic Conversion, we are discussing a transformational process in the life of a person's sexual history where there is a horizon adjustment toward the erotic energy of the person and away from erotophobia. The person is led to embrace the erotic through insights and shifts in understanding. In alignment with sex-positive theologies, Erotic Conversion leads to a rejection of the hierarchical approach to the human person found in the dualistic system and drives toward the importance of embodiment within the experience of striving for authenticity and integration.

Erotic Conversion requires the person to wrestle with the ways in which erotophobia has affected his or her personal understanding about sexuality and the individual judgments he or she makes on an ongoing basis about relationships with others and sexuality itself.

Shifting from the fear and control of sex and sexuality found in the Christian tradition toward a sexually positive and, even, erotic theology is a challenge that requires not simply one insight alone or a singular change in belief. It ne-cessitates a larger conversion process that involves sexual integration.[23] This kind of change is not easy. It is profound. It is uprooting the negative past into a new present that makes the future beyond what the person could have ever expected. Challenging this reality involves a radical shift from an ideology trapped by denial, guilt, and shame toward one of sexual celebration, indi-vidual pride, and embodiment. Despite its label as a vice within Christianity, I use pride to note the positive aspect of self-love that promotes caring for the self in multiple ways, including one's physical, emotional, and sexual needs.[24]

Lonergan rested his epistemology on the notion of insight that encourages a path toward deeper levels of understanding. Lonergan understands insight as an "aha" moment that occurs through reflection on a collection of data. The insights necessary for Erotic Conversion involve the person collecting data about Eros and embodiment in his or her life.[25] The path of this conversion necessitates activities that involve embracing the body-self; these moments would be found within and through lived experience. The person might live through and interpret the good and even wholesome qualities of the erotic and/or experiences of the body that affect him or her negatively and teach him or her about the body's impact on the self (i.e., the strong and enjoyable physi-cal feelings that lead to greater fulfillment and unity, the joy of Eros and the liminal qualities of pleasure, the stimulation of bodily exercise, the benefits of healthy eating, the negatives of suppressing healthy behavior and feelings, the challenges of a body that is ill, and all those practices that help us to honor and enjoy the body as gift). All of these data may lead the person to say: "I am my body, the body is fundamentally good, the body should not be subordinated to the soul, treating the body as sinful is inappropriate and unhealthy." Having arrived at these notions and shifted erotic horizons, the person can further develop his or her understanding of what it means to be a sexual, erotic, and embodied person and begin to strip away the many biases that confront this kind of position.

Erotic Conversion is a process of self-discovery and the optimization of one's erotic energy. What one discovers is something new about the self that is actually a treasure that was always there. This kind of adjustment of horizon can free up sexual desire to be understood as responsible behavior that focuses on pleasure in a manner to include loving and wanting beyond one's self.[26] No longer does desire, in its physical and sexual definitions, need to be associated with being dirty, guilty, and shameful.

To adjust these kinds of notions requires commitment to a process that includes profound human experiences. Therefore, it is an activity-based con-version that depends upon the experiences of the body and its erotic energies.

Initially, Erotic Conversion may be caused by a climactic event of the body-self that moves the person to rethink erotic fears and the sexual ethics of his or her youth. Erotic insights will likely include sexual experience, although they are not limited to this type of awakening alone.

Sexual activity and other activities that lead us on the process of conversion are those that are informed by the person's embodiment. Positively, the intensity of embodied sexual activity can potentially help the person break through erotophobia. At the same time, erotically converted individuals may never live a life that is fully devoid of this fear. As stated previously, since erotophobia is so deep in the psyche, individuals may find it a life journey to confront the fear and guilt associated with it.[27] Fighting the bias that exists by allowing bodily and sexual experiences to enliven judgments and understanding is a never-ending challenge. While erotic moments along the way can be magical and assist individuals in altering their paths for the good, we still must acknowledge that persons who start this journey bring all the baggage of the past with them. The mystery of conversion is that individuals become new persons while still remaining who they are.[28]

Since it is a process that results in a change of course and direction, Erotic Conversion is not a singular event although it might include momentous judgments and decisions.[29] It might not have an obvious turning point or moment of exhilarating change. Instead, it will tend to have ebbs and flows of satisfaction and dissatisfaction, of slips back into erotophobic responses that are taught throughout one's life and steps forward toward more positive moments of ecstatic embrace of the sexual self. After early erotic insights that lead to reflection about a more positive view of sexuality, further insights can help to sustain the initial ones and lead to greater self-awareness, more responsible actions, and a more nuanced appreciation of the erotic body-self.[30] The person cannot simply say that he or she believes in embodiment and the principles of body theology and expect to move forward without the biases of the past influencing him or her.[31] In fact, after embracing Erotic Conversion, the person may notice how he or she still communicates language and takes on behavior that still express erotophobia.[32] While individuals may give credit to the power of the erotic for shifting them away from fear and self-loathing and, in the process, recognize the wonder of sexual activities that can bring them to a new appreciation of their embodiment, they will still need to acknowledge that the insidious problem of erotophobia remains. It is not something that can be easily pushed aside. Like religious conversion, it requires work.

By explaining sexual awakening and confrontation of the taboo of sexuality in our culture with conversion language, I propose it as a process that needs ongoing reminders, reflection, and new activities that reinforce the new stance of embracing Eros.[33] As with the other conversions in Lonergan's method, Erotic Conversion will also create new criteria for the way we evaluate issues and develop future ways of thinking. The shifting and changed worldview will lead us to new openness and new directions in the way we evaluate sexual issues, look at sexual diversity, and consider the placement of Eros in the life of persons.[34] As Lonergan states, "Conversion, as lived, affects all of man's conscious and intentional operations. It directs his gaze, pervades his imagination, releases the symbols that penetrate to the depths of his psyche. It enriches his understanding, guides his judgments, reinforces his decisions."[35]

Eventually, foundations will be formed by the person that positively influence choices in the future and shape the way he or she interacts with the world in a more permanent way. Erotic Conversion will not only result in shifting the person's thoughts, feelings, and beliefs, it will shift the way in which he or she makes decisions and acts.[36]

By embracing an ideology that affirms Eros and embodiment, the person allows all future deliberations to be influenced and directed by erotic energies and the influential and persuasive belief that the body-self is united and good.

Conversion may also alter the individuals with whom we spend time. Individuals who experience conversion are drawn to create and join social groups that reflect their new view of the world and support their continual path of conversion.[37] This has certainly been apparent with lesbian and gay individuals who often come to an understanding of their sexual orientation through interaction with others and benefit from establishing social and political communities that support, sustain, and affirm them.[38] Communities that flow from an experience of Erotic Conversion help to exemplify the notion that there are political consequences that result from seemingly private decisions. And, besides the social consequences that go beyond one's self toward the larger community and culture, Lonergan believes that there are historical consequences that transcend the time in which the person lives. In other words, later generations will benefit or experience burden because of the choices we make today.

Happily, within Christian theology, recent focus on body theology, the concept of embodiment, and other new sexual theologies have attempted to direct a new historical course and provide assistance to individuals who seek to deepen their reflection on this issue. Many sexual liberation thinkers have compiled a tremendous amount of data regarding dualism and erotophobia in philosophy, theology, the churches, government, and society. Of course, many sociologists and psychologists have also gathered relevant data for this discussion. Thinkers associated with liberating Eros have created a school of thought that confronts Christian bias against sexuality while building a thematic, instructive, and inclusive sexual ethics. These theologies have walked as partners with the civil rights movement and more progressive psychological schools that speak about sexuality as a core component of human behavior.

LGBTQ theologies not only assist homosexual persons in articulating the possibility of reconciling Christian faith with their sexual desires, it helps them to counter erotophobia as it is experienced through the systems of heterosexism and the bias of homophobia. The overall gay liberation movement, the legal and societal advancements, and the new challenges to orthodox Christianity create new possibilities in the life of gay people that makes coming out as sexually different more possible. More than any other time, gay people are liberated, protected, and supported through community efforts, created and shared social space, and the enactment of new laws and support systems. The notion of Erotic Conversion can be a helpful way for understanding the process experienced by lesbian or gay persons when they come out of the closet. In turn, I suggest that coming out of the closet is an instructive example for those who face Christian erotophobia and desire Erotic Conversion.

Coming Out of the Closet as a Form of Erotic Conversion

Erotic Conversion is a process that shifts the person from a worldview that devalues sexual pleasure and operates out of an erotophobic ethics toward a worldview that embraces the power of sexual pleasure and liberates sexuality from the narrow views of traditional Christian ethics. As this requires changing the relative horizon of the person, Erotic Conversion is not a once in a lifetime event and requires openness to the process of growth and a degree of discipline in the effort to change. Similarly, coming out of the closet for the homosexual person includes stages along the way and an ongoing commitment to a new worldview that is adopted. In that it is an embrace of the power of Eros in one's life and a shift of one's sexual horizon, coming out of the closet is a form of Erotic Conversion. It is a process incorporating stages of insight and reflection that eventually affect moral choices. In discussing coming out of the closet as a form of Erotic Conversion, I consider three stages of experience that the gay or lesbian person might engage: (1) self-discovery; (2) making the choice to verbalize one's same-sex orientation to another person(s) for the first time; and (3) being out of the closet over the rest of one's life.[39] In the gay community, there have been debates that coming out means one or more of these three actions. In my approach, I argue that coming out of the closet involves all of them.[40]

Coming Out as Self-Discovery

The initial insight that is necessary for coming out of the closet involves self-discovery: the person comes to know over time that she or he possesses same-sex desire. This self-discovery begins with the collection of data that makes the gay person aware of his or her orientation.[41] The data or information that informs this insight may include deep emotions, erotic dreams, visuals that attract one's attention, and sexual fantasies.[42] Interactions with other gay people and positive images of gay people in the media might help to inform the person about his or her own orientation.[43]

Eventually, the insights may include experimental sexual encounters. Typically, individuals with same-sex desire can find themselves having same-sex encounters and yet, at least initially, resisting quite strongly the identification of being a homosexual. Such a person may want to resist having such encounters, but ends up having them anyway. Only with time and great personal effort does the person gradually come, if he or she does, to accept her orientation, to view it as a given, to identify its capacities and limitations. The person then begins to act in accordance with his or her orientation and its capacities, seeing its actualization as a requisite for an integrated personality and as a central component of personal well-being. As a result, the experience of coming out to oneself has for gays the basic structure of a self-discovery more than the structure of a choice.[44]

Following this initial insight of self-discovery, the person creates deeper and more penetrating notions of who he or she is and how sexuality is tied up with this self-knowledge.[45] The lesbian or gay man may also need to wrestle with internalized homophobia, which can be insidious without the person even knowing it.[46] One of the greatest challenges in this process can be understanding one's homoerotic desire over and against what heteronormative society teaches us about gay people.[47]

Gay persons must not only confront the issues that others in society have with their sexual orientation, they must challenge the models of sexuality that they have learned throughout their lives, including gay stereotypes, religious notions of homosexuality as sinful, and the normality of heterosexuality based on gender complementarity.[48]

We have found that four powerful magical beliefs exist in the implicit learning of homophobia and self-hatred among gay and lesbian youths. First is the idea that homosexuals are crazy and heterosexuals are sane. Unlearning this idea involves giving up the assumption of heterosexual normalcy in favor of positive attitudes. Second is the idea that the problem with same-sex desire is the self, not the society. Unlearning this belief means recognizing cultural homophobia and discovering that the problem with hatred lies not in the self, but in society. Third is the magical belief that to have same-gender desires always means giving up gendered roles as they were previously known and acting as a gender-transformed person, a boy acting or dressing as a girl, a girl living as a boy, or either living as an androgyne. Some will feel gender transformation is the right path for them based on their desires, experiences, and needs. However, having same-sex desire does not necessitate gender inversion or living by the social standards of gender that are socially constructed. Fourth is the belief that if one is to be gay, there are necessary goals, rules, roles, and political and social beliefs that must be performed or expressed. The fact is there is not one way to be gay, there are many divergent ways.[49] Overcoming magical myths involves confronting homophobic and heteronormative bias that creates standards and definitions that organize hierarchies that oppress LGBTQ persons. The gay person who reaches self-identification as a gay person is forced to confront the definition of homosexuality provided to him or her throughout the course of life and, for the first time, change that understanding by including one's self in that definition.

The Erotic Conversion that the gay person experiences in the process of this self-discovery is a turn with or movement toward the sexual self that the person is despite what society might say about same-sex orientation.[50] Eventually, the person has the insight that he or she needs to embrace his or her sexuality and not be controlled by the negative attitudes of other people and larger institutions. At the same time, gay people who come to know their sexual orientation as real will arrive at the conclusion that they are different from the mainstream in multiple ways.[51] This point of view leads many lesbians and gay men to see the world through distinct lenses and to experience unique challenges.[52] Beyond the process of self-discovery, the gay person will be forced to ask the question about how she or he should live in the world. Coming out to oneself by way of labeling oneself as gay is the first step toward communicating this knowledge to another person and making choices about one's future.[53]

The Choice to Come Out

After the process of self-discovery and self-identification, a decision needs to be made whether to deliberately share this information with others or stay closeted.[54] This decision-making process is unique to gay people and often feels more like a burden than a gift.[55] It often begins with gays and lesbians reflecting upon what it would mean to speak to others about their erotic feelings. Many also consider the implications of silence about this core aspect of themselves.[56] What would it mean to hide? Will I ever fall in love? Can I pass as heterosexual in the way I behave on a daily basis? Would I be able to simulate my sexual desires with a person of the opposite sex?[57]

In the decision-making process, there is also the consideration of the implications associated with coming out of the closet. Perhaps, in this decision-making process, more insights are required to enable the person to make effective decisions regarding coming out of the closet in a healthy way. Perhaps the person will realize that it is more devastating to be silent, hidden, and full of shame than it would be to reveal one's self to friends and family. Upon further reflection on the implications of decisions to be in or out of the closet and a healthy dose of self-acceptance, the lesbian or gay person can reach the conclusion that it is better to name this orientation to others and make choices based upon this desire.[58] The gay person can test the waters of this process by choosing someone close to her or him who would be more likely to be accepting and supportive.[59] This can lead to more challenging conversations with others who may need more persuasion.

Discussing same-sex orientation with another person, the lesbian or gay man comes out of the dark into the light of new possibilities and new self-acceptance. This is a step toward confronting the shame associated with homosexual erotic desire. Because this self-discovery and process of coming out of the closet is so intense and necessary for gaining self-acceptance, it tends to be a shared experience within the gay community that creates connections between individuals. Gay people often share their coming out stories with each other in an act of bonding.[60] The bond between individuals with same-sex desire occurs in light of the intensity of the decision to come out and the profound memories that arise from this experience. Meanwhile, part of the coming out process often includes meeting other gay people for the first time in a shared setting. Here, homosocialization often enables the gay person to grow in self-acceptance since he or she is often presented with positive homosexual role models for the first time in his or her life.[61]

Coming out of the closet requires a tremendous amount of courage as the person will face rejection and forms of bias from members of a homophobic society.[62] Even those friends and family members who verbalize acceptance of a gay person's decision may question the reasoning process and the conclusions he or she has reached. The so-called accepting friend or family member may also express deep regret that the gay person has turned out this way and, in the future, choose to be distant.[63] For the gay person, this is an experience of being a marginalized person or a member of a minority group within one's own family or group of friends.[64]

There will also be choices related to sexual activity: the sexual desires of the lesbian or gay person will continue to push for realization.[65] The individual will face the choice to suppress erotic feelings, act upon them in secret and shame, or incorporate them into his or her life in a more integrated manner. Of course, because one is out of the closet or identifies as homosexual does not preclude that a person will choose healthy or integrated sexual behavior. It is one thing to come out of the closet by giving this secret the light of day. It is another thing to make continual choices regarding communicating this part of one's self and to make sexual choices throughout one's life.

Coming Out as Being Out

While an individual's initial coming out is a life-altering and radical moral decision with huge implications, the person will be forced to face new and difficult choices in light of his or her orientation. The gay person will need to continually choose future behavior that corresponds or fails to correspond to this initial decision.[66] Like Erotic Conversion, coming out of the closet is not a onetime event. The courage to come out to more individuals at different levels of relationship, embrace one's sexuality, live openly, and make challenging life choices in light of sexual orientation will continue throughout the life of the gay person. Should I tell co-workers? Should I tell neighbors? Do I discuss it with an old high school friend who contacts me twenty years later? Do I share a bank account with my domestic partner? Do I bring my domestic partner to a family or work event? Do I tell customers when it may mean that I lose their business? If the gay person chooses to be out in life, she or he opens up about the person she or he is in the public domain and faces the ramifications of that honesty.

Meanwhile, gay people who are out will face the possibility of experiencing forms of violence and hate that will confront them in different ways throughout life. This negativity is the very thing that creates potential barriers regarding the choice to come out or not come out over and over again.

We must be forthright everywhere. We must remember the basic truth of the coming out process, an experience that itself offers a model for a politics of dignity. Coming out is not chiefly a means to happiness. It is a conscious giving up of power, a subjection to an increased prospect of discrimination, and an opening to heightened awareness of the ways by which society despises gays—these are not the near occasions of happiness. Yet coming out—even in the face of social interdict—gives people a sense of self, a sense that for better or worse their lives are their own, that their lives have a ground. We must let our love and emotions show publicly; we must resist attempts to make us clean up our act—to live by the standards of others.[67]

Conversations on the topic of the closet too often present a binary opposition between being in the closet and out of the closet. This is problematic in that it fails to correctly interpret the processive and repetitive aspects of coming out and allows the notion of the closet to fall into a discursive contest between the good of sharing one's secret and the issues related to keeping it private.[68] There is a distinction between coming out and being out.[69] Gay people do not simply come out of the closet, they decide *how* they will come out and to what level they will be outspoken regarding their orientation when involved in different levels of social intercourse. Being out ends up shaping the way one will live his or her life, it creates a moral stance in relationship to the world, it becomes an identity choice.[70] Queer identity politics have helped to drive the notion that the individual must make the choice to be homosexual instead of simply accept a homosexual identity.[71] Queers see sexual orientation as an opportunity for self-transformation and a potential for actualizing the person whom they want to become. They believe that "queer marks the very site of gay becoming."[72]

Different ends result from choices related to being out of the closet. For one thing, individuals have a chance at experiencing positive forms of pleasure and relationship with others in their lives by embracing the persons they are and experiencing an integration of their erotic dimension.[73] Second, they can also build self-esteem by living up to the challenges that being different from the mainstream presents, by facing the painful aspects of being out head-on, and by experiencing successes along the way. Third, the more individuals come out and discuss their orientation, the more heterosexuals are exposed to gay people who can help to break down some stereotypes and develop more familiarity and support.[74] Fourth, closeted gay people would be more exposed to the many gay people around them if more people with same-sex desire come out of the closet. This could embolden closeted individuals to make future positive choices regarding their own sexuality. Homosocialization, friendships and acquaintances with other gay men and lesbians, is considered one of the most effective ways toward helping individuals feel positive about their orientation.[75]

The latter notions speak directly to the political implications of coming out of the closet. Not only does the gay or lesbian person decide to change his or her life fundamentally by being out of the closet, he or she makes a political decision to affect and confront the larger society by way of personal moral choices. Coming out as a performative act becomes a political strategy that both joins the gay person to a constituency group and presents challenges to those who oppose homosexuality and want to see it silenced.[76] In the past, many gay people would join their identity group by flocking to gay ghettos where they would be able to demonstrate their sexual orientation with more acceptance and physical safety. Today, when individuals move to gay ghettos, it tends to be more about lifestyle choice than freedom and safety. In effect, gay identity is not as defined today by where one lives.[77] More options exist and many gay people are choosing to stay where they are at the time of their coming out and living within more traditional communities. The gay person as neighbor within a straight community presents its own political challenges and stereotype disruptions.

The fact that gay and lesbian individuals are choosing to be out seems positive and effective in responding to contemporary heterosexism and homophobia. But, in order to experience this process of conversion, same-sex oriented persons need to have insights along the way that it would be good to make this courageous step. They are led to the adoption of a stance, a foundation, from which they approach the world.[78]

The homosexual experience of Erotic Conversion is a positive example to others who need, want, and hope for Erotic Conversion in their lives. In a sense, gay individuals teach us that we can make a transformational change that is based on the value of sexual pleasure. Then, once discovering this in ourselves, building self-esteem in light of this reality, and choosing a stance that places value on the erotic, we can make moral choices that correspond to the pleasure we need and want.

For Christianity to come out of the closet as erotic, it must begin to reconcile the place of pleasure in the human experience and positively incorporate Eros in the everyday of life. For Christians to come out of the closet as erotic, they must turn away from the forms of erotophobia that make up the dominant discourse and turn toward the value and power of erotic pleasure for human living.

Conclusion: Toward a Christian Form of Hedonism

The good news is that the relative horizon of erotophobia can be adjusted, challenged, and changed. It requires a "turning with" the body and its erotic power. At the level of responsibility, we can also interpret just how an embrace of embodiment and the erotic positively affects the decision making of the human subject. One should not assume that this shift of horizon results in an embrace of an absolute hedonism that has no regard for responsibility and the other or the end of all sexual ethics. The accountability for our sexual choices includes an awareness, embrace, and understanding of the fullness of ourselves, the whole person, embodied.

At the same time, Erotic Conversion can open the possibility of a *Christian form of hedonism* where pleasure is embraced as good and sexuality no longer needs to be controlled in a dangerous way.[79] Pleasure is balanced with responsibility, concern for the other, and a consideration for the other values traditionally found within the Christian tradition (e.g., charity, love, communion, reconciliation).[80] Since it incorporates a concern for responsibility and the relationships we have outside of ourselves, the search for pleasure by the Christian hedonist includes a consideration for the consequences of his or her activity. In evaluating sexual choices of others, this form of hedonism includes an adequate consideration for the persons involved in a moral decision.[81]

Meanwhile, when doing ethics from this perspective, Eros is understood, before reflecting on individual sexual issues, as a positive and powerful force that opens a doorway to the divine and our own body-self.[82] This experience of the sacred includes intense "feelings of wholeness, oneness, transcendence, and ecstasy" that evoke a liminal or transforming erotic quality.[83] This form of hedonism requires an integrated approach; it requires Erotic Conversion. Having been erotically converted, individuals can make judgments for erotic pleasure that deepen their level of responsibility with sexual, physical, and, even, environmental choices.[84] Choosing the erotic does not mean, as Christian churches often tell us, that we have chosen selfishness, evil, and/or sin. Instead, this can be the very choice that propels moral growth and development as a responsible individual or Christian. In other words, a person can seek sexual pleasure and have moral character at the same time.[85] Such a belief is a new worldview, a transformational value, a balanced hedonism, a hallmark of Erotic Conversion.

Notes

1. Historian Mark Jordan has noted that while much criticism of the Catholic Church's relationship to sexuality has focused on the confessional as an instrument of oppression, there is a long history of both the Catholic and Protestant traditions using the pulpit in a proactive way to present their moral stance against sexual pleasure. In these traditions, marriage becomes a way to control that pleasure. See Mark D. Jordan, *The Ethics of Sex* (London: Blackwell, 2002), 4–5, 114–17.

2. For an overview on this topic, see Beverley Clack, *Sex and Death* (Cambridge: Blackwell, 2002). An essential figure in this view is Augustine, for whom sexual desire was connected to original sin. Even the baptized suffer from a propensity

toward sin because of the presence of original sin. This theory is often connected to gender, because of Eve's role, and sex, the apple being a symbol of sexuality. In the creation story, the shame of being naked results in the sin. Augustine discussed how eternal damnation was possible for those who succumbed to the sin of sexual pleasure. See his *On Marriage and Concupiscence* 1.13. For more on Augustine's view, see Peter Brown, *Body and Society: Men, Women, and Sexual Renunciation in Early Christianity* (New York: Columbia University Press, 1988), 387–42. With Thomas Aquinas, damnation was the result of mortal sin, which was the identification he used for many sexual sins. It was considered a "self-imposed destruction" and loss of relationship with God fully chosen by the person. See Eileen Sweeney's commentary on the first and second parts of the *Summa Theologiae* in *The Ethics of Aquinas*, ed. Stephen Pope (Washington, DC: Georgetown University Press, 2002), 154. Martin Luther saw sex outside of marriage as a giving into lust and necessarily sinful. It damages one's relationship with God. See Jordan's analysis of his view of Luther's *Large Catechism* in *Ethics of Sex*, 118–19. Luther's dependence on Augustine's connection of sex and the fall should also be noted. See James Nelson's discussion of Luther in *Embodiment: An Approach to Sexuality and Christian Theology* (Minneapolis: Augsburg, 1978), 55.

3. Christine Gudorf wisely calls the churches' approach to sexuality a "sexual moral minimalism" that focuses almost exclusively on those sexual acts to be avoided. She writes, "this moral minimalism gives no guidance in or opportunities for reflection on sexual virtue as the process of constructing sexual relations, genital and non-genital, which are just, loving, and promotive of individual and social growth." See *Body, Sex, and Pleasure* (Cleveland: The Pilgrim Press, 1994), 15.

4. Sex in marriage was more often focused on procreation. Marriage as a vocation was morally less than the celibate life in both Catholic and Protestant traditions. It served as a place to control sexual energies and not a place to celebrate the sexual dimension of the person. See Jordan's overview of the topic in *Ethics of Sex*, 108–25, and his specific treatment of John Calvin's view that marriage was a protection against unlawful lusts in the same text (61).

5. This is the approach taken by Aquinas and his subsequent followers. See Diana Fritz Cates, "The Virtue of Temperance," in *Ethics of Aquinas*, 322.

6. For a good resource on this topic, see Joanne Carlson Brown and Carole Bohn, eds., *Christianity, Patriarchy and Abuse: A Feminist Critique* (Cleveland: The Pilgrim Press, 1989).

7. Jennifer Manlowe observes that religious approaches to sexuality are often damaging to the psychological and physical well-being of women. See *Faith Born of Seduction: Sexual Trauma, Body Image, and Religion* (New York: New York University Press, 1995), 76. Also see Gudorf, *Body, Sex, and Pleasure*, who discusses how penile-vaginal sex often leaves women without orgasmic experience since that form of sexual act cannot bring them to orgasm on its own (31).

8. Marvin Ellison, *Erotic Justice: A Liberating Ethic of Sexuality* (Louisville: Westminster John Knox Press, 1996), 49–54.

9. See Manlowe, *Faith Born*, 70. She speaks of the sin of being an embodied female. The stereotype associated is the woman who cannot control her own erotic desires.

10. Rosemary Radford Reuther discusses how the severe punishment of women is associated with the legacy of women bringing sin and death into the world because of Eve. See "The Western Tradition and Violence Against Women," in *Christianity, Patriarchy and Abuse: A Feminist Critique*, ed. Joanne Carlson Brown and Carole Bohn (Cleveland: The Pilgrim Press, 1989), 32. Also see Elaine Pagels, *Adam, Eve and the Serpent* (New York: Random House, 1988), which includes analysis of Tertullian's view of women based on this story. She includes his infamous quote, "You are the devil's gateway" (63).

11. My analysis of procreationism in this paragraph is largely dependent upon Gudorf, *Body, Sex, and Pleasure*. See page 29 for the definition quoted above.

12. June Price Taugney, Patricia Wagner, and Richard Granzow, "Proneness to Shame, Proneness to Guilt and Psychopathology," *Abnormal Psychology* 101 (August 1992): 470.

13. Psychologists Paul Abramson and Steve Pinkerton reference a study that analyzes the academic performance of human sexuality class students. The studies show that individuals trained to be negative about sexuality as children tend to develop distortions in adolescents and adulthood that affect their ability to listen effectively to any information about sex including contraception. See their *With Pleasure: Thoughts on the Nature of Human Sexuality* (Oxford: Oxford University Press, 1995), 133.

14. R. W. Southern, *Western Society and the Church in the Middle Ages* (New York: Penguin Books, 1970), 226–28.

15. For background, see Gustavo Gutierrez, *A Theology of Liberation* (Maryknoll, NY: Orbis, 1973); Otto Maduro, "Christian Faith and Socialism: A Latin American Perspective," in *Struggles for Solidarity: Liberation Theologies in Tensions*, ed. Lorine Getz and Ruy Costa (Minneapolis: Fortress, 1992); Juan Luis Segundo, *The Liberation of Theology*, trans. John Drury (Maryknoll, NY: Orbis Books, 1979); Leonardo Boff, *Liberating Grace*, trans. John Drury (Maryknoll, NY: Orbis Books, 1987); Ada Maria Isasi-Diaz, *En La Lucha: Elaborating a Mujerista Theology* (Minneapolis: Fortress Press, 1993).

16. Rosemary Radford Reuther, "Feminist Theology and Interclass/Interracial Solidarity," in *Struggles for Solidarity: Liberation Theologies in Tensions*, ed. Lorine Getz and Ruy Costa (Minneapolis: Fortress, 1992), 57. Marcella Althaus-Reid believes that liberation theologians in Latin American have not been concerned enough with the poverty of women and analysis of economic status. See *Indecent Theology: Theological Perversions of Sex, Gender and Politics* (London: Routledge, 2000), 33–37.

17. Althaus-Reid brings together liberation theology, queer theory, and post-Marxism and postcolonial analysis to challenge the marginalization of sexuality. See Althaus-Reid, *Indecent Theology*.

18. Kwok Pui-lan endorses this perspective in her commentary on Althaus-Reid's work. See "Theology as Sexual Act?" *Feminist Theology* 11:2 (January 2003), 149–56.

19. Nelson's two most important texts are *Embodiment* and *Body Theology* (Louisville: Westminster John Knox Press, 1992).

20. Carter Heyward, *Touching Our Strength* (San Francisco: Harper & Row, 1989), 123–24.

21. See Elizabeth Stuart, *Gay and Lesbian Theologies: Repetitions with Critical Difference* (Hampshire, UK: Ashgate, 2003).

22. In Lonerganian terms, "authenticity" refers to the dynamic human spirit embracing the call of the transcendental precepts. The person is attentive, intelligent, reasonable, responsible, and loving. "Integration" refers to the goal of human development to be self-aware, self-constituting, and responsible in one's relationship to the world. Daniel Helminiak, a Lonerganian scholar, updates Lonergan's view and corrects dualistic tendencies by discussing a unified person being made up of organism, psyche, and spirit. See Daniel Helminiak, *The Human Core of Spirituality: Mind as Psyche and Spirit* (New York: State University of New York Press, 1996), 171–72.

23. Nelson enjoys the usage of theological terms within Christianity to explain this kind of change process. For instance, he uses the term "reconciliation" to describe shifting toward a focus on the unity of the body-self. See *Embodiment*, 73.

24. See Joseph Kramer, "Sexual Healing: Healing the Heart-Genital Split in Men," in *Sex and Spirit: Exploring Gay Men's Spirituality*, ed. Robert Barzan (San Francisco: White Crane, 1995), 32. For a feminist perspective on this issue, see Sheila Briggs, "Sexual Justice and the 'Righteousness of God,'" in *Sex and God: Some Varieties of Women's Religious Experience*, ed. Linda Hurcombe (New York: Routledge and Kegan Paul, 1988), 275.

25. While it might seem overly rational to discuss sexuality in such a way, there is tremendous evidence that the brain is key in the human's interest and response to sexual stimuli. In fact, the brain has "pleasure centers" that influence the person's search for sexually pleasurable experiences. See Abramson and Pinkerton, *With Pleasure*, 88–94.

26. Elaine Graham has argued that desire is too often understood as subversion, threat, or manipulation within the Christian tradition. She wants desire to be understood in less cynical terms and as instructive of the person's relationship to the self, world, and others. See "Toward a Theology of Desire," *Theology and Sexuality* 1 (September 1994): 13–30.

27. Lonergan understands conversion to be a lifelong process. See Bernard Lonergan, *Method in Theology* (Toronto: University of Toronto Press, 1971), 118.

28. In discussing an intellectual conversion toward feminist positions and away from male-dominated bias, Tad Dunne makes a similar argument. He writes that "the mind does not begin from a clean slate and gradually add pieces of knowledge." We start "where we find ourselves" and move forward with a more enlivened

and effective process for taking on the next step in the journey toward self-transcendence. See "Authentic Feminist Doctrines," in *Lonergan and Feminism*, ed. Cynthia Crysdale (Toronto: University of Toronto Press, 1994), 117–18.

29. Lonergan, *Method in Theology*, 130.
30. The implications of one's conversion for future conclusions comprise one central aspect of the way conversion changes one's direction. Lonergan believes that it "transforms the concrete individual to make him capable of grasping not merely conclusions but principles as well" (*Method in Theology*, 338). This makes the case for more potential growth in values and principles related to embodiment for the erotically converted person.
31. Ibid., 122. In discussing growth after conversion experience, in this case the choice for scholarship as an outgrowth of intellectual conversion, Lonergan speaks of a "continuous renewal of that dedication" as the way individuals can "achieve the goals they have set themselves."
32. An example would be to claim erotic freedom but still call sex dirty in common language and humor.
33. In a sense, insights are a dime a dozen. They need to be checked, reflected upon, and given the ability to influence us if they are to be worthwhile. More effective judgments can be made if the person accumulates insights in order to make commonsense judgments that are effective in concrete situations. See Bernard Lonergan, *Insight: A Study of Human Understanding*, 5th ed. (Toronto: University of Toronto Press, 1997), 323. More insights that are reflected upon are essential. Less oversights and insights accepted on face value without questioning their authenticity are not helpful and can lead toward problematic judgments. To sustain, reaffirm, and develop a worldview that endorses embodiment and Eros as a power for good, the person should seek out more insights and reflective understanding of their meaning.
34. Lonergan argues that moral conversion leads to changes in "the criterion of one's decisions and choices from satisfactions to values." See *Method in Theology*, 240.
35. Ibid., 131.
36. This includes the person's tendency to write "scripts" that direct future behavioral responses. So deep within the person, they are difficult to rewrite and erase. See Abramson and Pinkerton, *With Pleasure*, 144.
37. Lonergan understands community as the gathering of people with "a common field of experience, with a common or at least complementary way of understanding people and things, with common judgments and aims." See Bernard Lonergan, *A Third Collection*, ed. Frederick Crowe (New York: Paulist Press, 1985), 5–6.
38. The religious aspects of gay ghetto living are explained well by Ronald Long, "The Sacrality of Male Beauty and Homosex: A Neglected Factor in the Understanding of Contemporary Gay Life," in *Que(e)rying Religion: A Critical Anthology*, ed. Gary David Comstock and Susan Henking (New York: Continuum, 1997), 266–85.

39. I do not claim that this is highly original in its design. In fact, it's very similar to the way John McNeill describes it in *Freedom Glorious Freedom: The Spiritual Journey to the Fullness of Life for Gays, Lesbians and Everybody Else* (Boston: Beacon Press, 1995), 61–91. What I am attempting to do is bring together two schools of thought within the gay community: the idea that we are born gay and need to accept that fact and the idea that we choose to be gay. This is often the difference between people who identify as gay and people who identify as queer. It is also a debate between genders: gay men tend to focus on identity, while lesbians focus on choice. My integration of these views is similar to the conclusion of Stanley Siegel and Ed Lowe, *Uncharted Lives: Understanding the Life Passages of Gay Men* (New York: Penguin, 1994), 113–14.

40. The academic debate in the gay community over the topic of sexual identity has been between essentialist and social constructionist theories. The latter have mostly defined this debate resisting the idea that fixed identities should be applied to persons. They believe society and culture, not nature, define identities, and force confessions from individuals regarding which identity is theirs. By making individuals see themselves in terms of their sexuality, they believe that the dominant discourse enters into a process of social control. Essentialists are believed to be more focused on sexuality as a result of nature and in the realm of biology. My approach is "both/and" in that I argue about same-sex orientation using aspects of both theories. I find that both of these together enable a positive understanding of how one experiences himself or herself sexually. I do not believe they are necessarily diametrically opposed. This approach is often called "social interactionism," a viewpoint that attempts to combine the two schools. For an excellent collection of writings on this topic, see Edward Stein, ed., *Forms of Desire: Sexual Orientation and the Social Constructionist Controversy* (New York: Routledge, 1992). Within this collection, James Weinrich defines the social interactionist approach in his essay, "Reality or Social Construction," 182–208.

41. There have been differences noted by psychologists and gay and lesbian scholars regarding the way gay men and lesbians arrive at self-discovery of their orientation differently. In general, lesbians are more likely to include some focus on the discovery of attraction through friendship and community. Conversely, gay males are more likely to describe self-discovery through imagery, genital stimulation, and homoerotic desire. While these tendencies may be true, we should be careful to note that there is a diversity of experience in both gay men and women when it comes to self-discovery and the points of data that are collected in this process. It is never clear-cut because of gender, living condition, or sexual orientation. I include erotic and genital stimulation in my analysis since we are ultimately discussing sexual expression. I choose to keep our focus on sex, sexuality, and the experience of being different from the heterosexual norm. For further reading on this topic, see Laura Brown, "Lesbian Identities: Concepts and Issues," and John Gonsiorek, "Gay Male Identities: Concepts and Issues," both in *Lesbian, Gay, and Bisexual Identities over the Lifespan: Psychological Perspectives,*

ed. Anthony D'Augelli and Charlotte Patterson (Oxford: Oxford University Press, 1995), 3–47.

42. Richard Isay, *Being Homosexual: Gay Men and Their Development* (New York: Avon Books, 1989), 48. Isay argues that, for men, adolescence includes the development of sexual identity that includes homoerotic imagery, sexual attraction to other boys, and sexual experiences. This usually leads to coming out to oneself. Women tend to have a different experience of coming out that does not tend to be linear and goal oriented. Instead, they are more process oriented and continue with self-discovery through changing social contexts. See Theo Sandfort, "Homosexuality, Psychology and Gay Studies," in *Lesbian and Gay Studies*, ed. Jan Willem Duyvendak (London: Sage Publications, 2000), 23.

43. The exposure of gay people and the large number of people who are out is positively affecting the ability of others to come out as well. Psychologists predict this will change the coming out process, making it easier for future gay adolescents. See Sandfort, "Homosexuality," 34. For information on how meeting gay people can enable individuals to embrace their orientation, see Robert Rhoads, *Coming Out in College: The Struggle for a Queer Identity* (Westport, CT: Bergin and Garvey, 1994), 59. For poll information regarding how socialization with a gay person changes people's attitudes, see Dee Bridgewater, "Effective Coming Out: Self-Disclosure Strategies to Reduce Sexual Identity Bias," in *Overcoming Heterosexism and Homophobia*, ed. James Sear (New York: Columbia University Press, 1997), 66.

44. Richard Mohr, *Gays/Justice: A Study of Ethics, Society and Law* (New York: Columbia University Press, 1988), 40.

45. A large number of gay men and lesbians seek out therapy for assistance in working through the process of self-discovery. See Richard Isay, *Becoming Gay: The Journey to Self-Acceptance* (New York: Henry Holt and Company, 1996).

46. Internalized homophobia is defined as "the conscious or subconscious adoption and acceptance of negative feelings and attitudes about homosexuals or homosexuality by gay men and lesbians" (James Sears, "Thinking Critically/ Intervening Effectively About Homophobia and Heterosexism," in *Overcoming Heterosexism*, 15).

47. Janis Bohan, *Psychology and Sexual Orientation: Coming to Terms* (London: Routledge, 1996), 95.

48. Stereotypes are often used as an instrument of systematic oppression. In the case of lesbians and gays, they have been used to support the case that homosexuality is evil. See Gilbert Herdt, *Same Sex, Different Cultures: Exploring Gay and Lesbian Lives* (Boulder, CO: Westview Press, 1997). 57. Also see Laura Markowe, *Redefining the Self: Coming Out as a Lesbian* (Cambridge, MA: Polity Press, 1996), 44–60.

49. Herdt, *Same Sex*, 133.

50. By conversion here we do not imply the ability to change sexual orientation through conversion therapies.

51. Interestingly, gay men and lesbians are often mocked when young for being different. At the stage of coming out, they own this difference in a more empowered way. See Bohan, *Psychology and Sexual*, 143.

52. Herdt believes that the process of coming out itself has profoundly affected the worldview of lesbian and gay people. Beyond how powerful this process is and how much it influences gay culture and the point of view of gay people, he argues for a deeper move toward developing a "moral voice" that can influence the way one sees the world (we might call this "stance") and responds to activity choices. See *Same Sex*, 167–68.

53. Isay claims that this often happens in late adolescence and typically happens with great pain and significant delay. Each gay person discovers this about herself or himself through sexual fantasies and has to negotiate those feelings and discover their meaning. This is a period of forming one's sexual identity. See *Being Homosexual*, 48.

54. Typically, gays and lesbians think through their coming out processes carefully and choose selectively who will be the first person they tell and what other individuals will be told later. This is sometimes called "managed disclosure." See Gonsiorek, "Gay Male," 33.

55. Jeffrey Weeks effectively demonstrates how choice can be a burden and feel undesirable when a lack of freedom is associated with it. In his view, it is naive to celebrate the idea that a person has a choice since this ignores the fact that many choices can be painful. This is helpful for understanding the psychology of coming out of the closet. See Jeffrey Weeks, *Invented Moralities: Sexual Values in an Age of Uncertainty* (New York: Columbia University, 1995), 61–64.

56. Steven Seidman notes that it takes a lot of work to stay silent about one's same-sex desire and to pass as heterosexual. "Passing is not a simple, effortless act: it's not just about denial or suppression. The closeted individual closely monitors his or her speech, emotional expression, and behavior in order to avoid unwanted suspicion." See *Beyond the Closet: The Transformation of Gay and Lesbian Life* (New York: Routledge, 2002), 21.

57. Many gay men have attempted to live a married heterosexual life to avoid the issue of their sexual orientation. See Michael Ross, *The Married Homosexual Man* (London: Routledge, 1983), 47–65.

58. A process for transforming gay shame into gay pride is explained by Gershen Kaufman and Lev Raphael, *Coming Out of Shame: Transforming Gay and Lesbian Lives* (New York: Doubleday, 1996), 122–86.

59. Ritch Savin-Williams discusses how adolescents often choose individuals they know will be supportive first to build up toward more difficult coming out conversations. See "Lesbian, Gay Male, and Bisexual Adolescents," in *Lesbian, Gay, and Bisexual Identities*, 171.

60. A good example of this kind of experience is captured in group interviews found in Mark Thompson's *Gay Spirit: Myth and Meaning* (New York: St. Martin's Press, 1987), 237–57.

61. Isay, *Being Homosexual*, 62.

62. Carol Thorpe Tully describes the courage of gay teenagers who face coming out in a homophobic society. In her text, she includes many studies regarding coming out at different stages in life. See *Lesbians, Gays and the Empowerment Perspective* (New York: Columbia University Press, 2000), 118.

63. Kristin Hancock, "Psychotherapy with Lesbians and Gay Men," in *Lesbian, Gay, and Bisexual Identities*, 416–19. Hancock discusses how families of origin reacted differently to the self-disclosure of their children as homosexual. Much of this involves their common perception and moral evaluation of homosexuality. Those who are more apt to be against homosexuality because of morality and religion may vocalize support for their child but will continue to agree with their prior convictions.

64. Tully, *Lesbians, Gays*, 122. She writes that the younger people are when they come out the more likely parents are to deny, reject, and question the conclusions of their child. It can also lead parents to lay blame on themselves for past behavior. This is sometimes called the mother's lament.

65. Mohr argues that sexual experience is an important part of the coming out process. Sometimes individuals have homosexual encounters and deny being homosexual. However, the desire for homosex remains, and the individual begins to identify his or her identity with the sexual desire. For this reason, Mohr is uncomfortable in calling homosexuality a choice. See *Gays/Justice*, 40–41.

66. Steven Barbone and Lee Rice, "Coming Out, Being Out and Acts of Virtue," in *Gay Ethics: Controversies in Outing, Civil Rights and Sexual Sciences*, ed. Timothy Murphy (Binghamton, NY: Harrington Park Press, 1994), 95.

67. Richard Mohr, *Gay Ideas: Outing and Other Controversies* (Boston: Beacon Press, 1992), 97.

68. Eve Kosofsky Sedgwick, *Epistemology of the Closet* (Los Angeles: University of California Press, 1990), 11.

69. Barbone and Rice, "Coming Out," 94–95.

70. Seidman, *Beyond the Closet*, 86. In writing about the contemporary situation, Seidman notes that gay men and lesbians are more likely today to make this choice and stay in their home town or local area. In the past, identity choice often meant moving in proximity to others who made similar choices. For more conversation on the change in this regard, see Gilbert Herdt, "'Coming Out' as a Right of Passage: A Chicago Study," in *Gay Culture in America: Essays from the Field* (Boston: Beacon Press, 1992), 61. Herdt writes that coming out used to mean that the person entered a secret society of other homosexuals. Today, it means that they present a "gay self" to the larger public.

71. For a very approachable overview of the queer point of view, see Richard Dyer, *The Culture of Queers* (London: Routledge, 2002).

72. David Halperin, *Saint Foucault: Towards A Gay Hagiography* (Oxford: Oxford University Press, 1995), 79.

73. James Reid presents psychological studies that not only prove that coming out is a major transformational life experience but that individuals who enter into it typically develop stronger senses of their self and higher levels of ego-strength that help them when they are older. He writes, "the outcome of this developmental transition has profound implications for self-worth, self-esteem, coping mechanisms, and mental health. As a result, there is a tremendous potential for personal growth and development." See "Development in Late Life: Older Lesbians and Gay Lives," in *Lesbian, Gay, and Bisexual Identities*, 219–20.
74. Rob Eichberg, *Coming Out: An Act of Love* (New York Penguin, 1990), 60. Eichberg argues that if more people come out they disabuse people of their stereotypical views of gay people and lay the foundation for a broader view.
75. Isay, *Being Homosexual*, 61–66.
76. Michael Warner, *Fear of a Queer Planet* (Minneapolis: University of Minnesota Press, 1993), xxv.
77. See Seidman, *Beyond the Closet*, 88–89. While I agree with Seidman on this topic, we should also state that different parts of the country and world accept homosexual behavior to a different degree. This may make staying within tradition communities more challenging to some than others.
78. The term "stance," sometimes defined as fundamental option, was understood by Lonergan as a worldview or foundation. I am using this logic in discussing the gay and lesbian choice to come out and embrace identity. After all, the basic definition of stance in Catholic theology is that stance expresses "the sort of person we have chosen to be, the fundamental direction we have chosen for our lives." This definition has a lot of utility when discussing the decision to be in or out of the closet. See Richard Gula, *Reason Informed by Faith: Foundations in Catholic Morality* (New York: Paulist Press, 1989), 79.
79. Gudorf, *Body, Sex and Pleasure*, 99.
80. Remember that hedonism is associated with the move toward pleasure and the avoidance of pain. The person's interest in these activities appears to be associated with evolutionary aspects of human psychology. Here, we are attempting to redefine hedonism as part of the person's natural search for pleasure balanced with behavioral consequences. It can also be argued that the evolution of rational thought is connected to pleasure and pain in such a way that they become integral components of general intelligence. Abramson and Pinkerton help to explain the science associated with the human search for pleasure in *With Pleasure*, 45–50 and 228.
81. I am using the Catholic moral theology framework of Charles Curran to modify hedonism. He takes a relationship/responsibility approach to moral problems. For a good overview of his view, see James Keenan, "The Moral Agent: Actions and Normative Decision Making," in *A Call to Fidelity: On the Moral Theology of Charles Curran*, ed. James Walter, Timothy O'Connell, and Thomas Shannon (Washington, DC: Georgetown University Press, 2002), 37–55.
82. Kramer, "Sexual Healing," 32.

83. Donald Boisvert, *Out on Holy Ground: Meditations on Gay Men's Spirituality* (Cleveland: The Pilgrim Press, 2000), 92. Boisvert uses Emile Durkheim's understanding of "sacred" in describing gay religious experience, including the spiritual experience of sexual ecstasy.

84. Many feminist scholars have connected sexist dualism to our poor treatment of the Earth. See Rosemary Radford Ruether, *Gaia and God: An Ecofeminist Theology of Earth Healing* (San Francisco: Harper, 1992). We have also noted gay scholar Daniel T. Spencer, *Gay and Gaia: Ethics, Ecology, and the Erotic* (Cleveland: Pilgrim Press, 1996), which discusses an erotic environmentalism. Also see J. Michael Clarke, *Beyond Our Ghettos: Gay Theology in Ecological Perspectives* (Cleveland: The Pilgrim Press, 1993).

85. Latin American liberation theologian Gustavo Gutierrez made the point that the poor, considered unintelligent, have the right to think since liberation theology privileges their experience. Similarly, we are including the voice and thoughts of the sexually oppressed in our theology since they have the right to be considered moral persons. Gustavo Gutierrez, *The Power of the Poor in History* (Maryknoll, NY: Orbis Books, 1984), 87.

Chapter 3

Lesbian Feminist Pioneers in Religion

Mary E. Hunt

The story of lesbian feminist pioneers is an important chapter in the history of queer religion. This version of it is confined to the U.S. Christian scene since there is more than enough there to demonstrate the marvelous contribution of lesbians to the field of feminist theology broadly conceived. The focus of this story is how the foundations of queer theology find their roots in feminist theology via the contributions of lesbians. The two approaches dovetail in terms of their content, dynamics, and trajectories. Of course, there are also places where they diverge. It is a story that is still unfolding.

Roots of Feminist Theology

Feminist theology is chronicled as beginning in the late 1890s, when Elizabeth Cady Stanton, Matilda Jocelyn Gage, and other suffrage leaders named patriarchal religion as one of the key sources of women's oppression.[1] Until and unless images and symbols of the divine were modified to include female as well as male, until ministry and worship were available to women as well as men, these women saw little hope in changing the social order. So, they did their theological work along with their political activity, convinced that they go hand in hand. History proved them to be correct.

There is no way to assess which if any of them were lesbians, or even exactly what the word "lesbian" meant in that period. But they established the political nature of theology, insisting that women's concerns about religion were intimately connected to women's social well-being. That dynamic became a regular dimension of feminist work in religion throughout the next hundred years and later in queer theology.

The first ordained women in ministry, including Congregationalist Antoinette Brown Blackwell (1853) and Methodist Anna Howard Shaw (1880), are not considered to have been lesbians. But their lives were typical of many of their generation. For example, Brown thought single women had an easier time of being taken seriously than married women. She changed her mind when she met her future husband, Mr. Blackwell, with whom she had seven children.

Shaw's *New York Times* obituary describes her death: "Her secretary, Miss Lucy E. Anthony, a niece of Susan B. Anthony, who has been with Dr. Shaw for thirty years, and two nieces, the Misses Lulu and Grace Greene, were at her bedside when she died." It also includes the fact that she never married and makes reference to "Dr. Shaw's most intimate friend, Susan B. Anthony."[2] These are the kinds of comments that lead researchers to wonder if the roots of lesbian feminist work in religion are even deeper than we will ever know.

By the 1960s, feminist theology took nascent shape in Valerie Saiving's classic article, "The Human Situation: A Feminine View."[3] She argued that men's sins were different than women's sins, thus establishing the first significant conversation about the gendered nature of religion. Men's sins are of pride and power, she said, while women's are of self-trivialization and distractedness. Religions like Christianity that told everyone to be meek and humble could in fact be morally helpful to men. But they are spiritually and even physically dangerous for women. Again, the matter of Saiving's sexuality is not at issue. What is important is that she laid the foundations for all subsequent work in religion to be evaluated in terms of sex and gender. This is a foundation of both feminist and queer theologies.

Georgia Harkness was the first woman theologian to teach in an American seminary.[4] Her more than thirty books of theology, ethics, prayers, hymns, and sermons established her as a pioneering figure in the field. She taught at Elmira College for Women, Mount Holyoke College, eventually on the graduate level at Garrett Biblical Institute, and later at Pacific School of Religion.

Harkness was not explicitly feminist in her outlook; she referred to herself as a liberal. Nonetheless, she experienced sexual discrimination in the 1940s when she was passed over for a position in systematic theology at Garrett. She eventually took a position at Pacific School of Religion in "applied theology," considered to be of lesser prestige than philosophical or systematic theology. The president of Garrett made clear that he did not want women on the faculty; equal pay for women and men was not an option. Harkness's reported reaction suggests some, however nascent, feminist consciousness.

Her subsequent work was done within the parameters of denominational theology. Harkness used her access to the inner sanctums of United Methodism at midcentury to push for the full ordination of Methodist women. She championed many social justice issues, including antiwar and antiracism efforts. She even spoke publicly in favor of same-sex love though not, as far as has been reported, about her own personal life.[5]

She lived with Verna Miller, both in Berkeley when she taught at Pacific School of Religion, and later in Claremont, California, where they retired. She dedicated one of her books to Miller: "To Verna who shares my home and my life and to whom the book and its author owe much."[6]

The two women wished to move into a Christian retirement community, Pilgrim Place, in Claremont, California. Unfortunately, they were not welcome because Miller had not been a church worker as was required for entrance. This was waived of course if one entered as the spouse of a church worker. Many retired ministers and missionaries who lived there had spouses, mostly women, who had not been church workers either. Harkness and Miller solved the problem by moving near the progressive Pilgrim Place, which eventually changed its policies. But the important point is that they were treated as a same-sex couple insofar as they were discriminated against.

Many scholars have been careful not to out Harkness, given the negative history of the United Methodist Church on same-sex love and the delicacy of reading into any relationship more than those involved in it experienced and/or disclosed. Anecdotal evidence suggests that one could quite easily regard Harkness as a lesbian though she herself did not say so. This is why it is not done. I think it is safe, fair, appropriate, and enough to say that Harkness fit the pattern of other early feminist Christian theologians who made strong claims for women and lived in community with women while they did public work on social justice. In this sense, she contributed to the foundational work in both feminist and queer theologies.

Nelle Morton, a beloved professor at the Theological School of Drew University, is another such example.[7] She was a religious educator by training whose commitments to eradicate racism and to empower women infused her work. After her retirement from teaching, she became a feminist theologian whose work on the process of listening to women and developing theology accordingly was taken as axiomatic in the field. She lived a women-connected life though she did not speak publicly of herself as a lesbian.

Whether these women were lesbians in terms of their sexual lives is difficult to know and not of utmost relevance for this analysis. What is important is that they theologized on the basis of their experiences as women at a time when such was not part of the normative methodology. This experiential dynamic remains an integral part of both feminist and queer theologies.

Lesbian Feminist Theologians

Mary Daly left no such ambiguity about herself. She was an early feminist Catholic theologian who later called herself a philosopher when she found even the word "theology" intolerable. She lived the painful contradictions of that patriarchal religious tradition where women were treated as subordinate to men and barred from ordination and graduate theological studies. In the 1960s, Daly went to Europe to obtain two doctorates (in addition to an American one) with most of her classes in Latin. So she was well trained to confront a recalcitrant system on its own terms.

Daly created new intellectual and spiritual space for thinking about women and religion. With her classic text, *Beyond God the Father*, she encapsulated the problems of patriarchy by claiming, "if God is male, then the male is God."[8] As a result of her insight, virtually every subspecialty in religion was revised to take account of the now obvious patriarchal slant. Biblical interpretation, church history, ethics, preaching, pastoral counseling, as well as systematic theology itself were subject to intense feminist scrutiny. The field simply would not be the same again. Similar critical work using the lenses of race, class, and colonialism emerged beginning in the 1970s. When queer theology appeared in the 1990s, the ground was prepared because of these efforts to insist on particular, concrete issues of analysis.

Daly was a lesbian who expanded the meaning of the word. She came out in the early 1970s, spoke publicly then about her sexual identity, and later wrote about the inadequacy of male-defined terms for same-sex love. In her imaginative lexicon, she defined "Lesbian" (always with a capital "L") as "a Woman-Loving woman; a woman who has broken the Terrible Taboo against Women-Touching women on all levels . . . rejected false loyalties to men in every sphere."[9]

She never confined the idea of lesbian to a sexual reduction of the term. Rather, she saw it as a description, indeed as a form of encouragement for women to bond with one another, to break with patriarchal practices. At the same time, she appreciated, enjoyed, and loved women in every way and dimension, including the sexual. But her focus was always on "The Fire of Female Friendship," the "Gyn/affection" that is the source of strong feminist energy and a catalyst for feminist social change.

Daly rejected male-dominated gay liberation and insisted on women being protagonists regardless of their sexual partners. She was critical of early transgender options as a reinforcement of what she considered stereotypic binary sex roles. She lived out her commitments in the company of women friends and a few good men. She was persuaded that new ways of being are possible.

That Daly was a lesbian was never in doubt. But sexual identity was never a primary analytic category for her. She championed animal rights as much as human rights, mirroring other feminist theologians who always included more issues like race and class along with their concern for sex and gender. She was mystical in her concern for the planet, beginning with a piece of clover that she befriended as a child through which she had a primary experience of the world.

Daly loved community and disliked coupled relationships of any sort even though she lived for a period with a woman. She was never a strong proponent of same-sex marriage. In her view, marriage was a patriarchal, heterosexist construct that same-sex loving people would do well to avoid. This contrarian approach is echoed in the later work of many feminist and queer theologians who prefer to push the horizons rather than accept and conform to heterosexual givens even if it means postponing immediate social justice for longer-term structural change.[10]

Sally Miller Gearhart wrote the first explicit treatment of lesbians in the Christian tradition, "The Lesbian and God-the-Father Or All the Church Needs Is a Good Lay—On Its Side."[11] Gearhart was a professor of speech at San Francisco State University, not a theologian. But she had been raised a Bible-believing Protestant and taught in Christian colleges. She knew the tradition, biblical texts, and hymns that reinforced the oppressive theology in worship. Gearhart loved to belt out hymns, sometimes with a feminist rewriting of the lyrics that produced hilarious results. She became one of the first out lesbians tenured in a U.S. university, surely to the consternation of her previous employers in traditional Christian circles.

Gearhart delivered her famous essay as a lecture in February 1972, at a pastors' conference at Pacific School of Religion in Berkeley, California. When she was asked to share her essay for a church publication, the Program Agency of the United Presbyterian Church, which sponsored the publication in question, turned down the article for reasons of prejudice. Happily, the Philadelphia Task Force on Women in Religion published it as a pink supplement to *Genesis III*, their feminist newsletter that was edited by Nancy Krody, a longtime lesbian feminist activist in religious circles.

Gearhart's piece was passed hand-to-hand in mimeographed form in the early 1970s, amazing readers who simply had not dealt with such issues in a religious context. She claimed, "I cannot separate the lesbian from the woman," a clear affirmation of the need to leave aside male definitions and an invitation to all women to identify themselves on their own terms.[12] She went on to affirm, "being a lesbian involves for me some growing political consciousness. That means I am committed to assessing institutions like the church, which, as far as most women are concerned, takes the prize as the most influential and in itself the most insidiously oppressive institution in Western society."[13]

Gearhart, a Methodist turned Lutheran who eventually left Christianity altogether, set the pace for lesbian and later bisexual women to reject privatized, individualized analysis. She encouraged women to embrace an explicitly theo-political agenda, which included more than simply sex and gender but never left those aside.

Gearhart joined the Council on Religion and the Homosexual, a group that included the iconic lesbian couple Del Martin and Phyllis Lyon. That group formed in the mid-1960s after state officials in California assured activists that no legal changes would come about without support from religious organizations and their officials.[14] The council's work was reminiscent of the suffrage women's efforts, deconstructing religion so as to be able to reconstruct a new social order. It is always theo-political work that matters, not simply theology or politics. This is now a methodological given in both feminist theology and queer work in religion.

Gearhart and her friends came out against great odds even in the seeming safety of feminist circles. Lesbian women were encouraged to keep their sexual identity quiet lest all feminists be labeled "lesbian." Gearhart was not to be silenced. "The love that dares not speak its name" until then had been associated with men in religions settings. Thanks to her, it now had a beautiful female face.

Gearhart, like Daly, left Christianity in favor of Goddess and Earth-centered religion. She wrote science fiction.[15] Rarely in later years has she trifled with the churches. Nonetheless, she left an indelible mark on the field of feminist studies in religion. No longer would "gay" suffice to describe women and men. No longer were men the only spokespeople for queer religious people. Lesbian women had their own voices and their own contributions to make.

Another shaping feminist dynamic emerged as these two women and many others found the contradictions of sexism to be overwhelming. Whether lesbian or not, they chose not to continue to deal with the Christian tradition given its sexist nature and/or practice. The primary contradiction for them, and for many other colleagues, was as women in a patriarchal tradition and not as lesbians in a heterosexism tradition. Being a lesbian was seemingly secondary, no less important, but simply not as basic as being a woman.

This dynamic explains why so many Christian LGBTIQ groups in the period from 1965 through the present have been overwhelmingly male in their makeup and focus. Gay men simply have not had to cope with the root discrimination that all women, lesbian and otherwise, feel in patriarchal Christianity. As males, there is a place for them in the tradition. It is as gay men that they are marginalized. By contrast, in many Christian denominations, all women are marginalized. The exclusion of lesbians is a subset of that experience.

This is neither to trivialize the exclusion of gay men nor to exaggerate the oppression of women, especially since some notable Christians who are sexist and homohating are women. But it is to underscore that sexual discrimination was so widespread—to half or more of the Christian population—that it was not surprising that it preceded queer analysis. It also explains why lesbian feminists have insisted consistently that substantive structural changes take place in the Christian tradition rather than simply tweaking it to allow some queer people access.

Other Christian women leaders came out as well. One celebrated case was the Rev. Joan Clark, who paid dearly for her integrity. In 1979, after seven years in her job in the Women's Division of the Board of Global Ministries, she was fired for being honest about her sexuality.[16] Within a decade, enough churchwomen, mostly Protestant clergy, had come out that they could form the organization Christian Lesbians Out Together (CLOUT) in 1990. It is a supportive network of women, ordained and lay, who bond to eradicate abuses of power and who celebrate lesbian lives.[17]

Another Methodist, the Rev. Jean Audrey Powers, came out in 1995 with far less fanfare and fewer consequences. Hopefully this was because of some inroads made by her sisters. In each case, the common factor was women whose lives of dedication and service to a range of social justice issues naturally and logically extended to their own sexuality and their own integrity in assuming it. Integrity is a hallmark of queer and feminist theologies.

Several other scholars added their luster and credibility to the early work. Beverly Wildung Harrison, professor of ethics at Union Theological Seminary, established her professional credentials on issues of reproductive justice.[18] Widely considered the pivotal figure in the founding of the field of feminist religious ethics, Harrison urged a multifaceted analysis that included a substantive critique of heterosexism.[19] She educated the first cadre of feminist ethicists who went on to work on issues of family, economics, and sexuality. They built on her powerful analysis of structures not simply people, of systems and ideologies. She incorporated issues of heterosexism seamlessly into her critical work and insisted that it be an integral part of any social justice agenda.

Letty Russell, longtime professor at Yale Divinity School, wrote and lectured on new models of church based in the round. She urged attention to human liberation in all of its components.[20] Russell was an ordained Presbyterian minister who modeled ecumenism at its best. She nurtured many of the women who were part of the first significant cohort of women to be ordained in mainline Protestant churches. She encouraged women throughout the world to study theology, organizing a doctor of ministry program in feminist liberation theology at San Francisco Theological Seminary with her partner, Shannon Clarkson. Their hospitality was legendary, their home a welcoming place for all.

Russell's work was infused with a commitment to bring feminist values of equality and mutuality to the structures of ecclesial power, both denominations and ecumenical groups like the World Council of Churches. Hers was an effective institution-based strategy. As an open lesbian, she might have been rejected by many conservative Presbyterians. But her dedication in ministry and the consistence of her principles left little room for discussion.

These women, and many more whose names and stories remain untold, laid the groundwork for future forms of feminist theology that include lesbians explicitly, and for queer theology based on that work. Those who took on lesbian issues more explicitly could not have done so without the early signal contributions of the pioneers. It is hard to overemphasize the importance of the holistic analysis that emerged from this cohort of feminist theologians.

Lesbians on Lesbians

Carter Heyward is an important example of the next step in this work, lesbians writing on lesbians. She was ordained in the first group of Episcopal women priests in 1974. Her subsequent coming out only added luster to that group's pioneering reputation. Heyward taught at Episcopal Divinity School. She educated several generations on the "redemption of God," the important links between and among social justice issues, and the power of women's erotic love as a spiritual resource.[21]

Heyward's feminist theological work was the first academic corpus to be thoroughly infused with lesbian identity and analysis. Her Nicaraguan solidarity and antiracism work demonstrated once again the common feminist theological concern with a range of intersecting social justice issues. Heyward, with her life partner Beverly Harrison, wrote explicitly on issues of lesbian life and love.[22] She inspired several generations of graduate students who have gone on to do queer theology with a firm grasp of its feminist roots.

Bernadette J. Brooten is another lesbian academic who trained her talent on lesbian issues. She produced a landmark study on same-sex loving women in the early Christian period.[23] She argued that the later Christian opposition to same-sex love between women was based not so much on the matter of sexuality as on power. Since most male-male and male-female sexual relationships were based on power-over models, female-female sexual relationships presented the unique possibility of equality between partners. This, more than the actual sexual dimensions, upset the cultural applecart several millennia ago.

Mary E. Hunt wrote about lesbian feminist issues from a Catholic starting point. She focused on women's friendships as a paradigm for adult human relationships and community.[24] Her analysis of Catholic heterosexism helped to change the discourse from concern about homosexuality as such to equally vital concern with the root cause of the social problem, namely, heterosexism.[25] Like Heyward and other feminist theologians, Hunt developed a multifaceted analysis of race, class, colonialism, and ecological concerns that grounds her efforts to do queer work in religion with a lesbian feminist foundation.

Much of this generation's work, like that of the previous generation, was done by white women. Racism in society at large and in churches and academies in particular made coming out more complicated and costly for women of color. This is a painful reality among feminists, one that has resulted in a disproportionate number of early scholars being white. Nonetheless, those women have woven antiracism into their lesbian feminist work in an effort to eradicate the problem.

Rene Hill was the first African American Womanist theological colleague to come out. Hill is senior associate minister for Peace and Justice at All Saints Episcopal Church in Pasadena, California. She brings to her local work a broad social justice perspective and a particular focus on the needs of queer people of color.

African American Womanist scholar Emilie Townes is a leading ethicist and academic administrator whose poetic approach to theology is unique. She, too, weaves a complicated web of social and spiritual issues in her work, including the matter of a lesbian body that refuses to "perform a heteronormative drag show."[26] Her leadership as an ordained Baptist clergywoman, an Ivy League divinity school dean, and a colleague committed to sharing resources with Brazilians in theological education make her a central figure in this work.

Irene Monroe is another lesbian Womanist whose work as a public theologian rooted in African American and feminist theologies is her own brilliant brand of queer Womanism. She writes extensively in the secular gay press, always amazing her readers with her insight, her verve, and her rigorous demand that the world be more just and loving.[27] Monroe's influence is enormous because her column is syndicated in dozens of media outlets and she has come to the attention of Oprah Winfrey. Monroe teaches, engages in solidarity work, and lectures widely.

Queering Feminist Theologies

The development of queer theologies emerged from a combination of the feminist/Womanist work and the gay theologies that in their early manifestations were predominantly male. Gay scholars, including pioneers like John E. Fortunato, John Boswell, and John McNeill, were focused mainly on men's experiences, history viewed through a male lens, and church as a male-defined space to which out gay men wanted access. This was understandable given the historical context of the 1970s and 1980s. Happily, later gay male scholars, including Marvin Ellison and Robert Goss, began to read and be influenced by feminists. So as queer theologies came into being, these bridge builders were able to be explicit about the contribution of feminists that shaped gay men's work.

Virginia Ramey Mollenkott is a pivotal figure at the intersection of feminist and queer work in religion. She is an unlikely one since she comes from an evangelical background, and is a scholar of English literature and not theology by first training. But her mark is indelible on the field both for her pioneering work on scripture and for her courageous embrace of transgender people and concerns.

Mollenkott studied at Bob Jones University, where she learned the hard lessons of evangelical fundamentalism with its anti-feminist and anti-queer biases. For her personal angst about perhaps being a lesbian, she was counseled by a faculty member to get married and get over it. She married and went on to graduate studies, where she became an expert on John Milton. She was a highly regarded English professor at William Patterson University in New Jersey for three decades.

Mollenkott always harbored a special interest in the religion that had been so formative, if also so problematic, for her. She brought the same clear thinking and writing, careful attention to text, and delight in language and symbols to her second scholarly arena, theology and religion. Naturally, she gravitated toward the text, bringing to the Bible her keen sense of analysis, her detective skills at finding the women and queer people hidden away there, her faith in things seen and unseen. And just as naturally, she brought a feminist lens and gaydar to her work.

She has written more than a dozen books.[28] Her best-known work, *Is the Homosexual My Neighbor?* (1978/1994), co-authored with Letha Dawson Scanzoni, opened a conversation that many other evangelicals preferred to postpone.[29] It acted as a springboard for her own later coming out publicly and foreshadowed her courage and wisdom on trans issues. By the time she published *Sensuous Spirituality: Out from Fundamentalism*, she had established herself as a prominent theologian both feminist and evangelical, an unusual combination.[30] Along the way, she helped the National Council of Churches develop inclusive-language lectionaries that are used all over the world. She prodded the Evangelical and Ecumenical Women's Caucus, of which she is a stalwart member, to look critically at issues of sexuality and gender.

Gradually, she came to know and love many people who described themselves as trans—whether transsexuals, intersexed people, cross-dressers, transvestites, or the like. She published *Omni-gender: A Trans Religious Approach*, in which she demonstrated how transgender people destabilize all gender categories.[31] That carefully worked out sense of what it means to be gay/lesbian/bisexual that framed the many theo-political strategies to bring about inclusion in religions and society was subject to reconsideration due to this persuasive work. Feminists and queers alike went back to the drawing boards on what sex is, how to understand gender, and what it all means for making change in religion and in the world at large.

It is no accident that such transformational work was done by an evangelical lesbian feminist who describes herself as a trans woman. Who else would have the skills, insights, and necessity to do so? Mollenkott brought her humanities sensitivities to religion. Her evangelical background stood in sharp contrast to feminist theology, which was predominantly liberal to progressive to liberationist. She marshaled her commitments to social justice—economic, racial, and ecological as well as sexual. She lived her lesbian sexual identity in the crucible of human variety and found that trans people helped her make sense of her own embodied life. Most of all, she brought an impeccable integrity to the process, earning the trust and care of many fellow sexual outlaws as she lived the Christian values she espoused. She is a unique combination who, with the help of other colleagues, has produced queer feminist work that is now located at the edges of both feminist and queer theologies.

Feminist and Queer Trajectories

This overview of lesbian feminist unto queer work in religion is admittedly partial and incomplete. There are many more women whose contributions have shaped the enterprise. Many heterosexually identified allies have added their voices to the mix, making concern for gender justice normative in the field of feminist studies in religion. Christine Gudorf, for example, has described the problematic of sexual dimorphism in religious studies.[32] Elisabeth Schüssler Fiorenza and Rosemary Radford Ruether never miss an opportunity to include heterosexism in their scholarly work to overcome oppressions.

By contrast, some queer male scholars give little evidence of having read and/or incorporated feminist work into their efforts. But those who have bring the same kind of inter-structured analysis of oppression to their work. Still, for the most part, the connections between feminist and queer approaches remain to be solidified in future work by scholars yet to come.

The disconnects have understandable historical reasons. Queer work is far newer than feminist work. It is rooted in the social sciences with religion a relative latecomer to the issues. Many male scholars and even more gay male activists grew accustomed to a post-Stonewall world in which their bars, their sexual practices, and, tragically, their HIV/AIDS pandemic were normative. This was nowhere more obvious than in religion.

In mainline Christianity, the churches, which some considered the domestic sphere of public life, were run by men despite the preponderance of adherents being women. This is glaring in the Roman Catholic Church, where male-only clergy, many of whom are gay, pretend to lead congregations that are made up of mostly women. Many African American churches have similar dynamics. Those churches have rejected feminism and kept queer people at bay while cultivating male leadership as a way to keep at least some men in the fold. The resulting discrimination against women only set the stage for rejecting queers in leadership.

Next steps are complicated. First, all of the theologies that have been thought about as singular must now be understood as plural. Feminist theologies, queer theologies, and so forth make for a variegated and complex reality. Second, many competing claims, both other religious traditions and other social justice concerns beginning with poverty and war, shape the theo-ethical agenda. How feminist and queer concerns will fare in such an intellectually, morally, and spiritually "competitive" world remains to be seen.

Third, while feminists show many signs of queering their work, it is not clear that queers are engaging in an equally feminist approach to theirs. A good example of this is an ecofeminism that has not been complemented by a green movement that attends to feminist concerns. Fourth, the backlash against both feminist and queer religious efforts is fierce and growing as the religious right realizes the power of each, not to mention the power of the two taken together. The struggles will not get easier but they can be engaged in as a wider feminist queer movement.

This work is built on a firm foundation because lesbian feminist pioneers in religion spared no energy or courage to create it. With the same spirit and determination, contemporary colleagues can deepen and expand it.

Notes

1. See for example, Elizabeth Cady Stanton and the Revising Committee, *The Woman's Bible* (New York: European Publishing Company, 1895); see also Matilda Joslyn Gage, *Women, Church and State* (New York: The Truth Seeker Company, 1893).
2. "Dr. Anna H. Shaw, Suffragist, Dies," Obituary, July 3, 1919, *New York Times*, http://www.nytimes.com/learning/general/onthisday/bday/0214.html (accessed January 4, 2011).
3. Valerie Saiving, "The Human Situation: A Feminine View," *Journal of Religion* (April 1960).
4. Rosemary Skinner Keller wrote the definitive biography of Georgia Harkness. Rosemary Skinner Keller, *Georgia Harkness: For Such a Time as This* (Nashville: Abingdon, 1992).
5. Rebekah Miles, ed., *Georgia Harkness: The Remaking of a Liberal Theologian* (Louisville: Westminster John Knox Press, 1997).
6. Rebekah Miles points this out in a footnote. See ibid., 17. The reference is to Harkness's *The Modern Revival of Christian Faith: An Analysis of Secularism* (New York: Abingdon, 1952), 5.
7. Nelle Morton, *The Journey Is Home* (Boston: Beacon Press, 1985).
8. Mary Daly, *Beyond God the Father: Toward a Philosophy of Women's Liberation* (Boston: Beacon Press, 1973), 19.
9. Mary Daly, *Webster's First New Intergalactic Wickedary of the English Language* (Boston: Beacon Press, 1987), 78. Written "in cahoots with Jane Caputi."
10. See Roundtable on "Same-Sex Marriage and Relational Justice," *Journal of Feminist Studies in Religion* 20:2 (Fall 2004). See especially Martha Ackelsberg and Judith Plaskow's contribution, as well as Mary E. Hunt's lead piece.
11. Sally Miller Gearhart, "The Lesbian and God-the-Father Or All the Church Needs Is A Good Lay—On Its Side," 1973, http://www.lgbtran.org/Exhibits/Sampler/View.aspx?ID=LAG&Page=1. It was later published in *Loving Women/Loving Men: Gay Liberation and the Church*, ed. Sally Miller Gearhart and William R. Johnson (San Francisco: Glide Publications, 1974), 119–52.
12. Ibid., 1.
13. Ibid., 2.
14. See Sally Miller Gearhart's profile in the Lesbian, Gay, Bisexual, Transgender Religious Archives Network, http://www.lgbtran.org/Profile.aspx?ID=29 (accessed January 5, 2011).
15. Sally Gearhart, *The Wanderground* (Watertown, MA: Persephone Press, 1978). This is her best-known work.

16. Joan L. Clark, "Coming Out: The Process and Its Price," *Christianity and Crisis* 39 (June 1979): 149–53.

17. See Christian Lesbians Out Together (CLOUT) History, http://www.cloutsisters .org/about_us/clout_herstory/ (accessed January 5, 2011).

18. Beverly Wildung Harrison, *Our Right to Choose: Toward a New Ethics of Abortion* (Boston: Beacon Press, 1983).

19. Beverly Harrison, *Justice in the Making: Feminist Social Ethics*, ed. Elizabeth M. Bounds, Pamela K. Brubaker, Jane E. Hicks, Marilyn J. Legge, Rebecca Todd Peters, and Traci C. West (Louisville: Westminster John Knox Press, 2004).

20. Letty M. Russell, *Church in the Round: Feminist Interpretation of the Church* (Louisville: Westminster John Knox Press, 1993), and *Human Liberation in a Feminist Perspective: A Theology* (Philadelphia: Westminster Press, 1974).

21. Carter Heyward, *The Redemption of God: A Theology of Mutual Relation* (Lanham, MD: University Press of America, 1982), and *Our Passion for Justice: Images of Power, Sexuality, and Liberation* (Cleveland: The Pilgrim Press, 1984).

22. Beverly Wildung Harrison and Carter Heyward, "Pain and Pleasure: Avoiding the Confusions of Christian Tradition in Feminist Theory," in *Sexuality and the Sacred: Sources for Theological Reflection*, ed. James B. Nelson and Sandra P. Longfellow (Louisville: Westminster John Knox Press, 1994).

23. Bernadette J. Brooten, *Love Between Women: Early Christian Responses to Female Homoeroticism* (Chicago: University of Chicago Press, 1996).

24. Mary E. Hunt, *Fierce Tenderness: A Feminist Theology of Friendship* (New York: Crossroad, 1990).

25. Mary E. Hunt, "Eradicating the Sin of Heterosexism," in *Heterosexism in Contemporary World Religion: Problem and Prospect*, ed. Marvin M. Ellison and Judith Plaskow (Cleveland: The Pilgrim Press, 2007), 155–76.

26. Emilie Townes on "Embodiment," http://www.rsnonline.org/index.php?option =com_content&view=article&id=80&Itemid=138 (accessed January 6, 2011).

27. For a full listing of her articles, see http://www.irenemonroe.com/home/ (accessed January 6, 2011).

28. Virginia Ramey Mollenkott, *Women, Men, and the Bible* (Nashville: Abingdon Press, 1977 [revised 1988]), *The Divine Feminine: The Biblical Imagery of God as Female* (New York: Crossroad, 1983), and *Godding: Human Responsibility and the Bible* (New York: Crossroad, 1987).

29. Virginia Ramey Mollenkott and Letha Scanzoni, *Is the Homosexual My Neighbor? Another Christian View* (San Francisco: Harper and Row, 1978).

30. Virginia Ramey Mollenkott, *Sensuous Spirituality: Out from Fundamentalism* (New York: Crossroad, 1992).

31. Virginia Ramey Mollenkott, *Omni-gender: A Trans Religious Approach* (Cleveland: The Pilgrim Press, 2001).

32. Christine Gudorf, "The Erosion of Sexual Dimorphism: Challenge to Religions and Religious Ethics," *Journal of the American Academy of Religion* 69:4 (Fall 2001): 863–91.

Chapter 4

Listening to the Passion of Catholic *nu-tongzhi*

Developing a Catholic Lesbian Feminist Theology in Hong Kong[1]

Lai-shan Yip

Since the decolonization of Hong Kong in the 1980s, Hong Kong residents have been worrying about their freedom and basic human rights, democracy, and the rule of law after the handover of Hong Kong to China on July 1, 1997. Despite its efforts to address these concerns, the government passed antidiscrimination legislation in 1996 to cover only areas of sex, disability, and family responsibility.[2] In the 1980s, when the Hong Kong government initiated the decriminalization of male-male private sex between consenting adults, the Hong Kong Catholic Church supported such a position. The Church, together with other Christian organizations, also advocated for the inclusion of sexual orientation under the antidiscrimination legislation and to extend the coverage to harassment and harmful speech.[3]

However, some local Catholic groups have reservations about the antidiscrimination legislation regarding sexual orientation after a group disrupted a Sunday Mass at the Cathedral on August 17, 2003, to protest the 2003 Vatican document rejecting the legal status of same-sex unions and against the Hong Kong Catholic Church, whose weekly herald, *Kung Kao Pao*, published in its headline the Vatican document.[4] Despite its appropriation of the justice tradition in its antidiscrimination efforts and commitment toward human rights and democracy, the Hong Kong Catholic Church has been unaware of the impact of its heterosexist teachings on its own flock, that is, condemnation of homosexual acts and treating homosexual orientation as intrinsically disordered, though claiming to "accept the sinner."[5] Ultimately, the justice tradition is not meant for Catholic *tongzhi* in claiming their own dignity and empowerment within the Church.[6] To date, there is no Catholic *tongzhi* group formed within the Church.[7]

In this context, the Hong Kong Catholic *tongzhi* need to develop their own theology based on their experience and cultural context in order to counter the heterosexist Church teachings and claim their own empowerment and spirituality. While local Catholic theology has rarely dealt with the issue of *tongzhi*, Asian Catholic feminist theologian Sharon A. Bong has started to take up such a challenge by reflecting on the life experiences of LGBT people in Malaysia and Singapore from religiously, culturally, and ethnically diverse backgrounds. The topic is a huge taboo that their spirituality concerns myriad understandings of peace in their coming out experience.[8] Although this topic has not received the same kind of sensitivity in Hong Kong, Bong's approach in theologizing, in which the bodily experiences of LGBTQ people are treated as "an epistemology of sacred body," is also shared by a local Protestant feminist theologian, Rose Wu.[9] Being a local feminist and gay-rights activist, Wu is the only one who has produced a theological work based on her ministry with local Protestant *tongzhi*.[10] She also finds theological materials from local Protestant circles as well, where she draws largely on the experiences of North American churches and their LGBTQ theologies.[11]

I agree with Wu that most Asian Christians have adopted the traditional interpretations and the heterosexist teachings from the Western Church in understanding the issue of homosexuality, especially under the colonial influence of the past and, now, the neo-colonialism influence of present-day globalization. Hence, we can and need to draw on both Western and Eastern experiences for theological reflections as the differences are all shared within the same global ecumenical community.

In this essay, I propose a Catholic lesbian feminist theology in light of more local feminist theological resources for such a theological project. Moreover, as noted by Mary Hunt, the institutional Catholic Church has been shaped by "kyriarchy," an interlocking system of various oppressive lordship structures, so that eradicating heterosexism is an effort running in parallel to and in concerted effort with other liberation movements.[12] North American feminist and lesbian feminist theologies have been able to extend their reach beyond concern for gay rights in addressing the complex system of overlapping and interlocking oppressions, which is also critical for engaging the whole Hong Kong Catholic Church in such an initiative. Here I only touch on particularly relevant North American feminist and lesbian feminist theologies for addressing the experiences of local Catholic *nu-tongzhi* (female *tongzhi*) and with Wu's work and Bong's work. Then, from this dialogue, I offer my proposal for a local Catholic lesbian feminist theology.[13]

Experience of Catholic *nu-tongzhi* in Hong Kong

The relevance of the insights from North American feminist and lesbian feminist theologies for Hong Kong depends on the contextual experiences of the Catholic *nu-tongzhi*. There is no research primarily on the attitude of the Hong Kong Catholic Church toward *nu-tongzhi*. My own research has surfaced only a few stories of Catholic *nu-tongzhi*: a short interview of a *nu-tongzhi*, Bik-kei;[14] two stories of a *nu-tongzhi*, Stargazer (nickname);[15] and a father having a *nu-tongzhi* daughter[16] in two separate issues of a *tongzhi* association newsletter. I have also found a local female oral history project in which there is Catholic *nu-tongzhi*, Ho-lok, a twenty-seven-year-old teacher in a Catholic high school.[17] Acknowledging the limitation of the scarcity of information on Catholic *nu-tongzhi*, I attempt to construct a generalized picture from these few pieces.

The above three Catholic *nu-tongzhi* do not find that the Catholic faith contradicts their own sexual orientation. They also show a queer expression of Catholic faith. I use the term "queer" here to mean that there is no normative expression of their faith. While distancing herself from parish life, Bik-kei involves herself in queer advocacy in university campus life and cultivates her faith with feminist theologies. Stargazer has a strong affiliation with a parish group. Ho-lok has had a supportive Catholic *nu-tongzhi* circle since her college years. All three of them seem to be quite educated in that they are able to articulate arguments against heterosexist Church teachings. Yet, only Bik-kei seems to be involved in some forms of activism due to her formation in feminism. During the early development of the *tongzhi* movement in the 1980s, the *nu-tongzhi* groups have tended to identify with the gay-male-dominated movement, instead of the feminist movement. The feminist movement at that time did not address the issue of sexual identities. After the establishment of Queer Sisters in 1995, the *nu-tongzhi* have started to address the double marginalization and shape a more inclusive movement.[18] Since 2000, two major queer women's and *nu-tongzhi* groups—F-Union, formed in 2001, and Women Coalition, founded in 2003—exhibit a strong feminist consciousness and political participation.[19] This may show that *nu-tongzhi* groups have broadened the local feminist movement whereas feminist consciousness has shaped *nu-tongzhi*'s political consciousness. While acknowledging the different sociopolitical context of the North American feminist and lesbian feminist movements, I think both the local *nu-tongzhi* and feminist movements and the ones in North America move in a similar direction, toward a more inclusive vision and political agenda, and that North American feminist and lesbian feminist theologies will provide helpful insights for the articulation of a local Catholic *nu-tongzhi* theology.

While Catholic *nu-tongzhi* share similar difficulties in coming out, their stories show that acceptance of *nu-tongzhi* in the Church simply cannot be taken for granted, despite the official teachings on love and friendship for homosexuals. Bik-kei stays away from parish life. Stargazer chooses to come out only to close friends from childhood in her parish group, but has to tackle a serious challenge to her identity from a friend in this group; only through her own study and more current information on sexual orientation can she address that challenge successfully. She gradually gains more acceptance from these friends, one of whom later comes out to her privately. Ho-lok has to hide her sexual orientation and her opposition to official Church teachings on homosexuality in school. She also avoids any intimate behavior with her partner in busy city districts lest her colleagues and students discover her same-sex love. She has been harassed by some colleagues due to her boyish appearance. Yet, during her college years, she associated with other Catholic *nu-tongzhi* in the Catholic Society without being stigmatized. Her Catholic father has also used all means to stop his daughter's same-sex love. Like all other *tongzhi* who cannot come out to their own families and have to find other living spaces for their partnership, Ho-lok and her partner maintain a half-cohabitation, in which they rent a room and only live there on weekends. In that sense, living a *nu-tongzhi* partnership relies on class privilege as only the middle- and upper-class people can afford to rent such an apartment.

Since local Catholic *nu-tongzhi* also face heterosexism from the Church and society as their North American sisters do, they will benefit from the insights from North American feminist and lesbian feminist theologies. Yet, Catholic *nu-tongzhi* may face stricter sexual codes and less tolerance due to a mutual malformation of Catholicism and Confucianism. In the examples noted here, these women do not struggle much with official Church teachings on homosexuality. I find that this kind of flexibility regarding ethical requirements reflects the non-absolutization of the Chinese yin-yang cosmology. Catholicism tends to equate moral wisdom as an absolute and lacks such flexibility; moral teachings become absolutized. Moreover, the diverse sexual expression in Chinese history, together with cultural wisdom, support diverse sexual expressions and various forms of committed love and caring relationships, which should not be regarded as Western cultural products only.[20] Furthermore, as a founder of Queer Sisters suggested, coming out as political activists, instead of *nu-tongzhi*, can be a local strategy of resistance and survival that can avoid adopting a universal LGBTQ movement and thus broaden the pursuit of justice.[21] I also find that this helps to strengthen the awareness of the interlocking character of various oppressions and a holistic struggle for the human rights of all. The experience of Catholic *nu-tongzhi* echo with what Sharon Bong identifies in the life experiences of LGBT people in Malaysia and Singapore in the sense that they reconcile the binary between their religious identity and their sexuality imposed by their respective religious traditions.[22]

To summarize this general picture, educational background, income, and class status are key factors for Catholic *nu-tongzhi* to claim their identity and pursue their partnerships. Knowledge in feminism, queer theory, and feminist theologies also facilitates their political participation to combat sexual and gender oppressions as well as working toward a more holistic struggle for human rights. In addition to North American feminist and lesbian feminist theologies, cultural wisdom concerning non-absolutization for ethical issues and a tolerance of diverse sexual expressions offer additional and important dimensions for articulating local Catholic *nu-tongzhi* theology.

North American Feminist and Lesbian Feminist Theologies

North American feminist and lesbian feminist theologies offer helpful dialogue partners for the experiences of local Catholic *nu-tongzhi*. The contributions of feminist theologies in the 1970s have precipitated in later lesbian feminist theologies. These feminist theologies from Mary Daly, Rosemary Radford Ruether, Elisabeth Schüssler Fiorenza, and others have started to examine the interactions of sex, class, and race in both theological and societal realms. During the LGBT liberation movement of the late 1960s and the early 1970s, gay theological and pastoral work focused primarily on gay male experiences, which concerned individual identity and coming out in the public arena. Sally Miller Gearhart, however, from her lesbian experience identifying with women, highlighted the political implications of LGBT issues and the patriarchal evils of Christianity, thus rejecting individualistic discourses.[23] During the 1980s, feminist theologians reclaimed the feminist erotic for theologically countering the masculine, phallocentric, and individualistic discourses on sexuality and continued the feminist critique of structural oppressions, countering the privatizing of sexual discourses.[24] Carter Heyward, an Episcopal priest and theologian, and Mary Hunt, a Catholic lay theologian, both integrated feminist consciousness with lesbian experience in their theologies. The former developed a theology of power in right relation whereas the latter developed a theology of friendship.[25] Both works represent lesbian feminist theologies that counter heterosexist theological discourses as they offered new relational discourses linking the personal with the political. A brief review of their work, along with other key figures, will set the stage for a more contextual theology in Hong Kong.

From the Erotic to Passion of the Heart

While basing her work on Audre Lorde's reclamation of the erotic as a deep bodily knowledge, the deepest passion, and a yearning for joy and self-fulfillment, Heyward highlights the erotic as power in relation and identifies this erotic power with God. God will become our relational power when we let the Spirit dwell in "the quality of our lives in relation, the authenticity of our mutuality and the strength of our relational matrix."[26] We are called to live in right relation with others in mutuality. While equality means the same status of two parties, mutuality is different in the way that it calls people of unequal relations into a vision of justice, relational growth, and working together for a liberative future.[27] "Our erotic power is sacred power because it is transcendent."[28]

In view of the heterosexism embedded in Western culture and Christian theology, Heyward finds that we are always exposed and shaped by alienating power and the "power-over" structures and that we live in the tension between erotic power and alienating power. Using the Marxist critique of global capitalism, she also argues that we are not valued as nonmonetary human beings and thus lose our capacity to love ourselves and our bodies, and others. Eventually, we lose ourselves as a people, surrendering to alienation. Erotic power helps us to sense and challenge the alienating power.[29] The divine as erotic power implies sex-affirming, body-affirming, and relation-focused ethics in which non-abusive sexual pleasure is a moral good and friendship is the basis for sharing goodness.[30] Friendship requires faithfulness that one needs to be real, honest, open, and present, to seek the welfare of the other. This faithfulness opens us to the transformation of the erotic. The courage to love under the power of the divine erotic helps to overcome self-bound satisfaction and opens us to various commitment levels in sexual friendships. The right relation in all these relationships will exhibit courage, compassion, anger, forgiveness, touching, healing, and faith.[31]

I find that Heyward's emphasis on mutuality and the sex-affirming, body-affirming, and relational ethics of sex and her Marxist critique of alienation created by capitalism helpful in countering the compulsory heterosexuality and the commodification of women's bodies and sexualities. However, as pointed out by Elizabeth Stuart, the possible danger in identifying the erotic power with the divine lies in the false identification of the divine with our own feelings and in using the language of mutuality and faithfulness to justify our will-to-power in relationships. This seems evident in Heyward's refusal to accept the professional boundaries in a therapeutic relationship as her therapist rejected friendship with her after therapy. Heyward felt erotic power between her and her therapist and regarded the rejection as abusive.[32] Saying "yes" to our erotic power should not become a means of controlling others' response to that power; this will mean learning openness and vulnerability.

To avoid the danger of reducing sex to privatized and individualized experience based on pleasure and satisfaction and of reducing the power of the erotic to individual sexual experience, Linda Woodhead points to authentic erotic power as generative and transformative power in a wider relational matrix.[33] Mary Hunt also advocates the inclusion of justice in sexual ethics to address injustices caused by private pleasure.[34]

While white feminist theologians have reclaimed the feminist erotic in theological discourses, Kwok Pui-lan has warned of the difficulty for Asian women to talk about sex and the erotic because of the heavy yoke of compulsory heterosexuality—decent women are not allowed to do so in public and a lot of Asian women work as prostitutes.[35] Rosemary Hennessy points out that in the capitalist production of new desiring subjects, the claiming of sexual desire relies heavily on class and economic status.[36] Hortense Spillers also points to class privilege in the claiming of female sexual agency as something most women still cannot enjoy.[37] In that light, I would argue for a sustained critical analysis of different classes of women, *nu-tongzhi*, and Catholic *nu-tongzhi*, and to make this a priority in our theological articulation and political agenda. I would also propose replacing the term "erotic" with "passion" to overcome the simplistic identification of the feminist erotic desire with sex and to remind us of the tragic side of attempts to love under structural sin.[38] I find the language of passion is more suitable, especially when passion in Chinese culture is applied to all relations, including the cosmic. Rita Nakashima Brock has articulated the erotic in the metaphor of the heart that may address the difficulty of talking about the erotic among Asian women.

In *Journeys by Heart*, Brock uses the metaphor of the heart for the self and the capacity for intimacy and how heart knowledge functions for the union of body, spirit, reason, and passion.[39] The power of our primal interrelatedness is the erotic power, the incarnation of divine love. Divine erotic power is the life-giving power of the universe leading us to a greater sense of the whole of life as sacred and of love in its fullness.[40] Brock finds that Jesus participates centrally in the Christa/Community for the co-creation of erotic power. The image of Christa refers to the female Christ and expands the identification of Christ from Jesus to the members of Jesus' community. The fullness of humanity is the presence of erotic power in each individual-in-community. The whole Christa/Community embodies the God/dess and has a transformative impact on Jesus as well. That Jesus is capable of profound love and concern for others implies his being loved by others in his life. Jesus' vision of the community of Goddess grows to include marginal people in encounters with their "real presence." They co-create liberation and healing of heartbroken-ness. Relationships create the possibility of a new vision, for in the power of real presence, erotic power works.[41]

Brock also points out that Jesus' acts in the passion narrative are politi-cal acts for a choice of life for himself and the people he loved by challeng-ing oppressive powers. While Jesus' death is a tragedy caused by patriarchal evils, it is the call to risk a commitment as a caring community, to the promise of the community of God/dess, which is domination-free. The resurrection comes through the witnesses who refuse defeat by death or oppressive powers and whose vision leads them to explore the new territories of erotic power. Filled with the grace of the Spirit, the community of God/dess generates life through living persons. The resurrection affirms that no one person alone can overcome brokenness, but needs the community of heart, or erotic power.[42]

Brock's metaphor of the heart and the language of connectedness and heartbrokenness stretch the focus of the erotic from its sexual aspect to all the passions in life. This metaphor is easier for Asian women when discussing the erotic. Moreover, Brock's image of individual-in-community allows different ways of participation in the community of erotic power and can help to rec-tify the heroism solely resting on the Jesus figure. Brock does not romanticize the community of erotic power and addresses the heartbrokenness or tragedy under political tyranny, the risk in the struggle for justice, and the challenge of the dangerous memory of domination and violence. While Brock's concept of erotic power does not directly address economic issues, it does give the basis and momentum for transformation in economic and political life.

Contextualizing Friendship toward "Erotic Celibacy"

While the Church and modern society have devalued friendship, Mary Hunt finds in friendship the love and justice of many possible relational matrices—including friendly connections with animals and the Earth—to counter heterosexism and patriarchal dualism. Treating friendship as the relational norm, she points to the constitutive qualities of right relation, namely, love, power, embodiment, and spirituality. Love is the attitude that creates and sustains connections with others and the world. Power has to be kept in bal-ance in friendship for its continual development, as friends need to be able to make choices for themselves and their significant others and with the commu-nity. The commitment of friends in equalizing power includes the struggles against systemic oppression and the empowerment of individuals. Relation is a sexual expression involving the interaction of bodies. When it is consenting, caring, and conducive to the well-being of the parties involved, it generates love between them and beyond them. Spirituality is the choice-making for the quality of life of the individual and the community. Friendship as a relational norm is helpful in the way that it is available to all, but can also be built from pre-existing relationships. Yet, Hunt points to the limitations of her model, as it has not dealt with the mysterious part of friendship, its relevance to male experiences, and its practicability.[43]

Hunt also emphasizes the need to sacramentalize friendship through public expression of celebrating its formation and commemorating its loss. People are called to be "justice-seeking friends" for liberative struggles and communal survival.[44] God is a divine friend, a personable yet nonintrusive image, expressed in both singular and plural forms. The generativity, attention, and community in women's friendships produce justice, which reveals the divine nature.[45]

Much like passion, I find the language of friendship is much easier for Asian women to understand and use. However, as Elizabeth Stuart has cautioned, such a process of seeing God as friend has a similar problem to Heyward's erotic power as God in that the identification of God with human action and agency will dismiss the divine element. Stuart also finds that only modern Christianity devalues friendship. Another difficulty I find in using friendship as the relational norm is that poor people have become socially and politically excluded when lacking resources for social activities. During the de-colonization in the 1990s, a lot of grassroots organizing projects were terminated by the Hong Kong government. Hence, the class factor continues to be an important concern in local theological reflection. Moreover, as noted by bell hooks, the academy has dominated feminist thinking such that grassroots approaches to feminist sharing is separated from the feminist movement.[46] The local feminist movement has experienced a similar problem. Grassroots community building is thus needed to strengthen both friendship building and the feminist movement.

While Stuart finds that Hunt's work offers little theological reflection, I find that the issue is more about the recognition of using women's experience as a kind of theological language.[47] I do think it is beneficial to have the dialogue with traditional theological and biblical languages in Stuart's theology of "just good friends." She builds on the tradition of the Spirit/Paraclete in the people and the community of Jesus' followers, the wisdom tradition of Sophia, the Trinity as a community of non-hierarchal friendships, and the advance of God's will in sexual subversion in biblical stories about Ruth and Naomi, Tamar, and David and Bathsheba. I find in Stuart's reflection on gay and lesbian relationships two important highlights: the rejection of the hierarchal distinction between *agape* and *eros*; and the understanding of the erotic as power generated between people, instead of an essential nature.[48]

Parallel to this theology of friendship, Hunt also proposes a Catholic lesbian feminist theology based on women's experiences and wisdom on moral agency and bodily integrity, community focus, feminist erotic, justice connections, and feminist relationships. This latter theology includes three dimensions. First, lesbian sexual expression, which is conducive to community, is affirmed. Second, "shared motherhood" is a better expression for same-sex committed relationships than "same-sex marriage" as it produces more social benefits in adopting children. Third, Hunt issues a call to holiness, as the theology of Vatican II encouraged, and the pursuit of justice as practiced in an increasingly pluralistic religious context.[49] These dimensions lay the foundation for the development of Catholic lesbian feminist theology as rooted in both lesbian experiences and the Catholic tradition. Hunt has also advocated for the public recognition of various forms of committed love, to expand the notion of "shared motherhood" to other forms of caring and committed relation.[50] These reflections on friendship and an expanded view of various relationships are enhanced with reflections, rather queerly, on celibacy.

In view of the celibacy campaign advocated by evangelical Protestants in the United States since the 1990s and its distortion of the biblical understanding of purity, Lisa Isherwood finds in the Catholic tradition and history of celibacy and the biblical teachings on family their challenge to heteropatriarchy, in which marriage has been a means for the wealthy to maximize their profits. She also points to the resistance to established societal order in both contemporary and medieval celibate life, in which erotic embrace of the world dissolves heteropatriarchy. Echoing the feminist theology of the erotic, Isherwood finds in the erotic Jesus a life of fully embodied humanity, which is Christic. Celibacy, indeed, is a space for embodying *eros* and moving beyond Otherness and a life of profound vulnerability and intimacy. The celibate Christ formed a countercultural community to transgress heteropatriarchy.[51]

I consider this notion of erotic celibacy an important addition to erotic theology as it widens the understanding of sexual diversity and expression— the embodiment of the erotic without genital activity transgresses sexual obsession and retains autonomy for those who can freely connect to God and all others. Mark Jordan argues, for example, that the highly erotic language in the mystical tradition expresses the intensity of union with God and that prayer experiences can provide insights and a guide for sexual ethics.[52] Isherwood provides a complementary effort in using contemplative life and celibacy to articulate a sexual ethics of erotic connections that challenges heteropatriarchy.

As discussed above, from the North American lesbian feminist theologies, a community of erotic power building, grassroots interconnections, committed and caring relations, and erotic celibacy are important insights for countering the heterosexism in the largely Western Catholic tradition. Yet, contextualized revisions are required to attend to the specific cultural issues or conditions in Hong Kong in terms of the use of language and the class factor.

Wu: A Liberation Theology of Right Relation

In order to draw more insights from local theological work, the theological reflections of Rose Wu, based on her ministry with local Christian *nu-tongzhi*, can serve as a good supplement to the lack of documented information on Catholic *nu-tongzhi*.

Owing to the double marginalization of *nu-tongzhi* in the 1980s and the eventual forming of Queer Sisters, Wu sees the need to address the oppressions of *nu-tongzhi*. In her review of lesbian feminism and queer theory before incorporating them into her theological proposal, she describes how lesbian feminism has identified the entangled relation of sexism and heterosexism and its impact on women's erotic love and relationships. Its political expression also renders a holistic vision of liberation that matches the call for political participation from lesbian activists. She disagrees with the rejection of heterosexual relationships in lesbian separatism as she sees compulsory heterosexuality as the systemic cause for oppression, rather than heterosexual relationships. She also disagrees with lesbian separatism in its claim for representation of all women and its call for all women becoming lesbians in order to be feminists.[53]

Regarding queer theory, Wu finds it helpful in deconstructing the binarism of identity labels and unfolding the plurality and fluidity of identity. She also finds in queer politics the creativity for resistance strategies. However, she notes that erasing identity will risk de-politicalization and loss in the critique of privilege. She calls for the exploration of differences under a critical social analysis so as to build solidarity with the marginalized. She suggests shifting from the politics of identity to the politics of identification.[54] I agree with Wu's evaluation of lesbian feminism and queer theory and find the critical appropriation of lessons learned from them as helpful for local theological reflection.

Wu finds the sole use of *nu-tongzhi* experiences for analysis as insufficient and expands the analysis with feminist notions of liberation. To tackle heterosexism in the Christian tradition, she emphasizes the use of liberation theology. In her theology of Right Relation, she not only draws on Heyward's erotic theology of right relation, but also Leonardo Boff's theology of the Triune God, in which the Trinitarian communion points to the social and integral liberation of both the Church and society. Wu also draws on Elizabeth Johnson's work to reclaim the female imagery of the Divine to counter the masculine and patriarchal understanding of relationships and to recover radical equality and community in diversity, as shown in Johnson's Trinitarian theology. These two Catholic theologians only strengthen the tenets of a Catholic lesbian feminist theology based on the experiences in the North American Catholic Church. The recovery of diversity as a characteristic of Trinitarian theology is important in affirming the diversity of sexual expressions and the variety of human relationships.[55] The queer expression of faith among the Catholic *nu-tongzhi* is supported by a Trinitarian theology of valuing diversity in union.

However, Marcella Althaus-Reid has pointed to the failure of liberation theology in Latin America and the basic ecclesial communities to change the society from the grassroots. She has criticized the unexamined heterosexual ideology in religious symbols and the safe and decent location of these theologians who produce decent theology and ethics, but who are irrelevant to the lives of poor women. She argues for women's gaze—"a penetration by what we call the female phallus into the sexualization of the enterprise confronted it . . . (and) erotic desires"—as a tool to do theology.[56] She also argues for the realization of women's sexual storytelling as the agency in sociopolitical changes.[57] I agree with Althaus-Reid's critique of liberation theology and the importance of women's sexual storytelling in sociopolitical transformation. While I find her use of sexual and fetish language to articulate a sexual theology in *Indecent Theology* as liberating our theological imagination, such language presents the same kind of difficulty posed by the language of the erotic. In traditional Chinese society, same-sex activities were understood in socially different ways and often non-sexually. For example, there were homosocial roles such as *xiang gong* (male prostitute), *duan xiu* (cut sleeve), and *fen tao* (shared peach), and homosocial relations such as *jinlan zimei* (golden orchid sisters), *qidi* and *qixiong* (adopted brothers), and *hanlu yingxiong* (stranded heroes). Terms for sexual acts were poetic without any condemnation, such as *mou dou fu* (grinding bean curd), *hou ting hwa* (the backyard flower), *dui si* (paired eating), and *chui xiao* (playing a vertical flute).[58] I would argue for a sexual theology rooted in this rich, local, and contextual language in the storytelling of *nu-tongzhi*.

To reunite sexuality and spirituality, Wu includes an incarnational theology that sees God's incarnation in a relational manner, countering the hierarchal dualism in theological and philosophical discourses and the divine impassivity in human life. She also includes the integration of spirit and body as one totality of human experience. Moreover, in order to counter homophobia, she proposes a sexual theology that connects sexual relations with justice making and tackles the interlocking system of oppressions. This part of Wu's theological proposal echoes Catholic lesbian feminist theology as well.[59] Although we do not see in these Catholic *nu-tongzhi* the linking of sexuality with spirituality, Asian women's spirituality, which does not operate from a distinction between the sacred and the profane, may indicate the absence of duality between sexuality and spirituality.[60] The Catholic *nu-tongzhi* have not shown any problem in integrating their faith with sexuality, which may indicate that Wu's work is compatible with their understanding of the Catholic faith.

Wu then proposes four "re-imagings" in articulating a prophetic vision of a liberating and inclusive Christian community for the Hong Kong Blessed Minority Christian Fellowship (HKBMCF). First, the HKBMCF needs to develop from a people in exile to an exodus community, which witnesses with an alternative culture, rather than a refuge, and engages in collective political participation. Second, a hermeneutics of dangerous memories is practiced to re-examine Christian traditions and look for resistance and liberation. Third, a ministry of equal discipleship is practiced to break from the kyriarchal model of leadership. Fourth, celebrating the Eucharist at a table of hospitality and solidarity is to build communion across boundaries.[61]

Although there is no formal *tongzhi* group or ministry at the Hong Kong Catholic Church at this moment, I find this vision of a liberating and inclusive Christian community as a good guideline if Catholic *tongzhi* organize among themselves. Indeed, I do not think it is helpful to form *tongzhi* groups under the hierarchal Church. Creating a new space for practicing a new vision of church is more possible outside the hierarchy. Thus I would draw from Brock the image of Christa/Community witnessing to the resurrection and spreading the faith of resurrection and add this as the fifth "re-imaging."

A Local Catholic Feminist Theology

Owing to the political context of Hong Kong, I believe Catholic *nu-tongzhi* need to come out as political activists. I also believe—even though *nu-tongzhi* need to create a new model of Church outside the hierarchy—that the extensive network of women existing beyond hierarchy offers a transgressive challenge and urges transformation to the hierarchy. By incorporating insights from North American lesbian feminist theology as well as from the Asian Catholic feminist theologizing of Sharon Bong and from the local theologizing of Wu, my proposal for a local Catholic feminist theology includes the following tenets.

First, passionate friendship of mutuality and equality is the basis for community building and justice seeking and serves for creating a new Church community of liberation and inclusivity outside the hierarchy. Reaching out to the poor and facilitating their organizing is an important entry point and special efforts for grassroots organizing are needed to counter the social and political exclusion of the poor. Second, sex affirming, body affirming, desiring the well-being of others, and justice doing in sexual relations link sexuality with spirituality with the freedom in erotic celibacy for one's whole making also included in such spirituality. There is no distinction between the profane and the sacred in human life. Third, diverse sexual expression is affirmed as reflecting the Triune God. Continual critical analysis of how the class affects the sexual expressions of various groups is conducted for theological reflection. Cultural resources and wisdom on affirming diverse sexual expression are to be included, drawing on the language used in the sexual storytelling of *nu-tongzhi* in order to identify culturally appropriate language, narrative, and imagery for articulating sexual theology. Fourth, various forms of committed love and caring responsibilities should be recognized. The notion of extended family in Chinese society has included various forms of committed love and caring relationships. This should be recovered and affirmed in combating the domination of the nuclear family as the norm. Fifth, coming out as a political activist is a calling to the pursuit of justice and building solidarity with the marginalized across cultures and faith traditions to combat all forms of oppression, including heterosexism and class oppression of the kyriarchal Church and society. The gay rights struggle is part of a much larger and holistic struggle for human rights.

This proposal is intended only as an offering to spur deeper and more theological reflections. Only when more Catholic *nu-tongzhi* as a community engage in such a theological conversation can we really develop a more mature Catholic lesbian feminist theology.

Notes

1. An earlier and truncated version of this essay appeared in the journal *In God's Image* 29:3 (September 2010). The original version of this essay won the inaugural Marcella Althaus-Reid award at Pacific School of Religion, May 2009.
2. Wahshan Chou, *Tongzhi: Politics of Same-Sex Eroticism in Chinese Societies* (New York: Haworth Press, 2000), 78, 272–74; Kwok-wah Shaw, "The Meaning of Legislation on Discrimination against Sexual Orientation for Hong Kong," in *Xing Zheng Zhi*, ed. Ching Yau (Xianggang: Tian di tu shu you xian gong si, 2006).

3. A statement on antidiscrimination legislation was submitted to the Hong Kong government jointly by the Justice and Peace Commission of the Hong Kong Catholic Diocese, the Hong Kong Christian Council, the Hong Kong Women Christian Council, and the Hong Kong Student Christian Movement in March 1996.

4. Union of Catholic Asian News, *Cathedral Denies Gay Activists Entry during Sunday Mass after Previous Disruption*, HK4618.1251 (2003, accessed August 25, 2003); available from http://www.ucanews.com/2003/08/25/cathedral-denies-gay-activists-entry-during-sunday-mass-after-previous-disruption/.

5. See Mary E. Hunt, "Eradicating the Sin of Heterosexism," in *Heterosexism in Contemporary World Religion: Problem and Prospect*, ed. Marvin Mahan Ellison and Judith Plaskow (Cleveland: Cleveland Press, 2007).

6. *Tongzhi* is the English pronunciation of a Chinese term for LGBTQ people, originally translated from the communist Soviet term "comrade"—a title for the revolutionaries. The term first appeared in the Republic of China in the early twentieth century. In the first Lesbian and Gay Film Festival in Hong Kong in 1989, a local gay activist was the first to appropriate the term for same-sex eroticism. This appropriation soon gained popularity in Hong Kong, Taiwan, and Mainland China as it was regarded as gender-neutral, desexualized, fluid yet relational, transcendent from the homo-hetero binarism, culturally compatible in its integration of the sexual into the social, and free from medical and cultural stigmatization. With the approach of 1997, the adoption of the most respectable title in China by *tongzhi* rendered them the subversiveness of indigenizing sexual politics in the reclamation of their cultural identity; Chou, *Tongzhi* 1–3, 78–84.

7. The Diocese organized three seminars in June 2006 on ministry to homosexuals and announced its plan to start such a specific ministry; Hong Kong Diocesan Audio Visual Center, "Homosexuality: Counselling and Pastoral Care from a Catholic Perspective" (Hong Kong, 2006). At present, no group or ministry is established. I do know that the Blessed Minorities Christian Fellowship from a Protestant tradition and the cell group at Rainbow Hong Kong (a local *tongzhi* association) have a few Catholic members.

8. Sharon A. Bong, "Not 'For the Sake of Peace': Towards an Epistemology of the Sacred Body," *Asian Christian Review* 3:1 (Spring 2009). Bong's first article reflected on the lesbian experiences within the Catholic tradition. It was presented at the Second Biennial Conference of the Ecclesia of Women in Asia held at Yogyakarta, Indonesia, on November 16–19, 2004. Most Asian feminist theologians in the same conference have reflected on the issue of women's sexuality from their specific cultural contexts in their theological articulation, and, at the same time, draw largely on Western feminist theologies as conversation partners; Sharon A. Bong, "Queer Revisions of Christianity," in *Body and Sexuality*, ed. Agnes M. Brazal and Andrea Lizares Si (Quezon City, Philippines: Ateneo de Manila University Press, 2007).

9. Bong, "Queer Revisions," 64–66.

10. Rose Wu worked at the Hong Kong Women Council previously. In 1994, the council and the "Ten Percent" (the first local *tongzhi* group) co-organized the

first *tongzhi* theology course. Some of the lecture materials were published in the council's *Liberation* magazine in issue no. 13 in 1995.

11. Rose Wu, *Liberating the Church from Fear: The Story of Hong Kong's Sexual Minorities* (Hong Kong: Hong Kong Women Christian Council, 2000), 64–65. In view of the negativity toward sexuality, in particular women's sexuality, and the dichotomy between sexuality and spirituality, Asian Women's Resource Center for Culture and Theology, based in Malaysia, also conducted a workshop on sexuality in July 2001 and published workshop papers in its journal, *In God's Image* 20:3 (September 2001). The title of this issue was "Sexuality and Spirituality." Most papers analyzed the systemic factors that affect women's sexuality and some also dealt with LGBTQ issues. It has been a good start for theologizing the issue of sexuality in the multi-cultural and multi-faith Asian context, but still needs deeper and more elaborate theological reflections.

12. Mary E. Hunt, "The Heart of the Matter: A Feminist Perspective, Part 2: A New Framework," *Catholic New Times* (December 15, 2002).

13. I have to note that my proposal indeed incorporates an ecumenical dimension, drawing from both Catholic and Protestant theologians. It is Catholic only in the sense that I draw on more resources from the Catholic tradition to dialogue with Wu's work.

14. Wing Huen Lee, *Sexual Orientation Forum* (February 6, 2006); available from http://lesgay.info/viewtopic.php?t=356 (accessed June 9, 2008).

15. Stargazer, "Come Out Guerilla," *Lesbo* (June 15, 2005).

16. Father of Star, "My Daughter Is a Homosexual," *Lesbo* (April 15, 2005).

17. Siu-kwui and Wai-wai Law, "The Same-Sex Love of a Religion and Ethics Teacher: Ho-Lok," in *I Love Women: Oral History of Hong Kong Women Who Love Women*, ed. Siu-yin et al. (Hong Kong: FLY Media Limited, 2008).

18. Wu, *Liberating the Church*, 32–33.

19. Women Coalition website, http://www.wchk.org/index_news.html; F-Union website, http://hk.geocities.com/funionhk/.

20. Chou, *Tongzhi*, 20–41.

21. Wu, *Liberating the Church*, 20–21.

22. Bong, "'Not' For the Sake of Peace."

23. Mary E. Hunt, "Lesbian and Bisexual Issues in Religion," in *The Encyclopedia of Women and Religion in North America*, ed. Rosemary Skinner Keller, Rosemary Radford Ruether, and Marie Cantlon (Bloomington: Indiana University Press, 2006), 1215–16; Elizabeth Stuart, *Gay and Lesbian Theologies:: Repetitions with Critical Difference* (Burlington, VT: Ashgate, 2003), 15–31.

24. Alexander C. Irwin, *Eros toward the World: Paul Tillich and the Theology of the Erotic* (Minneapolis: Fortress Press, 1991), 123–33.

25. Hunt, "Lesbian and Bisexual Issues in Religion," 1216–17; Stuart, *Gay and Lesbian Theologies*, 51–63.

26. Carter Heyward, *Touching Our Strength: The Erotic as Power and the Love of God* (San Francisco: Harper & Row, 1989), 24.

27. Ibid., 34.

28. Ibid., 103.

29. Ibid., 48–60.

30. Ibid., 129.

31. Ibid., 136–55.

32. Stuart, *Gay and Lesbian Theologies*, 54.

33. Lisa Isherwood and Elizabeth Stuart, "Queering the Body," in *Introducing Body Theology*, Introductions in Feminist Theology (Sheffield: Sheffield Academic Press, 1998), 107–9.

34. Mary E. Hunt, "Just Good Sex: Feminist Catholicism and Human Rights," in *Good Sex: Feminist Perspectives from the World's Religions*, ed. Patricia Beattie Jung, Mary E. Hunt, and Radhika Balakrishnan (New Brunswick, NJ: Rutgers University Press, 2001).

35. Pui-lan Kwok, "The Future of Feminist Theology: An Asian Perspective," in *Feminist Theology from the Third World: A Reader*, ed. Ursula King (Maryknoll, NY: Orbis Books, 1994; reprint, 1996), 72–74.

36. Rosemary Hennessy, *Profit and Pleasure: Sexual Identities in Late Capitalism* (New York: Routledge, 2000), 201–2.

37. Hortense Spillers, "Stuart Hall, Cultural Studies, and Marxism," in *Changing Our Own Words: Essays on Criticism, Theory, and Writing by Black Women*, ed. Cheryl A. Wall (New Brunswick, NJ: Rutgers University Press, 1989), 94.

38. Elizabeth Stuart and Adrian Thatcher, "Desire," in *People of Passion: What the Churches Teach About Sex* (London and Herndon, VA: Mowbray, 1997), 212.

39. Rita Nakashima Brock, *Journeys by Heart: A Christology of Erotic Power* (New York: Crossroad, 1988), xiv.

40. Ibid., 26, 46–48, 67.

41. Ibid., 63–67.

42. Ibid., 93–103.

43. Mary E. Hunt, *Fierce Tenderness: A Feminist Theology of Friendship* (New York: Crossroad, 1994), 14, 100–106, 113–14.

44. Ibid., 115–64.

45. Ibid., 165–76.

46. bell hooks, "Feminism: A Transformational Politic," in *Feminist Theory: A Reader*, ed. Wendy K. Kolmar and Frances Bartkowski (Boston: McGraw-Hill Higher Education, 2005), 467–68.

47. Stuart, *Gay and Lesbian Theologies*, 58.

48. Ibid., 58–61.

49. Mary E. Hunt, "Catholic Lesbian Feminist Theology," in *Sexual Diversity and Catholicism: Toward the Development of Moral Theology*, ed. Patricia Beattie Jung and Joseph A. Coray (Collegeville, MN: Liturgical Press, 2001).

50. Mary E. Hunt, "Committed Love and Relational Justice," *Concilium* 1 (2008).

51. Lisa Isherwood, *The Power of Erotic Celibacy: Queering Heteropatriarchy*, Queering Theology Series (London and New York: T & T Clark, 2006).

52. Mark D. Jordan, *The Ethics of Sex* (Oxford and Malden, MA: Blackwell Publishers, 2002), 163–72.
53. Wu, *Liberating the Church*, 51–52.
54. Ibid., 52–55.
55. Ibid., 78–83.
56. Marcella Althaus-Reid, *Indecent Theology: Theological Perversions in Sex, Gender and Politics* (London and New York: Routledge, 2000), 38.
57. Marcella Althaus-Reid, *From Feminist Theology to Indecent Theology: Readings on Poverty, Sexual Identity and God* (London: SCM Press, 2004), 92–93.
58. Chou, *Tongzhi*, 22–24.
59. Wu, *Liberating the Church*, 84–88.
60. Agnes M. Brazal and Andrea Lizares Si, eds., *Body and Sexuality* (Quezon City, Philippines: Ateneo de Manila University Press, 2007), 194.
61. Wu, *Liberating the Church*, 100–115.

Chapter 5

Man-Boy and Daddy-God

*A Sacred S/M Reading of Ezekiel's
Call to Prophecy*[1]

David Dunn Bauer

The proliferation of queer or at least "queerer" approaches to religion and religious texts since the 1990s has carried gay and lesbian people of faith well
beyond questions of tolerance and acceptance in their own faith communities.
Queer people (whether lesbian, gay, bisexual, transgender, or some other form
of sexual or gender marginalization) are engaged in retrieving vital aspects of
their religious traditions to meet today's circumstances, not only for the sake
of revitalizing those traditions. Moreover, they do this work of retrieval, not
in spite of but precisely *because* of their queerness.

This shift from seeking tolerance and acceptance toward constructive and
original contribution to religious life has emerged quite distinctly in relation
to biblical interpretation. Apologetic arguments concerning familiar biblical
texts that have in the past been used to condemn "homosexuals" have given
way to a much broader engagement with the peculiarities if not the outright
"queerness" of most any passage of scripture. A website devoted to *"Torah
Queeries,"* for example, appeared in published form in 2009.[2] A similar anthology constructed through a queer hermeneutical lens of both Jewish and
Christian testaments appeared in 2006.[3] These are just two examples on a
growing list of publications marking fresh, innovative, disorienting, and more
generally queer engagements with sacred texts. Engaging with text means engaging with the communities shaped and informed by text. Too long, allowing
oneself to be respectfully informed by a religious text necessitated conforming
to a religious norm. Queerness releases readers from such pressure.

If we relax into this queered reality, we find in the Hebrew Bible (as well
as in the Christian Testament) a remarkable range of what many today would

consider "non-normative" relational, sexual, and gendered patterns and practices—both explicit and implicit—operating within human communities but
also between humans and the divine. It's a "queeriable" phenomenon how
often these textual features have been missed—repressed? ignored?—by
most commentators and interpreters. Queerer still, perhaps, is to consider
how these many textual peculiarities, once noted and articulated, carry the
potential to transform and revitalize religious experience today. Once queer
readings are shared openly in religious communities, the focus on who is a
normative and who a non-normative faith practitioner becomes less relevant.
The result, I believe, is not a trivial enhancement of communal faith experience, rather nothing less than a new chance at salvation.

Reconstructionist Judaism—in which I live and work as a rabbi—could
be viewed in its origins as a kind of queer movement within a broader Jewish
world. Reconstructionism was the first major Jewish movement to originate
in North America and has developed in such a way as to include remarkably
diverse approaches to both theological questions and religious practice. While
we share a profound awe for Torah and a general agreement about its human
authorship, there is still a daintiness of approach to its interpretation in many
of our communities. Perhaps the intellectual nature of Reconstructionist
theology, viewing God as the non-supernatural power that makes for salvation, complicates the development of an intensely personal relationship to the
divine. Reconstructionism in general dismisses the concept of the personal
interventionist God, but it welcomes the powerful metaphors and dramatic
dynamics in sacred text as a means of "divining" a path to salvation. I posit
this now, in advance of exploring Ezekiel's call, but I take up this theme again
afterward.

Prophets, of course, and generally speaking, shimmer with a kind of queer
energy just by being prophets. As they call their own people to task or speak
"truth to power" (in today's idiom), prophetic figures often live on the edges
of their own communities or, in some cases, are expelled from the community in which their prophetic work is rooted. Life on the margins is queer.
Yet an additional layer of prophetic queerness should claim our attention and
imagination—the queer ways in which a prophet relates to the One in whose
name the prophecy is offered. This can yield insight and opportunity to faith
practitioners today in their own ongoing negotiations with the Divine and
the Sacred and, indeed, in their struggles with what "divinity" actually means.

In this essay, I probe the rather peculiar story of Ezekiel's call to prophecy,
a close reading of which I wish to offer here as just one marker—and a rather
small one at that—of what I take to be the inherent queerness of religion and
its potential for shaping and reshaping religious practice today. Ezekiel's call to

prophesy exhibits the dynamics of a consensual, contemporary sadomasochistic (S/M) encounter. Were these discerned between two humans in a sacred text, they could of course be dismissed as evidence (by some) of misguided or even "sinful" behavior; but these dynamics appear here in an encounter between a human and God. This, surely, cannot so easily be discounted.

Setting the Stage for a Divine S/M Encounter

Ezekiel's call to prophecy qualifies as "peculiar" for more than one reason, especially in light of the claim made by Abraham Joshua Heschel: "The prophet does not volunteer for his mission; it is forced upon him. He is seduced, he is overwhelmed. There is no choice. Yoked in the knowledge he is compelled to receive, he is also under stress of the necessity to declare it."[4] Heschel implies equivalence across the board among "not volunteering," "being forced," "being seduced," "being overwhelmed," "having no choice," and "being yoked." I contend that these terms themselves cannot be yoked as equals, and that Ezekiel's call and commissioning should be read as the consensual rather than the coerced subjugation of the male prophet to the stronger male God. The disparity in power does not automatically denote human unwillingness to participate, but proves instead to be the source of satisfaction for both parties in a very intimate covenant.

I start by reiterating the undeniable: we cannot know with any certainty what Ezekiel saw, experienced, thought, felt, or meant as he wrote his words. Ultimately we only witness the speeches and interaction of the figures on the page. It would be absurd to impute to Ezekiel any cultural awareness of consensual S/M practice or dynamic as portrayed in contemporary discourse. Nor can any overt, explicitly sexual engagement between him and Him be identified in the text. I would claim, however, that the prophet's encounter with God, as recounted, is erotically fueled. His experience of the Divine in the moment of his call is stronger for his having deliberately acted out the role of Man-Boy to the God-Daddy, ultimate bottom to the Eternal Top.

Ezekiel's famed silence is a significant part of his service. Although in 3:4–7, Ezekiel is charged to speak for God, in 3:25 God is heard to impose silence upon him. But Ezekiel's silence does not begin there; it has been constant since the beginning of the book. Ezekiel sees, hears, and falls upon his face, but never speaks throughout the entirety of his call and commissioning. Contrast strongly both Isaiah and Jeremiah in their initial encounters with God, as the one prophet (Isa. 6:5) protests his unclean lips and the other (Jer. 1:6) his youth as reasons why they are not ready to accept the service being imposed upon them.

David Halperin has written on this issue as well but in a different way. In his book, *Seeking Ezekiel,* and from the chapter entitled, appropriately enough, "Ezekiel's Dumbness," Halperin reviews a range of psychological explanations for the symptom of the prophet's silence:

> Given our approach, we can hardly avoid speaking of the dumbness as a symptom. But we cannot content ourselves with using it as an indicator of one medical condition or another. We must provide some explanation of its meaning for Ezekiel, and of its role within his psychic life. If we can do this successfully, and at the same time solve the long-acknowledged problems of the pertinent biblical texts, we may judge that our method has validated itself.[5]

While focusing on Ezekiel's silence toward the people to whom he was to act as prophet, Halperin seems to ignore Ezekiel's silence and speech in relation to God. I am not prepared to debate the psychological approach Halperin takes, any hermeneutic being potentially as revelatory as any other. I suggest, though, that Halperin's is the most extreme example of a common pathologizing view of Ezekiel—"Something must be wrong with the man!"—that derives from the unease of readers who know how reluctant other prophets were to being called by God. Moses, Jeremiah, Isaiah, and Jonah all initially express unwillingness to take God up on the Divine offer. The irony lies in our doubting the sanity of Ezekiel, the prophet who does *not* resist God's advances.

The first significant line that Halperin ignores is 4:14, where Ezekiel first speaks aloud in the book, protesting God's directive that he eat bread baked over human excrement: "And I said, 'You, YHWH, my Lord, see, my soul/self has never been impure; flesh of the dead and torn I never ate from my youth until this moment, nor has disgusting meat ever entered my mouth.'"

This respectful yet urgent utterance, made after the imposition of dumbness at the end of chapter 3, demonstrates how Ezekiel's silence is ultimately chosen and self-imposed. He retains the power to speak in his own behalf (and possibly as an *'ish mokhiakh,* or "reproving preacher," to his people [3:26]) if he desires. Through his deliberate, chosen silence, though, he cultivates and prolongs the dynamic of intimate and exclusive communication with God as long as possible. Like Sherlock Holmes's "curious incident of the dog in the night-time," we should note carefully what Ezekiel does *not* say at 4:14 or at any other moment; *he does not say "No."* In that chosen tacitness, he sets a boundary of safety for himself and marks the borders of safe play space. In the presence of his mystical Master, he defines the limits wherein he can maintain the fierce dynamic they build collaboratively.

With notable fluency, God accepts Ezekiel's friendly amendment and moves on: "He answered me, 'See, I allow you cow's dung instead of human excrement; prepare your bread on that'" (4:15). A happy symbiosis has been achieved whereby Ezekiel can participate in establishing the rules of play between him and God without undermining or challenging God's authority. In fact, he protects and preserves the relationship and allows it to function uninterrupted. Compare the biblical exchange with the following from psychotherapist and S/M expert, Guy Baldwin:

> This is what accounts for comments like, "Can the music be softer?" "May I move my arm?" "Sir, the light is shining in my eyes and it's hard to see you." "The right restraint isn't as tight as the left one." These sorts of remarks are made in the hopes that the bottom can adjust and perfect the environment of the endorphin pump, so that the scene can go to a "higher level" without distractions which might compete with the Top's stimulations for bottom's attention.[6]

Ezekiel does not ask to be freed from his bonds. He tweaks the terms of his servitude to keep himself from rebelling or rejecting the larger dynamic. He keeps the scene going.

A closer look at 1:26–3:3 offers further texture to this peculiar (queer?) relationship.

Textual Analysis: The Daddy-Boy Relationship

1:26   *dmut k'mareh adam*—**image like the appearance of a man.** Note the similarity here to 1:5—*d'mut arba' chayyot, v'zeh mare'hen, d'mut adam lahennah* [**the image of four beasts and this was their appearance, they had an image of a man**]. In verse 5, the term *adam* is possibly a misread of *achat*. Even were it correct, the essential nature of the creatures is established with *chayyot, v'zeh mare'hen,* the *d'mut adam* is applied to the apparition in the verse and in the vision. Verse 26, although also describing something apparently supernatural, explicitly identifies the apparition as of a man, not just having the aspects of one.

1:27   *chashmal*—This ultimately untranslatable word is used solely in Ezekiel and only in combination with *k'eyn*, meaning **like the color of.** According to BDB,[7] the etymology and exact meaning are dubious. It is understood to mean a fiery, burning energy, part of the mystery of Ezekiel's vision of God, which in some Jewish traditions is too intense to be studied at all. Given the early placement in this descriptive passage, *chashmal* is perhaps best understood as the sum of what follows in apposition in this verse and verse 28: *k'mareh-esh* **like the appearance of fire,** *v'nogah lo saviv* **a brightness around it,** *k'mareh hakkeshet* **like the appearance of a rainbow**—a composite picture of brightness.

motnav—**his loins.** This is the referential point in this vision by which Ezekiel describes the entire figure. Other uses of this word, especially those in

Ezekiel, emphasize Freudian associations of weaponry (carried at the waist), the phallus (covered up before God as in priestly garments mentioned in Ezekiel 44 and other books), and writing utensils (as in the scribal figure in chapter 9 who carries his writing tools *b'motnav*). In chapter 21 the unsheathed sword of God is contrasted with the *shivron motnayim* **breaking of loins** of Ezekiel himself (and by implication, the whole of Israel about to be confronted by the wrathful, sword-wielding God). The belted *motneihem* **their loins** of the Chaldeans is an erotic focus for Oholibah in chapter 23. BDB gives one subdefinition of *motnayim* as "seat of strength," which is at least consonant with the entire vision described in 1:27–28. The fire and glow seem to be centered around the loins of the man apparition.

1:28   *mareh d'mut k'vod-YHWH*—**the apparition of the image of the glory of YHWH.** It is hard to tell when Ezekiel becomes certain that this is a vision of God. In the opening verse of chapter 1 he prefaces the whole book with "the heavens opened and I saw apparitions of God." In 1:24 he likens the sound of the wings to a series of phenomena, including *kol shaddai* **voice/ sound of Shaddai** (a name of God), but it is expressed as simile *k'kol shaddai*, **like the voice of God,** as if Ezekiel were comparing the sound he actually heard to how he might imagine the voice or sound of God. (It may be significant that the words *k'kol shaddai* are missing from the Septuagint. The phrase could be spurious.) This verse (1:28) seems to mark the moment of Ezekiel's recognition of YHWH in the vision, since at this moment Ezekiel first falls onto his face.

va'eppol al-panai—**and I fell on my face.** Ezekiel falls prone four times, making him the closest rival to Moses in all of Tanakh for frequency of the gesture. The two later instances, 9:8 and 11:13, occur when Ezekiel comprehends the fatal nature of God's wrath upon Israel. The two early ones, though, 1:28 and 3:24, both fall within the call and commissioning and both precede and perhaps facilitate Ezekiel's being penetrated by a spirit that brings him from a prone to an erect posture. Ezekiel falls abject, perhaps inviting God to lift him up or, alternatively, intuiting that God will lift him. We can interpret Ezekiel's falling as a dance move whereby his show of weakness creates the opportunity for a demonstration of strength from his Divine partner.

We should note the economy of style from the end of 1:28 into 2:1: *va'ereh, va'eppol al-panai, va'eshma kol m'daber . . . vayyomer elai, ben-adam, amod al-ragleicha va'adabber otach.* **I saw, and I fell on my face, and I heard a voice speaking, and it said to me, Man-Boy, stand up on your legs that I may speak to you.** The absolute spareness of diction gives an elegance and a terseness to both the narration and to the character of God. Neither as narrator nor as character does Ezekiel digress into emotional response. The sequence of actions functions as smoothly as if both parties shared an instinctual understanding of how the scene should play. Verse 2:2 continues the *pas de deux* with Ezekiel's being entered and lifted by the spirit as discussed above.

ben-adam—**son of man, member of the human race, Man-Boy.** This is God's pet name for Ezekiel. According to Moshe Greenberg, it is used more than eighty times in the book. Ezekiel the narrator names YHWH to us his readers in 1:28 (he uses *elohim* in 1:1). When Ezekiel the character addresses God directly in 4:14, 9:8, and 11:13 (and elsewhere), he uses the name by which God signs off on many of the prophetic messages that Ezekiel is to carry: *adonai elohim (YHWH)*. We might label this "God's formal name." Conversely, *ben-adam*, the name by which God addresses Ezekiel, reduces Ezekiel's identity to his role within their private relationship. In the language of the S/M dynamic we are exploring, God looks down and says, "Boy"; Ezekiel looks up and answers, "Sir?" (Compare these nuances in naming with the passage cited above from Guy Baldwin where Top is spelled with a capital T, and bottom with a lower case b.)

2:5 *v'yadu ki navi hayah v'tocham*—**that they may know a prophet has been among them.** God, having reduced Ezekiel to *ben-adam*, now suavely, almost in passing, promotes him to Prophet. By introducing His boy's new title in this manner, we sense the careful, strategic nature of God's manipulation of Ezekiel. Favors come in the same peremptory manner as do commandments.

2:6 *v'attah ben-adam*—**and you, Man-Boy.** The function of the appellation has changed by this verse. Whereas initially it established the distance and power differential between God and Ezekiel, here it starts to function as a paternalism wherewith God offers comfort and encouragement to Ezekiel as He sends him off to address the rebellious house. Both this and verse 8 begin with the expanded form of the term "*v'attah, ben-adam*" with the clear rhetorical function of drawing Ezekiel's attention even more fully onto God as He speaks. As God asks more of Ezekiel and demands his full attention, He pulls Ezekiel closer rhetorically, demonstrating and offering an even more complete attention from Himself. Even this brief anaphora and other linguistic echoes here (for example, *im'yishm'u v'im-yekhdalu*) lend this part of God's speech (vv. 6–8) a hypnotic rhythm and feel, as He simultaneously frightens Ezekiel with the stinging metaphors for his mission and reassures him with growing intimacy. Ezekiel's inevitable anxiety over the painful thistles, thorns, and scorpions becomes indistinguishable from the pleasurable experience of God's rhetorical embrace.

2:7 *v'dibarta et-d'varai aleihem, im'yishm'u v'im-yekhdalu*—**You will speak my words to them if they listen or they cease [to listen]** (also in 2:5). God communicates with great clarity here that the intimacy now established between Him and Ezekiel will persist regardless of how Ezekiel's prophecy is received by rebellious Israel. God always directs Ezekiel's focus back to their relationship, not to the potentially painful mission. The hypnosis leads to the extraordinary ritual that consummates Ezekiel's commissioning—God's feeding Ezekiel the scroll.

2:8   The repetition of *v'attah, ben-adam* with the truncated reference to the mission leads smoothly to God's proffering of the scroll and command to eat.

p'tze fikha ve'echol et asher-ani noten eleicha—**open your mouth [part your mouth] and eat what I give you.** The verb *ptzeh* (part) has a stronger feel to it than *ptach* (open), and is used far less frequently in Tanakh. Moshe Greenberg's comment on this verse is charming in its blithe misreading of the scene being enacted: "The prophet, had, of course, no idea what was to be proffered him; he (and the reader) might well imagine it was some kind of food."[8] Not an attentive reader, one hopes. The clear intent of God's words here is to warn Ezekiel (and the reader) that whatever is coming will definitely not be food, but must be accepted and swallowed as if it were. Verses 9–10, as God by hand unrolls and displays the sorrowful scroll for Ezekiel, make clear that God is testing Ezekiel's commitment and loyalty. Nothing about the scroll is being concealed or ameliorated. Exactly what he sees is what he eats.

3:1   *vayyomer elai, ben-adam, et asher-timtza echol, echol et-hamm'gillah hazzot, v'lech dabber el-beit Israel*—**And He said to me, Man-Boy, that which you find [before you] eat; eat this scroll; and go speak to the House of Israel.** The intimate *v'attah* is again missing from this verse of imperatives. God toughens His speech, ordering Ezekiel to eat.

3:2   Ezekiel reverts to *ptach* **open** as he describes opening his mouth. He does not assume God's commanding vocabulary here, but keeps his speech appropriately milder. The final word of the verse, *hazzot*, missing from the Septuagint, is a deft touch. The word is unnecessary and even slightly out of place in the past-tense narration, except as the bottom's faithful echo of the Top's order as God brings the scroll to Ezekiel's lips.

When God first presents Ezekiel the scroll, it is rolled up and held in one hand. God unrolls it to show Ezekiel its contents, but the text does not record its being rerolled. For the obvious Freudian association, and supported by the diction of 3:3, I assume that Ezekiel takes in the scroll in its cylindrical form.

3:3   The more forceful style of address, *ben-adam* without the *v'attah*, is employed here. The image of Ezekiel's being orally penetrated by the phallic scroll is borne out by the sequence *vit'n'cha ta'achel umeeicha t'malle*—**you shall feed your stomach and fill your bowels**—tracing the progress of the scroll deeper into Ezekiel's gut. The phrase *et hammegillah hazzot* is repeated a third time, *asher ani noten lecha* a second time, giving God's words the resonance of ceremonial litany.

The final words of 3:3 *vatt'hi b'fi kid'vash l'matok*—**and it was [became] in my mouth like honey for its sweetness**—encapsulate Ezekiel's empowerment through his submission. Note this observation from Baldwin:

> Many bottoms seem to need the anxiety that happens as they approach and arrive face to face with their own capacity to deal with stimulation. As the stimulation levels increase, bottoms wrestle with the stimulation process as they struggle to *digest* that stimulation. It becomes a war between two parts of the bottom: one part wants to put a stop to the pushy stimulation, and the other wants to master it and get beyond it. "Can I take it or will it break me?"[9]

By giving in to God and taking in that which is apparently unpalatable, Ezekiel's own mouth becomes the setting and the agency for the bitter scroll's transformation into sweetness. Bottoming becomes its own reward.

Queer Readings and Thriving Communities

Well, so what? Where does a reading of this kind take any of us? And is it good for the Jews? Is any sacred ground gained by this reading?

Yes, I believe so. In explaining to a friend my intention in writing this essay, I said, "It's not that people don't read this way, it's that people don't *talk* about reading this way." Not only are we often reluctant to eroticize God in common discourse, *homo*-eroticizing Him or His prophet or their relationship sometimes sounds even to me like marginalizing the text, removing it from its central position of accessibility. Self-censure of that nature is the voice of my own internalized homophobia, declaring *treyf* my urge and my ability to find myself in my own sacred text.

The long history and tradition of connecting the mystical to the sexual in Judaism has been catalogued in countless venues and still deserves much attention, though it scarcely needs "proving." Tradition has read the deeply sensual and romantic Song of Songs as an allegory of Israel's relationship with God. The Zohar, were we to remove all its erotic imagery, would be one very dry, very brief pamphlet. The giving of permission to read Jewish religion not only erotically but from a queer and non-vanilla erotic perspective, however, needs to occur over and over. The lessons must be repeated until they are learned.

I believe myself not to be alone in having heard my erotic side call out invitingly to God long before I experienced my religion proffering a welcome to my sexuality. The problem has been to find a religious context where the religious/erotic sensation could be brought and explored. Consider this anecdote, again from Baldwin:

> One man in Texas said to me, "My buddies would laugh at me if I told them what happens in my mind sometimes when I [engage in SM erotic] play." So, he doesn't tell, and they don't laugh. As you may have guessed, he was referring to the spiritual—transcendental? mystical?—experiences he has when he plays. This guy is not alone. Many feel that it is not hot, or not butch to admit such thoughts. Leather dykes have been talking openly about the spiritual angles of the leather/SM scene for a long time, but most men are still shy about bringing them up.[10]

If in a queer context such thoughts are seldom hot or butch, in a Jewish one—in almost any organized religious one—they certainly are never kosher.

It is plausible to talk about the human response to God in S/M terms: if we can acknowledge that it sometimes feels good to be dominated, we can infer it feels divine to be dominated by God. What are the implications, though, of saying God wants to engage on this plane? If we say God reaches out to humanity through this channel, does that ennoble our erotic selves or degrade God? It is one thing to find God in kink; it is another to assert that God is *into* kink.

There is a particular poignancy to this issue within Reconstructionist Judaism. While the queer sexual dynamic may not be immediately welcome anywhere, the relationship to the personal God is a special challenge in a Jewish movement that prays to "the non-supernatural force that makes for salvation." And yet, the satisfaction of the close, sweaty dance with God is one that I find provocative, resonant, and deserving of reverential respect.

Not everyone will find this reading of Ezekiel persuasive, although I don't feel that I had to stretch the text to accommodate it.[11] The text carries these valences quite prominently. For those who find this approach too radical or too racy, I *guarantee* you that you know someone for whom it will be profoundly resonant. I hope that it liberates individuals and communities to look frankly at text, look frankly at religious experience. I believe with complete certainty that even this discrete angle of approach can open tremendous possibilities for individual and communal salvation.

I am a rabbi by calling, and only by accident any kind of academic. I am intrigued by grammar, syntax, and textual elasticity. My passionate concerns, though, are for human emancipation and salvation. Mordecai Kaplan, the founding philosopher/rabbi of Reconstructionism, wrote very sternly in his 1934 opus, *Judaism as a Civilization*.

> To sense the full significance of self-emancipation, it is necessary to look somewhat more deeply into the meaning of salvation. . . .The success of any proposed program of Jewish living will depend entirely on the extent to which it leads to

the salvation of the individual. . . . Once [humans] have learned to reckon with the individual as an end rather than a means in appraising the value of any social ideal or program, it is reactionary to ask the individual to sink back into [his/her/hir] former subservience.[12]

My reading of Ezekiel is certainly part of my larger intention of queer emancipation, to assure the full inclusion of LGBTQ individuals in Jewish religious community. However, the degree to which all of us can potentially relate to the erotic dynamic of biblical text, there is some part of everyone that has been closeted and subservient within traditional religious communities. Kaplan saw community as the essential factor in achieving individual salvation.

When we study the quest for salvation and the conditions of its fulfillment, we note that salvation presupposes a community which treats the individual as so organic a part of itself that in promoting [that person's] life it is aware that it promotes its own. The chief aim of such a community is to help [that person] attain those objectives which constitute . . . complete self-realization.[13]

I see salvation very much in Kaplanian terms: the complete realization of self. Here we see the limits of unqueered religion and how the act of queering creates new spiritual possibility. The heteronormative approach to religious sexual ethics that has dominated (in no attractive way) Western religious life for millennia created a sequence of Revelation > Prohibition > Inclusion > Salvation.

Each person's own experience of the divine through eros constitutes a significant, universally available instance of revelation. However, inclusion in religious community has been available only after conforming to norms of prohibition of most forms of queerness, certainly homoeroticism and kink. I contend that the intrusion of heteronormative prohibition between organic revelation and communal inclusion pre-empts the possibility of salvation for the queer many, and ultimately for the communal whole. How can a community hope to reach salvation for itself or to facilitate it for its constituents if it imposes and polices a silence about profound and shattering revelation even more strictly than God did for Ezekiel? God imposed silence as part of the play dynamic. Ezekiel spoke up when he needed to. There has been no aspect of play and it has been dangerous for queer practitioners to speak up within faith communities. Even in contemporary, progressive communities, queer readings are still often causes for alarm.

That is sad, because a queer reading of text in this manner creates a different sequence: Revelation > Permission > Inclusion > Salvation.

If queer readings occur with the permission of the community, a vast number of people who have turned away from formal religious community might come *back*. A large number of people within community might come *out*.

Permission for honest discourse within community does not deprive a community of the opportunity to set a communal sexual ethics. In fact, only once this permission to speak is granted can a true value-based communal process occur. The obsolescence of a prohibition-based discourse is, in my view, self-evident. If people doubt that the potential for change through queer reading is significant, I encourage them to consider the impact of stifling one's most passionate and organic experience of God. Ultimately, queer reading is not about the kink, it's about the community. More truly spoken, there is no real community without the kink. Sir.

Notes

1. With thanks and respect to Rev. R.N.
2. Gregg Drinkwater, Joshua Lesser, and David Shneer, eds., *Torah Queeries: Weekly Commentaries on the Hebrew Bible* (New York: New York University Press, 2009).
3. Deryn Guest, Robert E. Goss, Mona West, and Thomas Bohoache, eds., *Queer Bible Commentary* (London: SCM Press, 2006).
4. Abraham J. Heschel, *The Prophets*, vol. 2 (New York: Harper Torchbooks, 1962), 224.
5. David Halperin, *Seeking Ezekiel* (University Park: Pennsylvania State University Press, 1993), 185.
6. Guy Baldwin, *Ties That Bind: The SM/Leather/Fetish Erotic Style—Issues, Commentaries and Advice* (New York: Daedalus Books, 1993), 227–28.
7. *Brown-Driver-Briggs Hebrew-English Lexicon* (BDB) is the generally recognized standard reference for biblical Hebrew.
8. Moshe Greenberg, *Ezekiel 1–20*, Anchor Bible Series (New York: Doubleday & Co., 1983), 67.
9. Baldwin, *Ties That Bind*, 223; emphasis added.
10. Ibid., 237.
11. As a pianist friend once said to a singer who had lost her place in the score and wanted to blame the accompanist, "Just keep reading what's on the page, ma'am."
12. Mordecai M. Kaplan, *Judaism as a Civilization* (Philadelphia, PA: Jewish Publication Society, 1994), 282.
13. Ibid., 283.

Chapter 6

Sadomasochism and Spirituality

A Queerly Religious Challenge to the Gay Marriage Paradigm

Patrick Califia

> *Marriage, n. The state or condition of a community consisting of a master, a mistress and two slaves, making in all, two.*
> —Ambrose Bierce[1]

The first decade of the twenty-first century has witnessed an astonishing surge forward for full civil marriage equality. In the United States, this campaign for gay marriage, however, has gone far beyond a demand for the legalization of same-sex relationships. Whether intentional or not, marriage equality has quickly become a single-issue movement, pushing all the other forms of inequality and mistreatment suffered by lesbians and gay men to the side. The complex question of the need for nonjudgmental and affordable health care, for example, has been reduced to the plea for permission to put one partner on the other's health insurance policy. Rather than the notion of "LGBT rights," marriage has become a *gay* campaign, applying only to rights needed by same-sex couples.

The dangerously ambiguous status of the relationships of transgendered people is never mentioned in gay marriage press releases or political rallies. Concern about national security adds a further layer of complexity to transgendered relationships. Justifying a host of intrusions into the private lives of American citizens under the rubric of "security," the federal government has made it even more difficult for transpeople to change legal documents to reflect their true gender status. Employers are required to check social security numbers, thus outing many Americans of transgendered experience. The State

Department is refusing to recognize even male/female marriages between U.S. citizens and foreign nationals if one of the partners is transgendered.[2]

Progress in securing legal status for same-sex relationships has of course generated a vicious backlash from various conservative organizations. Scrambling to mount a defense against that backlash, activists funnel much-needed energy and financial resources away from equally urgent concerns.[3] LGBT opponents of gay marriage argue that the media storm obscures their attempts to make progress in a host of other areas, including antigay violence; research on AIDS and other health concerns such as breast cancer; discrimination in the areas of employment, housing, and access to public services; homophobia in the mental health profession; opposition to full social equality bolstered by religious fundamentalists; the harsh treatment of gay youth, which often leads to their being rejected by their families, peers, and communities; and the invisibility of lesbian and gay elders.

Meanwhile, queer theorists note that marriage as a heterosexual model is failing even male/female couples more than half of the time. Many are likewise troubled by trying to comply with a social form that originated in male dominance over and ownership of women. A good number of gay men wonder whether monogamy is essential for marriage and, if so, if it will work for them. In short, is there space within LGBT communities to lobby for other ways to guarantee social recognition for uniquely queer romantic and sexual bonds, and equality that is not dependent on marital status?[4]

Marriage equality advocates will often insist that equal civil status depends on proving that we are morally or spiritually deserving of full citizenship. Committed, monogamous, long-term relationships are held out as the gold standard of gay maturity and thus necessary for securing our civil rights; Bruce Bawer and Gabriel Rotello are just two among many making this argument.[5] Christian theologians defending the sanctification of same-sex relationships usually assume that monogamy defines relationships that can be blessed. Eugene F. Rogers Jr. illustrates this theological approach to the significance of marriage by arguing that

> marriage shares with celibacy the end of sanctifying the body, of permitting it something *more* to be about, something *further* to mean, something *better* to desire, until finally it gets taken up into the life in which God loves God.... Sexual activity does not make sanctification any "easier" than celibacy does. As traditional marriage and childrearing are gifts of grace more than human achievements, and means of sanctification rather than satisfaction, so too monogamous, committed gay and lesbian relationships are also gifts of grace, means of sanctification, upholding of the community of the people of God. They are means, bodily means, that God can use to catch human beings up into

less and less conditional acts of self-donation, finally into that unconditional response to God's self-donation that God's self gives to the Trinity.[6]

Conservative groups have ridiculed the idea that same-sex relationships (especially those of gay men) could ever be monogamous. Because of this perceived moral failure, critics argue that same-sex couples would change the definition of the institution, opening the door to legalization of polygamous unions or multi-partnered arrangements.[7] Such charges raise the specter of a public relations nightmare, despite the fact that adultery and patronization of the sex industry are common behaviors among married heterosexuals. If some lesbians and gay men can demonstrate worthiness by being able to live up to the monogamous ideal of legal marriage and the responsibilities of parenthood, those of us who fail to do so embody the very public relations nightmare marriage equality advocates so deeply fear, and this nightmare is often perceived as a direct result of our own willful and self-indulgent behavior. Some gay men insist that their marriages are valid (or would be) despite sex with outside partners, yet many defenders of same-sex marriage have condemned such deviance from social expectations.[8]

In addition to questions of monogamy and multiple sex partners, another and somewhat surprising target of concern are communities that engage in sadomasochistic or more generally non-vanilla sexual practices. Conservative groups often capitalize on images of leather queens from gay pride parades or stories about purportedly bizarre sexual practices and relationships as a way to demonize non-heterosexual people more broadly. Yet the critique also comes from LGBT-identified people themselves, perhaps reflecting a concern for how these otherwise marginal practices could derail our full inclusion in both civic and religious institutions—including marriage.

A significant by-product of the marriage equality debate, I would argue, is the division of LGBT people into those who are socially and religiously acceptable (monogamous couples) and those who fail to achieve such respectability (mostly the non-monogamous and those engaged in non-vanilla sex). In this essay, I want to propose that the failure of the latter group relies on supposing that non-vanilla (especially sadomasochistic) sexual practices do not admit any moral or spiritual value. By offering just a snapshot of those sexual practices here, and the ways in which they can surface a profound spirituality, I want to urge not only a reassessment of non-monogamous, non-vanilla sexuality; I also want to suggest how such a reassessment can broaden the reach of LGBT movements for liberation beyond marriage equality alone. Indeed, what seems the queerest may well prove to be the most spiritually and politically liberating.

Locating the Critique

The critique of non-monogamy (often referred to as "promiscuity" by its critics) and of non-vanilla sexual practices takes a variety of forms, whether in
terms of morality, psychology, or theology. The critique also comes from a
wide range of groups and perspectives, including LGBT people themselves.
Despite her efforts to defend the sacredness of same-sex eroticism, Christian
theologian Carter Heyward, for example, locates multiple sex partners and
sadomasochism within the very systems of oppression from which we seek
liberation. "Each time we are captivated in a power-laded struggle for domination and control," she writes, "or for submission and being controlled, whether
in bed or in church, we short-circuit the yearning for relationship . . . and the
process of becoming at one with God and creation itself."[9]

Heyward further links sadomasochistic practices to domestic violence and
the troubling dynamic of abused partners finding sexual pleasure in their pain:

> We have learned, generation upon generation, to take pleasure in pain—that is,
> to respect our distress and appreciate our bruises as signs of our blessedness. . . .
> A battered spouse is a victim of a battering spouse but also, I think, of a per-
> vasive mentality in which battering is related to justification or "setting things
> right." Sadomasochism is testimony to the same cult of battering, pain, and
> suffering. And not only in the sadomasochism of leather and chains, bond-
> age and discipline, slave and master, but also the sadomasochism many of us
> experience in the connections between sexual coerciveness/overpowering and
> genital titillation and pleasure, or simply in our attachments to the very people
> who treat us worst.[10]

Heyward also locates gay male promiscuity within a larger social-economics
of "body worship" by noting that

> As a lesbian, I must admit my anxiety about the body cults/body worship I see
> every day in television commercials, magazines, films, and store windows. The
> sexist and heterosexist cult of body worship is a multibillion-dollar-per-annum
> enterprise, and it is also a people-eating machine that devours the flesh and
> spirit of girls and women, boys and men . . . I cannot say any more for the gay
> male "meat racks" and what I hear about the gay male cult of body worship.[11]

Heyward's analysis is apparently informed by the writings of anti-porn
feminists, many of them lesbians, who began attacking sadomasochism in the
late 1970s.[12] While lesbianism was upheld as the ultimate form of feminism,
sadomasochism was demonized as its evil opposite, the lived form of patriarchy
and racism, predicated on female self-hatred and male violence.[13] Male feminists like John Stoltenberg also attacked gay male sexuality using the language

of anti-porn feminism.[14] This ideology spread far beyond Christian theology. Even some aspects of pagan theology, as expressed by Arthur Evans,[15] among others, were and are explicitly opposed to sadomasochistic practices and to the kind of public sex Heyward sums up as "meat rack" cruising.

The rejoinder to these attacks came from lesbians and other feminists who were opponents of censorship. They felt that the liberation of female sexuality was an important component of gaining equality for women. Some of them believed that in the context of woman-to-woman eroticism, both pornography and sadomasochism could be freed of patriarchal toxicity and transformed into something with value for women. Others were prepared to argue against the censorship of any sexually explicit media, and defended the entire leather community, gay men, and heterosexuals, as well as lesbians.[16] My own work in this area grows out of my experience as a sex-positive feminist and sex radical—experience that has, quite queerly for some, taught me a great deal about being "spiritual."

Locating the Spirit in a BDSM World

For my purposes in this essay, sadomasochism (SM) is defined (based on my personal participation and observation) as a form of sexual fantasy play engaged in by mutually consenting adults. That play can take many forms, including dominant/submissive role-playing, the use of fetish costumes or substances, physical restraint, sensory deprivation, emotional ordeals, or the careful application of intense physical sensation. The rather wide range of activities, roles, practices, and postures in this kind of play is often summarized with the compound acronym BDSM, which evokes elements of bondage and discipline, dominance and submission, and sadism and masochism.

A BDSM encounter typically includes a preliminary conversation or negotiation in which desires and limits are clarified. A code phrase or gesture that either party can use to take a break and leave the frame of the fantasy is chosen. Constant communication (both verbal and nonverbal) continues during the enactment, which is referred to as a scene or session, to distinguish that time from ordinary reality, where different rules prevail. There is a community-wide expectation that all parties will be in contact after the encounter, to reaffirm its positive aspects and do any needed aftercare. A BDSM scene may or may not include genital sex.

In recent years, BDSM play rather routinely takes place within the context of a community that provides continuing education in the safe and imaginative use of various techniques. There are a plethora of identities available to people in that community, depending on specific fantasies and fetishes. The three most popular archetypes are top, bottom, and switch. The top is the person who prefers to orchestrate or conduct the fantasy. It is the top who makes use of the equipment and initiates dialogue. A bottom prefers to be the subject of the encounter. A switch is capable of functioning in either role. There are a growing number of players who like mutual intense stimulation or physical restraint and frequent switching during the course of their time together. There may be a competitive theme, to see who can out-do whom, or the dynamic may be one of mutuality—mirroring one another and glorying in this validation.

There are also scenes in which one person functions more as a guide than as a dominant top who expresses control or a sadist who monitors or inflicts levels of pain. The focus of this type of scene is to create a spiritually meaningful ordeal or journey for the partner. Rather than relishing the flow of power between them, the guide strives to facilitate the partners' internal state by manipulating their physical experience. The goal is transcendence, entering a state beyond the limits of material existence. The annual Black Leather Wings gathering, part of the Radical Faerie movement, offers a good example of this strive toward transcendence.

The Radical Faeries emerged in tandem with a gay civil rights movement in the 1970s and tapped into a broader countercultural energy. Rather than relying on an apologetic posture or seeking "inclusion" in mainstream social institutions and religious communities, Radical Faeries adopted a proactive and constructive approach to their queer sexualities and gender expressions. By turning to a variety of sources—such as the mythopoetic men's movement, feminism, and pagan and neo-pagan Earth-based traditions—Radical Faeries sought not only to critique the patriarchal and hierarchical dynamics of the wider society, but also to embrace what they understood as the fundamental connection between spirituality and sexuality. This queerly creative mix of traditions and practices generated a host of ritualized forms of sexuality and relational bonds, including a number of distinct groupings within this loosely affiliated and now worldwide network.

Among those groupings, the Black Leather Wings celebrates and ritualizes BDSM as a spiritual practice, as their annual ball dances demonstrate. This multi-gendered gathering is a celebration in which nude or costumed people are pierced and decorated. Oranges and lemons or brightly colored balls and bells are hung from sterile sutures in their chest, arms, or legs. The celebration includes a group dance that goes on for hours until everyone is in a state of ecstasy. There is no power division between piercers and dancers because they all take turns ornamenting one another and then joining the ritual.

Embodied experience within BDSM blurs the line between supposedly perverse sexuality and mainstream spirituality. Used here, the term "spirituality" is equally complex. It can be used to describe any human activity or value that goes beyond meeting our basic survival needs. (This is only true in cultures where ritual magic or worship is not needed to help people to meet urgent needs for food, water, shelter, and other life-giving resources.) Spirituality can also refer to the many ways in which one finds or makes meaning, or a search for guidelines and values to govern how one lives. It can be a search for entities or forces beyond the human sphere of experience. This may be framed as a need to experience oneness with a deity or other supernatural entity; a sense of oneness or unity with other living things or the world or universe as a whole; extended ecstatic states that go beyond the mundane physical pleasures of food and sex; or simple confirmation that we are not alone, that our lives matter.

Spirituality may overlap with religion, but it is not identical to it. In my own work, I find Rudolf Otto's concept of "the numinous" helpful[17] as well as William James's term "personal religion." As James describes it:

> The personal religion will prove itself more fundamental than either theology or ecclesiasticism. Churches, when once established, live at second-hand upon tradition; but the *founders* of every church owed their power originally to the fact of their direct personal communion with the divine. Not only the super-human founders, the Christ, the Buddha, Mahomet, but all the originators of Christian sects have been in this case—so personal religion should still seem the primordial thing even to those who continue to esteem it incomplete.[18]

According to James, religion is the codification and institutionalization of one charismatic individual's spiritual experiences. By following that individual's precepts, members hope to become better people and win value in the Other World. Or they may seek to duplicate the founder's transcendent states. Most religions have a hierarchy; there are clergy and laypeople. Generally speaking, spirituality does not recognize these divisions as knowledge is shared along a horizontal plane of power. Religions, by contrast, are based on polarized values: this is true, that is not; this is virtue, and that is sin. As James suggested: "Personal religion, even without theology or ritual, would prove to embody some elements that morality pure and simple does not contain."[19]

As Valerie Lesniak has observed, spirituality may encompass contradictions or borrow from any tradition:

> As the complexity of the pluralistic present-day world permeates human consciousness and ordinary life, individuals find themselves seeking ways to ... find some meaning in their multifaceted yet fragmented world. The appeal to spirituality has captured the religious imagination of contemporary people as encompassing these spiritual quests more than an appeal to organized religion or systematic theology. By centering attention on practical lived

human experience, spirituality is viewed as a more inclusive, tolerant and flexible canopy under which to pursue the mysteries of the human spirit and the
Sacred. Spirituality has become ecumenical and interreligious and not the re-
serve of any one tradition.[20]

Patrick D. Hopkins attempts to push the academic discourse about sadomasochism beyond the logjam between anti-porn feminists and the libertarian
claims of BDSM practitioners that any sexual behavior between consenting
adults must be permissible. He defines BDSM as "simulation" rather than
"replication of patriarchal dominant/submissive activities," and calls on radical feminists to reassess their opposition based on this "important epistemological and ethical distinction."[21]

Replication and simulation are very different. Replication implies that SM
encounters merely reproduce patriarchal activity in a different physical area.
Simulation implies that SM selectively replays surface patriarchal behaviors
onto a different contextual field. As Hopkins notes, that contextual field
makes a profound difference: "SM is constructed as a performance, as a staging, a production, a simulation in which participants are writers, producers, . . .
actors, and audience." Just like any performance, there are elements that appear to be similar to the "real" activity being staged. But as Hopkins likewise
notes, "similarity is not sufficient for replication."[22]

If Hopkins is correct, an argument could be made that all sex is a form
of simulation. The masculine heterosexual man performs virility for his girl-
friend or spouse. She in turn mirrors him with a polarized performance or
simulation of femininity. Vanilla sex requires a simulation of affection, respect, gentleness, and equality. BDSM works for the same reasons that any
form of human sexuality works. It satisfies people's need for an attractive and
arousing partner, a fantasy about the emotional dynamic between the participants, activities that are exciting and gratifying, and a context that feels
appropriate in its level of risk or safety.

All of this can, and I hope will, lead to a reassessment of non-vanilla sexual
practices, not only for the sake of dismantling stereotypes but also for the
profound spirituality one can access in the BDSM world. But what does any
of this have to do with marriage?

Broadening the Horizon beyond Marriage

As Mark Jordan has pointed out, the fight about gay marriage is essentially a
religious one masked by the rhetoric of secular legalism.[23] On a deeper level,
it is implicitly about whether gay men and lesbians have spiritual value. By
making a monogamous commitment to only one other person, the same-sex

participants are supposedly promising to follow the same moral code as their heterosexual counterparts, and thereby prove that they have the discipline to be faithful. Because marriage will demonstrate that same-sex couples have spiritual value, by that token, all homosexual men and women will supposedly be potentially decent and responsible citizens who deserve equal rights.

There is an unspoken assumption that the sex within these idealized relationships will not be kinky. For one thing, many of these couples are or plan to become parents. The United States is already prone to moral panics if anyone under the age of eighteen is exposed to the sight of a living homosexual. A living homosexual with a vanilla sex life is bad enough. People in the BDSM community are presumed to be unfit parents, and child custody cases are one of the most frequent breaches of our civil rights. With the constant looming threat of family court, people who do BDSM who are also parents live in terror of losing their children, no matter how scrupulous they are about keeping their sex lives as invisible as possible.

No convincing argument has yet been made that the practitioners of sadomasochism are significantly different than their peers in terms of education level, job satisfaction, values, participation in a stable relationship, or any other marker of a mature human being. The lack of any good research on this topic has led experts in the fields of medicine, mental health, and sexology to call for removal of the categories of "sexual sadist" and "sexual masochist" from the *Diagnostic and Statistical Manual-IV-TR*, the authoritative text on mental disorders, published by the American Psychiatric Association.[24]

Moreover, BDSM people have participated in virtually every aspect of the spiritual life, no matter how it is defined. A broad and secular definition might be the performance of activities that benefit others more than oneself or a demonstration of stewardship toward the community or the Earth itself. The leather community has passed this test time and time again with its relentless and stalwart fundraising for AIDS education and direct services, breast cancer, nonprofit agencies that serve LGBT people, and a host of charities too numerous to catalogue here.

If we broaden the meaning of spirituality even further, then we might say that it consists of a set of values or ethics that prevent one from harming others. Here, too, the leather community demonstrates consistent concern with the well-being of its members. No other sexual minority offers as many gateway organizations or as much education to newcomers. The BDSM community's standards include rigorous training in various techniques, so that both top and bottom are educated about how to enact fantasies safely that on the surface may seem dangerous. This community was one of the first to adopt safer sex practices for the prevention of HIV, and they are enforced at public events, along with an injunction to avoid playing while intoxicated. The negotiation process and use of safe words are embedded in a culture where it is understood that everyone in a scene should leave it feeling better than when the encounter began. If the terms "slave" and "master" were not in use, you would think that BDSM was an attempt to live out the most stringent feminist concerns for equality both in the bedroom and out of it.

But BDSM people do call themselves slaves or masters and a host of other names denoting their fantasy role in either wielding or ceding power. There are whips and chains. There are piercing needles and hoists and racks. Their luggage is heavily packed with slings, paddles, nipple clamps, masks, leather chaps, corsets, collars, handcuffs, and a long list of other toys or equipment that Homeland Security officers love to confiscate in airports. And the community-wide standards described above are most often taught at public sex events. Play parties, as they are commonly known, are often an evening attraction at leather conferences or contests.

An encounter between a top and a bottom, or a room full of people engaged in flirting, cruising, and playing, can just be dirty, good fun. Yet to my pagan way of thinking, this constitutes a spiritual activity in and of itself. By enjoying the pleasures of the flesh, we give thanks to the sacred forces that created us. This is numinous bounty, a generosity that is meant to compensate us, at least a little, for the harsh fact of death. The knowledge that life is short almost requires us to enjoy it as much as we can now because we do not know what pleasures will be afforded to us in the "Western Lands." We hope for healing and rest there, but our knowledge does not extend that far, and so we focus on what we do know, and offer comfort and delight to our fellow travelers on Mother Earth.

What then do we need for an act to become sacred? Consecrated space is a beginning, found in many times and places as a preliminary for encounters with holy forces. The places where BDSM occur are often deliberately cleansed and blessed by community members. The apparently secular act of setting up equipment and inviting the community to gather also sets the space apart and marks it as the dancing ground of the gods. It is a temple they may enter, if they wish to see it that way. The typical play party includes atheists, Christians, pagans, Buddhists, and adherents of many other faiths. Each person or group of people will have a different experience there. Intention plays a key role. While the triad at the St. Andrew's cross may be chasing transcendence, allowing the bottom to assume the identity of the goddess Innana as she descends to the realm of death and comes back to life, the man in a cage may be content to lick books through the bars for an hour, and go home happy with nothing but dust on his tongue.

Virtually every BDSM technique—exposure to extremes of heat or cold, sensory deprivation, flogging, suspension, deliberate wounding, fasting, confession, yielding one's will to a higher power—has also been employed by shamans and other technicians of the sacred, probably for millions of years. Mircea Eliade catalogued the cross-cultural existence of these phenomena, and gay historian and mythologist Randy Conner has documented their special value to and association with gay and differently gendered men.[25] A plethora of authors have pawed over the sadomasochistic experiences of Christian saints and quarreled about the sublimated eroticism (or not) in these stories.[26]

As human beings evolved, we longed for something besides mere survival. We hoped for another world. We craved protection and direction from beings wiser and more powerful than ourselves. And we learned that we could use our limited, weak bodies to acquire a vision of that Other World. Pain is a horse that can be ridden to heaven, with the subject's body serving as the beaten drum. And these visions are not for the bottom alone. The preparation for a scene, laying out of equipment, dedication of the victim, and the mortification or manipulation of their experience is tiring and exhilarating enough to deliver the top as well into an altered state.

What then and exactly is it that people experience when they have an extraphysical or ecstatic experience during a scene? There may be a sense of connection with all other living beings. The energy that creates life and sustains the universe may become visible as a rhythmic presence, pulsing in the background or infusing human beings with harmony. There may be a new sense of respect for life and an immense consciousness of unconditional love, given and received. Fear may be confronted and forced to flee. Beyond that, each individual's experience is unique and private. Ultimately, the value and meaning of these experiences are discerned by their effect on the given person's life—not by whether they took place in a monastery or a dungeon. The sublime does not disdain the squalid.

The spiritual value of non-monogamous relationships is less gaudy, but no less significant. It develops character in mundane domestic life more often than it opens one's eyes to the face of the divine. This relationship style can include casual sex with strangers, open relationships with a commitment to a primary partner, polyamory that gives each lover his or her own space in an extended family, triads that may or may not be open, the supposedly monogamous relationship with occasional nights out, and other configurations. On the surface, it would seem that the mindless promiscuity of anonymous, casual sex would be the most difficult to defend. But I have heard too many stories about lovers who met in bathhouses, crisis counseling offered to a trick, and comfort extended to a troubled married man to dismiss these encounters as soulless or selfish. Without the bathhouse culture of the 1970s, there may never have been such a thing as gay liberation. This sharing of sex generated a sharing of information and a sense of community. Casual sex can, at least on occasion, represent hospitality offered to a stranger, welcome extended to the outcast, generosity held out to someone who suffers. Eros is compatible with the practice of compassion. For sexual minorities, it is a holy sanctuary. It is not the only sanctuary, but it is one we shut down at our peril.

Parting ways with a stranger is easy compared to ongoing, committed, open relationships. The stereotype of orgiastic, irresponsible, impulsive days and nights filled with every manner of sexual position and technique could not be further from the truth, alas. Instead, polyamory (which involves multiple romantic relationships) and other types of non-monogamy (which generally distinguish between the primary partner and lesser connections) are a good deal of trouble. Many people assume that jealousy is only a problem for monogamous couples. But the fact that one has made a commitment to enjoying sex or love with more than one person does not eliminate jealousy. Facing the events that trigger toxic insecurity and taking care of one's self in the process makes for a braver, more generous spirit. A healthy self-love is strengthened, as well as love for one's partner and even for the person or people one is dating.

Being monogamous does not eliminate jealousy, either. All people, whether monogamous or not, doubt that we deserve to be loved. We all fear abandonment. We all hold a secret belief that there is not enough affection or sex to go around. Non-monogamy requires us to face those irrational beliefs and struggle toward a more balanced worldview and psyche. And any time we engage in an effort to love ourselves or others with more compassion, we are engaged in a spiritual practice. This sort of discipline does not necessarily rest upon a belief in supernatural forces. Until we can clean out the rain gutters of our souls and allow human love to fill our homes, we cannot perceive the love of our Creator(s), which flows effortlessly and abundantly all around us.

In my own experience, through non-monogamy, I have learned to value my partner for telling me the truth about what or whom he desires. I have learned to see the sexual experiences that do not include me as being central to his growth and development. One way to soothe jealousy is to unearth or define my own sexual needs and stand up for them by revealing them, even if they are things that my partner will not enjoy with me. I have also learned how to love more than one person.

These observations and experiences are precisely what the advocates for same-sex marriage equality fear. They are the ingredients for a public relations debacle. Yet what is undeniable for me and for so many involved in non-normative styles of relating is the spiritual value in the relationship structures and sexual institutions many of us have developed to help us survive in a very unfriendly world. To be clear, I am no foe of same-sex marriage. At the same time, and in ways similar to the call for gay men and lesbians to serve openly in the military, most LGBT people and our community organizations were woefully unprepared to deal with the panicked and vitriolic reaction of those who oppose us. This has only been exacerbated by the insistence from some in our communities that we strive for ordinary lives that differ as little as possible from the straight middle class, which has divided our energies and efforts.

Perhaps we have relied too much on a legalistic, civil rights model for gaining equality. The slow process of education, done on a one-to-one basis by queers who are brave enough to come out, might be the only thing that will allow such legislation to move forward, let alone be respected and upheld. Even then, the "lavender ceiling" will still be there, holding us back, as long as people hate and fear us. The answer to this quandary, however, will not be found by focusing on the least threatening segments of LGBT people and practices, which will only further stigmatize those deemed less acceptable by mainstream standards. Besides which, the profound diversity among us is no longer a secret. Effective public relations and education must address the complete spectrum of queer lives, or we risk looking dishonest and hypocritical.

Whether most same-sex couples would like to get married or not, it has unfortunately become a test of the power of the lesbian and gay male community. Every time a state amends its constitution to restrict marriage as between one man and one woman, we are seen as weak and thwarted. My fear is that we will internalize that mass media view of ourselves and give up if the battle for same-sex marriage turns out to be a lot more arduous than initial, small victories led us to believe. Yes—some of us are going to be happiest in relationship patterns that resemble those that were developed in patriarchal and racist societies. Maybe they can uplift marriage into something more beautiful and just. Meanwhile, others will continue to explore alternatives.

Is the gay man who lives alone but has a large network of ex-lovers and friends and is sexually busy on weekends in the city's parks truly single? What about the gay man who is parenting a child with a lesbian couple? How do we define ex-lovers who are sharing custody of their family? Then there is the leather "boy" who has a "Daddy" he sees once a month and entire clans of leather people who pledge allegiance to a dominant figure at its head, even though they may never have had sex or played with that person. Of course, there are many types of BDSM relationships, some of them even monogamous.

The gift queer people offer is to create a proliferation of choices, to refuse the married/single dichotomy. Yes, our relationships ought to be accorded equality and dignity, yet we also need to validate the rights of every individual. Eventually, that may mean that the worst fears of the Christian right wing will indeed come to pass, with the state *and* organized religions offering more than a one-size-fits-all approach to winning legal recognition and sacred blessings. Jeremy R. Carrette describes well what that kind of queerly religious and spiritual moment would entail:

> What I want to suggest is that intensity and intimacy are seen as political categories of a new theological exchange, not some romantic sharing or commercial product, but a new basis for Christian living in intense communities. Intensity demands intimacy, it demands self-disclosure, demands integration of mind, body and heart. Intimacy is intense because it demands the embodied reality of oneself in terms of fantasy enacted and a freedom in a pleasured exchange of the heart. . . . What is potentially dangerous about S&M . . . is precisely its intense exchange. Intense exchanges are dangerous to capitalism but not necessarily to a theology of loving power and humble reverence.[27]

Notes

1. Ambrose Bierce, *The Devil's Dictionary* (Owings Mills, MD: Stemmer House Publishers, Inc., 1978), 162.
2. Anonymous interview with "Adam" and "Eve," April 13, 2005. Adam is an American citizen; his partner is not. After changing all of his identification papers, including his birth certificate, and obtaining genital surgery, Adam was told that because he is transgendered, the federal government would not recognize his marriage or allow his wife to immigrate. They now live in her native land. Also see the immigration section in the National Center for Trans Equality website, http://transequality.org/federal_gov.html.
3. For both positive and negative assessments of this, see the anthology edited by Greg Wharton and Ian Philips, *I Do, I Don't: Queers on Marriage* (San Francisco: Suspect Thoughts Press, 2004).
4. Michael Bronski, "Over the Rainbow: Gay-Movement Organizers Obsessed with Fighting for Same-Sex Marriage Seem to Have Forgotten Their Roots in a Quest for a More Liberated World, One They Shared with Feminists Who Viewed Marriage as Hopelessly Patriarchal," in Wharton and Philips, eds., *I Do, I Don't*, 48–52. Non-monogamy is an issue for many lesbians as well; see Jackie Strano, "I Met My Wife at a Sex Party," in ibid., 326–28.
5. Bruce Bawer, *A Place at the Table: The Gay Individual in American Society* (New York: Touchstone, 1993); Gabriel Rotello, *Sexual Ecology: AIDS and the Destiny of Gay Men* (New York: Dutton, 1997).

6. Eugene F. Rogers Jr., "Sanctification, Homosexuality, and God's Triune Life," in *Theology and Sexuality: Classic and Contemporary Readings*, ed. Eugene F. Rogers Jr. (Malden, MA: Blackwell Publications, Ltd., 2002), 223–24.

7. David Benkof, "Monogamous Same-Sex Adultery," *San Francisco Chronicle*, (June 26, 2008), B-7. Also see Stanley Kurtz, "Beyond Gay Marriage," *The Weekly Standard* 8:45 (August 2008).

8. Dan Savage, "The Great Mate Debate," June 15, 2007, http://chemistry.type pad.com/the_great_male_debate/2007/06/re_gay_marriage_revisted. See also John Lyttle, "Like Homophobes, Some Homosexuals Regard Monogamy, Official Partnerships and Marriage as an Unnatural State for Gay Men," *The Independent* (April 11, 1997).

9. Carter Heyward, *Our Passion for Justice: Images of Power, Sexuality, and Liberation* (New York: The Pilgrim Press, 1984), 41.

10. Ibid., 129.

11. Ibid., 196–97.

12. While Heyward admits that the question of the morality of sadomasochism is a complicated one with no easy or fixed answer, she nonetheless argues that physically hurting one another is wrong, with or without consent. She further ties such behavior to the social systems of abuse, including racism and patriarchy, in which we are all embedded. See Carter Heyward, *Touching Our Strength: The Erotic as Power and the Love of God* (San Francisco: Harper and Row, 1989), 104–9.

13. See Robin Ruth Linden, Darlene R. Pagano, Diana E. H. Russell, and Susan Leigh Star, eds., *Against Sadomasochism: A Radical Feminist Analysis* (San Francisco: Frog in the Well, 1982).

14. John Stoltenberg, *Refusing to Be a Man: Essays on Sex and Justice* (London: Routledge, 2004).

15. Arthur Evans, *Witchcraft and the Gay Counterculture* (Boston: Fag Rag Books, 1981).

16. Carole S. Vance, ed., *Pleasure and Danger: Exploring Female Sexuality* (Boston and London: Routledge and Kegan Paul, 1984). Also see Samois, *Coming to Power: Writings and Graphics on Lesbian S/M*, 2nd ed. (Boston: Alyson Publications, 1982). I have written on this as well; see Patrick Califia, *Public Sex: The Culture of Radical Sex* (San Francisco: Cleis Press, 1982).

17. Rudolf Otto, *The Idea of the Holy* (London: Oxford University Press, 1923).

18. William James, *The Varieties of Religious Experience* (New York: The Modern Library, 1999), 35–36.

19. Ibid., 47.

20. Valerie Lesniak, "Contemporary Spirituality," in *The New Westminster Dictionary of Christian Spirituality*, ed. Philip Sheldrake (Louisville: Westminster John Knox Press, 2005), 8.

21. Patrick D. Hopkins, "Rethinking Sadomasochism: Feminism, Interpretation, and Simulation," *Hypatia* 9:1 (Winter 1994): 116.

22. Ibid., 123.
23. Mark D. Jordan, *Blessing Same-Sex Unions: The Perils of Queer Romance and the Confusions of Christian Marriage* (Chicago and London: University of Chicago Press, 2005).
24. See P. J. Kleinplatz and C. Moser, "Politics versus Science: An Addendum and Response to Drs. Spitzer and Fink," *Journal of Psychology and Human Sexuality* 17:3–4 (2005): 135–39.
25. Mircea Eliade, *Shamanism: Archaic Techniques of Ecstasy* (Princeton, NJ: Princeton University Press/Bollingen, 1964), 33–34; Randy Conner, *Blossom of Bone: Reclaiming the Connections Between Homoeroticism and the Sacred* (San Francisco: HarperSanFrancisco, 1993),184–85, 227, 229, 231, and elsewhere.
26. Virginia Burrus, *The Sex Lives of Saints: An Erotics of Ancient Hagiography* (Philadelphia: University of Pennsylvania Press, 2004).
27. Jeremy R. Carrette, "Intense Exchange: Sadomasochism, Theology and the Politics of Late Capitalism," *Theology and Sexuality* 11:2 (2005): 26.

Chapter 7

Not Just a Phase

Single Black Women in the Black Church

Kuukua Dzigbordi Yomekpe

Can a black Catholic woman from Ghana still be a "good churchwoman" if she's not married by a certain age? Would she have an easier time being one in the seemingly more liberating culture of the United States than in the traditional missionary Ghanaian culture? Who and what defines a "good churchwoman"? Why is the church so irrevocably empowered to define the status of women without actually listening to their life experiences? Do other single black churchwomen experience the pressure of this particular imposed status from the church? Where does the particular brand of U.S. racism factor into these questions? Is this pressure intensified for me because I have the added layer of Ghanaian cultural norms?

These are just a few of the questions marking my path forward into uncharted space—a space shaped simultaneously by faith, race, gender, and sexuality; a space populated by a growing number of black women refusing the confines of the very church that helped to liberate and empower them during post-slavery; a space where religion marks my body and its many (unmarried) desires nearly as much as race does in the U.S. racialized society. It is, in short, a genuinely queer space of resisting dichotomous identities without knowing precisely how to live into alternatives. It is also a genuinely queer space of doing the unthinkable: questioning religion and the church. Whether religion, and more specifically the black church, will help me chart and, even more, live in this queer space remains an open question.

This essay is an attempt to share my own formation as a woman of African descent in the black Catholic Church, first in the African context, and then in U.S. culture. Judging by my own background I suspect that many black women experience this type of formation by the church in similar ways, and have all aspired to the ideals that the church (and society) set for us.

As a first step, at least some historical backdrop for black women and the black church is necessary to set the stage for my own formation. Theories abound concerning why the black church is so central in the formation of black people, and why women especially are held to such high standards under which they are virtually guaranteed to fall short. In *The Souls of Black Folk*, W. E. B. Du Bois, one of the first black men to document the circumstances of the Negro in America, sheds some light on the prime influence of black church post-institutional slavery. He writes:

> The Negro church of to-day is the social centre of Negro life in the United States, and the most characteristic expression of African character. . . . At the same time this social, intellectual, and economic centre is a religious centre of great power. . . . Back of this more formal religion, the church often stands as a real conserver of morals, a strengthener of family life, and the final authority on what is Good and Right.[1]

To be sure, slavery was a major impetus in wanting to do things differently once slaves became freed people. The system of slavery that had branded black women chattel and allowed them to be raped, beaten, and sold by their white slave owners rendered them incapable of maintaining any semblance of moral standards. Katie Canon writes: "the legalization of chattel slavery meant that the overwhelming majority of blacks lived permanently in subhuman status."[2] Likewise, Sonia Sanchez, in her introduction to Ayana Byrd and Akiba Solomon's anthology of personal essays from black women about their bodies, writes:

> In this country from the very beginning, the slave masters put these black, often naked, women on auction blocks. What these white men saw was free access—a wildness, an exoticness in this very prudish society that was developing. . . . So the bodies of black women have written a history and herstory in America. A herstory that has placed black women not just as enslaved women who hated slavery, but as women who supposedly enjoyed the rape and pillage by their slave masters.[3]

Additionally, during slavery any semblance of a family unit was non-existent: "countless slave families were forcibly disrupted,"[4] as Katie Canon puts it. I purport that the goal, perhaps post-slavery, was to ensure that the women would never have to endure such lapse of morality again, and that the family structure was rebuilt and preserved at all costs. What better way to ensure such morality and stability than to anchor it to the church, which would act as the final, legitimizing authority? Of course, technically good moral standards applied to both men and women, but the Holy Book was used to keep women kowtowing to their husbands and to the church, and in some ways similar to the ideology they had all been subjected to by their slave owners. It would certainly be more than enough for women to deal with the legacy of slavery and the demands of society without the church also policing women's bodies as a result of the sordid history of slavery. Byrd and Solomon also note: "we . . . internalize unattainable beauty standards and hold warped notions of the purpose of our bodies. It's no secret that the most common way to talk about the female body in America is to discuss how it should be fixed or how much it appeals to men."[5] This quote brings me back to the idea I initially began with: the married churchwoman as a "fixed" set, and the single churchwoman and anything outside of this category as still "appealing to men" and needing to be "fixed."

My Experience: A Black Catholic Woman in Ghana

Growing up in a third-world country, in Ghana, West Africa, religion infused what everyone I knew did, and in my case, it was Roman Catholicism. Doing the missionary brand of the Roman Catholic tradition was a significant challenge, but my family had a head start. Several generations earlier, my maternal grandmother's side of the family used to belong to the Anglican tradition (now regarded as Protestant), which gave us the necessary roots to assimilate completely into Catholicism. My great-grandmother, daughter of an Anglican bishop, had converted from Anglicanism when she married a Roman Catholic Englishman.

Religion was presumably what kept people alive and gave them the courage to go on regardless of the challenges of each new day. The theology espoused in this culture spun out of a colonial structure—demanding that the natives live by a different set of rules from the colonizer, and creating two separate identities within the society, with the church defining what was acceptable and what was not. Similarly, in the time of slavery in the United States, Du Bois also notes how the Bible served as a means to sanction or denounce certain behaviors and actions. In Africa, the brand of Roman Catholic theology bartered by the missionaries, to the natives, preached the natural order of life drawing on the creation story to perpetuate systems of violence against women, as well as other forms of discrimination, even hate, claiming it was what God commanded. Laurel Schneider helpfully articulates the intersecting roots of discrimination and traces them precisely to the "natural ordering" that stems from the Abrahamic religions.[6] Looking back now, I can see why

Karl Marx would call religion the "opiate of the masses." We practiced what we were taught without questioning the authority of the church; we lived a theology that was not necessarily ours, but one that kept everyone in their place and supposedly happy.

In my experience, traditionally, women in my culture were sub-citizens, subordinate to men; as such, the colonizers and the missionaries merely capitalized on this structure and used it for their own ends. To be sure, women reigned over the house and the economics of physically running the family, but everyone knew men were in charge and made the decisions at home and in church. I attended Mass, bible study, and youth group religiously, all ensuring that I was taught my proper place as a woman in society and the church—being marriageable, raising children, and caring for a husband and aging parents. By all accounts, while growing up, those women who did not want to live out this identity were judged unfit in some way, and reprimanded, prayed over, or shunned.

My first sense of my family being made up of rather queer women came very early on. My family was one of the few in our neighborhood parish that was not a complete unit. My father and mother had split when I was four, my aunt and her husband after that, my grandmother and then her sister before that. Our women were known as the "independent thinkers," women who did not stay married if it did not suit them. Of all four generations that currently live, only two or three women are still coupled. We were the women who defied the traditions of the church as well as the societal norms. Of course, this also called into question our sexuality and sexual practices, each person drawing her or his own conclusions on why the Lyall and Riby-Williams women in my family refused to be tied down. What was truly queer about this was that these women in my family were not dying to remarry promptly. These attitudes and this theology shaped my formative years; I knew that if I wished to remain in the good graces of the church and society, I would need to marry and stay married, or join the convent (celibate singlehood). Divorcees, unwed mothers were barely acknowledged; second-marriage women were reinstated once the annulments cleared and they made those second set of vows.

My Experience: A Black Catholic Woman in the United States

Everything I had ever been taught, grown to know, and not question was thrown into a pot and stirred vigorously the minute I arrived in the United States. Never having been a minority before, I came face to face with the systemic effects of racism based solely on skin color and prejudice. My social and sexual body came into question both as a woman and as a person of color.

Suddenly, I was judged not on merit alone but heavily judged on appearance. I found that most of the churches I attended were not very welcoming and sometimes handshakes at sign-of-peace time were the most uncomfortable moments during the Mass. I discovered almost immediately what it meant to be black and Catholic at the same time; the black churches were not ministering to my Catholic body and soul, and the Catholic churches were not ministering to my black body and spirit. Arriving in the United States and living this experience gave me my first glimpses of a genuinely queer existence, of living with an imposed identity while struggling to remain resolutely me.

At first, the idea of the progressive U.S. Catholic Church and its lack of a missionary sensibility disturbed me; I was looking for stability in my culture shock. In hindsight, the U.S. Catholic Church is more progressive than most around the world, something I would come to appreciate later on as I struggled with my own sexuality. Slowly, I began learning what had shaped some of the theologies the colonial church in Ghana was espousing, and I began to question them, drawing some conclusions for myself. I had suspected all along that our lived experience as women within the church and society was not reflected in the ideals espoused. Be it ignoring the lived experience of an abused woman because she ought not to break the institution of marriage, denying abortion to women who are incapable of carrying a pregnancy to term for different pressing circumstances because it would be murder, or not providing condoms in AIDS-rampant countries because it would prevent the natural order of procreation, the church had me convinced that women's lived experiences were not taken into account.

My own experience as a black Roman Catholic growing up in a very rigid culture, church, and family structure in Ghana formed me to fear and thus retain my virginity until I was twenty-two and, before then, led me to kiss only two men, hoping to preserve my sexual body to give to my one true love. I lived most of my adult life believing that I needed to marry and procreate and it was better to do it quickly so as not to gather a trail of sexual partners that might cause me to fall into sin. A life of permanent healthy sexual singlehood was not espoused as an option. I suppressed my sexuality in different ways throughout most of my adult life in church. I believe that my experiences of church and society as a black woman are quite common for a good number of other black women. No doubt, many have grown up forced to live out values and ideals that were determined by church teachings and the Holy Book, handed down by men, and in households run by fathers and husbands. Even though many generations of black women have known that these ideals were unrealistic, they have strived to live by these, often to their detriment.

I believe the dichotomy between a good churchwoman and a single one hinges on notions of sexual defiance in the latter. A "good churchwoman" is married, compliant, and "fixed" and should be emulated; a single church-woman is noncompliant, and must certainly be avoided or converted at all costs. Rarely spoken—certainly not espoused—is a much queerer option: a permanent healthy sexual singlehood as a chosen vocation for some. But what does this queer liminal space look like?

I ponder this liminal space by bringing the formative experience I have shared above into conversation with my love for literature and film. For my purposes here, I have chosen the play *Woman Thou Art Loosed* and the film *Not Easily Broken*, both sponsored by Bishop T. D Jakes and his ministry, The Potter's House. I use the secular film *Deliver Us from Eva* by Gary Hardwick in an attempt to balance out the conversation. I believe these particular re-sources show espoused church ideals in juxtaposition with the lived realities of so-called black churchwomen. I want to argue that they relate more broadly to black women's experience of sexuality within and outside the church, es-pecially to the notion of a dichotomy between a married churchwoman and a single churchwoman; the latter is seen as only a transition to the former—"it's just a phase"—and sometimes even seen as a threat to the institution of marriage. Women are depicted as having only two choices: marriage and devout care for God and family or a devout celibate singlehood (until mar-ried). Anything outside of these two is cause for suspicion, policing, and/or "deliverance" through various means. Continuing to navigate the queer space I inhabit, I suggest that using women's own lived experience as a starting point, the church might be able to better care for the souls of *all* churchwomen. I realize that this might be a queer move for most mainline religions, but it might be one that could create space for engaging the dichotomies and living into the alternatives.

(Some) Black Women on Stage and in Film

Finding black women in the arts, especially on stage, whether in theater or film, offers rich resources for reflecting on the variety of queerly shaped lives of women who are black *and* religious. Although these resources are not al-ways negative, most highlight in bold relief the way in which church and so-ciety present as nearly self-evident the only two options for black women of faith: the good churchwoman, or the noncompliant or nonconforming single churchwoman. These depictions hardly represent the actual, complex, lived experience of black women and their interaction with the church. Their scripted lives—whether at the hands of a playwright or screenwriter—offer cautionary tales to those women who dare to upset the institutional norms of the church. The brief expositions that follow demonstrate, albeit rather painfully, that stark landscape.

I begin with the play by Bishop T. D. Jakes (to whom I will refer as the Bishop from here on), followed by the film he also sponsored, and end with one of my all-time bittersweet films from a completely different director and producer. I refrain from using the characters' real-life names to minimize confusion.

In *Woman, Thou Art Loosed*, the opening scene shows a single woman prisoner, Michelle, reliving through confession to the Bishop, the abusive life that landed her in prison. The Bishop is seen as a compassionate listener who asks prodding questions that allow the audience to focus on the sins of the woman who is eventually "loosed" by the Bishop's absolution. Michelle is in jail for the second time, this time facing manslaughter charges with a death penalty for shooting her stepfather, Reggie, who is her abuser. This carries significant irony as the shooting happens at the foot of the altar while Reggie is attempting to apologize to Michelle during a three-day revival led by the Bishop. In a flashback, Michelle begins to tell the story of "Uncle" Reggie's advances from age eight when he came into the family as her mother's boyfriend. "Uncle" Reggie eventually rapes a twelve-year-old Michelle in her mother's absence and leaves her bleeding in the closet. When Cassie, her mother, returns, she drags Michelle out of the closet, chastising her as she begins to cry and tell the story of the rape. She insists that Michelle is experiencing her first period, but later places blame on Michelle by accusing her of losing her virginity to a boy who took her for a "fast girl." Cassie instills shame in Michelle, threatening and silencing her with this fabricated story line.

Later, when Reggie arrives home, Cassie meets him with a knife, leading the audience to believe that justice will be served. Reggie fakes irritation at the accusations, threatens to leave her, and uses the same story lines Cassie used: "Michelle is a "fast girl" who is dressing provocatively and probably attracting attention from a neighborhood boy, thereby reinforcing Cassie's own fake story line. Cassie gives up the knife and begs Reggie not to leave her. Cassie goes on with life as usual, working a couple of jobs to support Reggie, who is a mooch the entire length of their relationship.

Meanwhile, the young Michelle has fallen into bad company, finding men and drugs to reassure her of her own self-worth, suffering more abuse at the hands of these men, and landing in jail for drug possession. We watch as Michelle, on probation, is reconnected with her old boyfriend, Todd, who asks her to join him at the revival. We watch as Michelle begins to rekindle the old flame, but also see her struggle with her old friends—the cocaine dealers, the pimps, and those to whom she owes favors. Michelle becomes the quint-essential messed-up black woman who needs to right her life with the Lord, which is where the revival comes in; her attendance proves that Michelle is willing to get right with God, and she receives the strength to resist tempta-tion, that is, until she succumbs and kills her stepfather (Reggie) on the last day of the revival.

The underlying theme throughout the entirety of this play is a good church-woman's faith and the power of the church to change women's lives. Every female presented (there are a few minor characters with their own mini-dramas), with the exception of Cassie, is single, and as a result needs to be saved and transformed. These single women, including Michelle, are shown as unstable, but redeemable if they are willing to learn to "live in the Lord." Michelle, silenced about the childhood abuse, continues to suffer; both Reg-gie's and her mother's denial of the abuse presents us with a clear view that Michelle is to be blamed by being a certain "type" of woman. I would argue that this certain "type" is the "single woman." The solution for Michelle is marriage—finding a good black man.

Meanwhile, the audience sees the subtlety of how by reconnecting with her old boyfriend, Todd, a "man of the Lord," Michelle might have a second chance at life. She loses that chance at being ushered into the realm of good married churchwoman when she fires that shot, taking revenge into her own hands; she was supposed to leave that up to God. Michelle is punished for re-fusing to wait for someone else (God/man) to manifest her destiny. Michelle's second trip to jail is almost akin to a lesson in obedience from the powers that be; she may have killed her abuser, but she is ruining her life once again because of a man.

On the other hand, her mother, Cassie, is seen as an exemplary good mar-ried churchwoman; she serves as an usher, a treasurer, and a prayerful woman vigilant in her prayers for Reggie's conversion to the Lord. Cassie is rewarded with Reggie's eventual "coming to the Lord" after several years of praying. We even witness the couple argue on a few occasions throughout the play, about "living in sin" by not blessing the marriage in church.

In the only scene where Cassie and Michelle confront the issue of the rape, Cassie, herself a teenage mother, sees the resemblance of Michelle's incident to her own abusive past. In Cassie's past, her father was not accused, thus enabling Cassie to quickly accuse her own daughter and save her man and her relationship as she had probably observed her own mother doing. In the scene when we watch Cassie confront Reggie, she chooses to believe her hus-band over her daughter, wanting desperately to hang onto the status of good married churchwoman. She keeps her man regardless of the sordid history he might have because she trusts in the Lord for his change of heart. Her contentment at being in the good graces of the church keeps her from the ultimate accusation that would result in her divorce. The abuse of the men and the secrecy surrounding the abuse even within the church are entirely ignored. There are a couple of other occasions where we see men doing drugs or prostituting, but the women are the ones who are caught and penalized for these actions. The men, though all flawed in varying ways, are not set up as foibles, because they are simply black men who need to be delivered from their ways, not necessarily to live up to an ideal.

In the film *Not Easily Broken*, also sponsored by the Bishop and his Potter's House Ministries, we see a slightly different scenario. The entire film is laced with a voice-over utilized at particular points. This voice is uttered through Dave, but represents the voice of the Bishop and, by extension, the voice of God. At critical points throughout the film, the voice is used to reflect on why women no longer "seem" to need men, or why the effort men put into relationships is never acknowledged. According to one such voice-over:

> Down through history, men have always been measured by how hard they have worked and cultivated, how well they protected their wife and children. In the old days, women saw their men as conquerors, providers, heroes. But somewhere along the line that changed; women started to become their own heroes; maybe it was because their man forgot to be heroic or because women don't want to be protected anymore or maybe women had to be their own heroes because of the pain they had to endure in life. But whatever the cause, the world took away a man's reasons for being a man. It told him he wasn't important anymore, and when that happened, it turns the whole world upside down.[7]

The story line opens with a couple, Clarice and Dave, on their wedding day with the minister wrapping a three-strand cord around both of them and stating the importance of having God as the third strand that will keep them together. We witness the couple hit rough waters after the honeymoon. Dave loses his chance at playing professional baseball when he splits his shins during a home run. Clarice begins to take a much more bread-winning role in the family because she has a well-paid job as a real estate agent. Depicting her as the "man" in the family is also inversely seen as emasculating the actual black male, Dave. The reversal of roles then sets the woman up to be derailed and brought back to her place of conforming to her role as wife and mother. Clarice is further shown as a career woman who has no desire to have children because of her ambition to climb the corporate ladder. We see Dave spend copious amounts of hours coaching Little League, and thanks to the voice-over, we know this is a direct result of Clarice's unwillingness to have children, her inability to conform to her role as a mother.

At the height of her career, and on the way to an awards ceremony, Clarice and Dave are involved in an accident that cripples Clarice. Dave was driving, but the scene showing the crash depicts Clarice berating Dave for his late arrival. The film then follows Clarice through her physical therapy, her equally bossy and nonconforming mother moving in, and Dave being "driven" to fall for Clarice's physical therapist, who happens to be a white woman. The disintegration of the relationship is skewed in Dave's favor. Clarice and her mother take over the house and care of Clarice, thus pushing Dave out of his role, house, and wife, into a white woman's arms. A few other scenes show a male-only gathering in which the men discuss their relationships rather dreamily as a testament to the "evil and controlling power" of a nonconforming woman. The couple returns to the minister to ask direction, and he admonishes them for leaving out God from that three-stranded cord. Throughout the session, Clarice is depicted as controlling, nagging, and nonconforming, and is compared to her mother.

The film grinds to a halt when Clarice, encouraged by her mother, puts Dave out of the home. Dave, who has been spending more time with the white woman, finally has a chance to act on his desires physically. When Clarice finds out, she has a major life crisis and attends another counseling session with the minister, who then pointedly asks her if her mother has replaced God in the relationship. Clarice returns home and puts her mother out, returns to her husband to beg his forgiveness and admit that her mother, being nonconforming herself, did not teach her how to be "a woman who holds on to her man's every word." She receives pardon, Dave returns home, and they make love for the first time in months. The film ends with Clarice announcing rather sheepishly that she is pregnant.

Clarice and her mother are portrayed within the dichotomy of good married churchwoman and single churchwoman, only this time, Clarice's mother, Mama, is divorced from her husband. Clarice begins as a successful real estate agent, who is happy amassing wealth and a big mansion, and having a freedom that comes with not raising a family. She is shown making several decisions without consulting her husband and withholding sex as punishment for a variety of minor infractions, like arriving late for Clarice's important event. All around, Clarice is the "man" of the house. She begrudges Dave for spending time with the Little League boys but still refuses to have a child. She allows her mother, who is equally nonconforming, to move into her house and dictate to Dave how the house ought to be run. In counseling, the minister warns Clarice about turning into a lonely, bitter woman like her mother because allowing her to replace God in that three-stranded cord is what is damaging her relationship. Replacing God with a nonconforming woman would be the worst possible thing Clarice could do. This admonition is the trigger that sends Clarice back to her mother, blaming her for not teaching her how to love her man "right" and accusing her of wanting her to be just as miserable as her. "Mama, I don't want to end up like you!" Clarice cries, voicing her fears and realization that there really are just two roles from which she can choose, and those who do not fit one end up in the other. The plot comes to a close with Clarice begging for her man back despite his infidelities, re-pledging her love and commitment to her role, and having sex that results in the pregnancy, thus, fulfilling her role as conforming black woman.

On the other hand, Clarice's mom, Mama, is depicted as nonconforming as well, but in a much harsher way because Mama appears to be beyond redemption; she threw her husband out for "no apparent reason" and never took him back. What does not become clear until the very end is the reason for Mama throwing out her husband—he was very abusive toward her and Clarice. This abuse shaped how Mama raised Clarice, which later comes into play when Mama reacts in the same way to Dave's cheating behavior, as she did with her own husband. However, this abuse is not the focus because it is just another flaw of an imperfect man that most conforming black women would know to ignore. The cost of taking care of herself and her child is dear: it leaves Mama bitter and lonely, and she is depicted as wanting to take her daughter down the same path. The focus is on her nonconformity rather than on the abuse and the silence that comes with the abuse. Mama is the woman in church that everyone smiles with but talks disapprovingly about at dinner tables.

In a similar way, the film Deliver Us from Eva, with a play on the words "Eva," "Evil," and "Eve," tells the story of the Dandridge sisters, three of whom are happily partnered. Eva, the oldest, is typecasted as the fussiest of them all with an attitude that "brings" a man so low he cannot live out his proper function as the head of the household. Eva is the quintessential bitch who is the choir director, but often shunned and the brunt of mean jokes because of her militant nature. Her sisters' partners are very infuriated with her because she is a meddler in their private lives.

Eva is a single, educated, and successful woman who makes her living as a State Department health inspector. She raised all three sisters single-handedly when her parents passed when she was eighteen. Eva is able to dish out researched advice along with data that ironically undermine the supposedly intelligent arguments of her brothers-in-law concerning their relationships with her sisters. Eva's influence on her sisters makes one of them study more, another to refuse to have children until she is ready, and yet another to refuse to have sex before marriage. Underlying this seemingly normal everyday life are the foiled attempts to set Eva up with various men. After the last attempt, Eva admits that she has been praying to God for the perfect man that God has destined for her to come along. She affirms what she knows to be true—the "man up there has my back."

As if to answer her prayer, or to show God's power to deliver, along comes a man, Ray, who fits her long laundry list. They meet at a church barbeque and everyone seems to think that he really is a God-sent. We discover that her sisters' partners have paid Ray a hefty sum of money to sweep Eva off her feet, and then leave her broken-hearted, forcing her to leave town. We watch as Ray indeed sweeps Eva off her feet after a rough start. Eva begins to relax and let her guard down and we see Ray also falling in love. All bets are off when Ray actually falls in love with Eva and wants to return the bribe. The partners capture Ray and fake a certificate of death and hold a pretend funeral; all the while Ray is locked away in an abandoned warehouse. Ray manages to escape and finally shows up at his own funeral and confesses the whole sham. Eva is disgusted by the whole ordeal and decides to take a job in another city to recuperate and start anew. We watch as Ray makes all attempts to win back her love and is rebuffed. Eventually, Ray shows up with a horse (Eva is an avid equestrian) and finally wins Eva back.

I believe Gary Hardwick, the director and producer, wants to communicate a rather simple message here: any woman who is fussy, militant, and independent will forever remain single, unhappy, and an outcast in society. All around her, the ideal woman is modeled for her, but initially, and even after the betrayal, Eva decides that her life is full and happy as is, and conforming to someone else's ideals is not necessarily her cup of tea. This film is bittersweet for me because Eva stands her ground and makes her own rules throughout the entire film, even while she and Ray are seriously involved, but in the end, he wins her back with a horse.

Dealing with this film by an entirely different director with what seems at first to have no church-related slant seemed at first to work as counterpoint to my overall argument. However, even here Eva is bought and made to conform to the religious/social ideal—a happy black woman equals a married one. Eva's sisters all play nonconforming female roles throughout the entire film, but the minute Eva leaves town they are all ready to play the role of conformed women, the lead among them being the one sister who had previously refused to have a baby. The film masquerades as forward thinking, yet still returns to the old ways of making women fit into traditional roles; Eva eventually conforms.

The men in this film are once again up to no good. They make jokes about Eva, hinting that if she did less talking and more lying on her back (sex) like everyone else she wouldn't be so mean and uptight. We watch as the men are consistently attempting to break up the strong sister-bond that the women have that makes them nonconforming. "God made Eva so we are Even" is one of the quotes from this movie, justifying their treatment of Eva. Ray is seen as the "messiah" for having worked his magic on Eva to make her fall in love. Every conversation in all of the gatherings among these women is centered on men and their flaws, which are then dismissed as God-given and forgivable. How then do I live; how then do we single black women live, either in or outside of the church?

Charting the Uncharted Space

All the women in the portrayals I have summarized above experience being Othered at various times. Michelle, Cassie, Clarice, Mama, Eva, and her sisters all have separate but strikingly similar experiences. For some, the opposite is true as well; they become the norm once they choose to conform. Each of the women who end up conforming begins as a nonconforming woman, and each is slowly reduced to the more befitting role; the process is strikingly similar for all of them. They are pitted against a conforming ideal or a nonconforming ideal, and then given an ultimatum: conform and live happily every after, or do not conform and remain single, bitter, and lonely. The cost for each of these women, conforming or not, is high: losing one's true self to conform to the ideals of church and society is equally high as losing friendship and community for being the nonconforming one.

More often than not—as each of these portrayals here and also in my own experience—church and, *by definition*, men are at the center of the turmoil. By dictating the criteria that signify conforming, they automatically "other" the groups who do not fit those criteria. For those for whom conforming is not a true option, one sees a kind of settling for the role of Other, as we see in Mama's case, and perhaps slightly in Michelle's—they are resigned to their fate as nonconforming and thus Other women within society and church.

In one of the final scenes of *Not Easily Broken*, Clarice tells her mother, "Mama, ama pray for you," to which Mama responds, "Chil' pray for yoself," prompting the audience to believe in a woman resigned to her fate. However, I see Mama as standing firm and using this moment to put forth a warning in the form of a challenge about the path that Clarice has chosen to take. Perhaps in the end, Clarice is going to be the one truly sacrificing herself and paying a high price for doing so. We may never be able to tell what the true meaning of

Mama's words are and what effect they have, but Clarice, along with Cassie, Eva, and the others, have made a choice to compromise by conforming.

I cannot fault real-life women who make the very same choices as the women above because whenever I do this, I in turn "other" them. The truth is, we are all part of the same system that oppresses women and pits us against each other. As I contemplate moving into the uncharted space before me, I wonder if I can do so as a "single woman" without being branded as dangerous or unfit. Can I truly live beyond the dichotomy of "good (married)/nonconforming (single)"? Is singleness "just a phase" on the road to being a good churchwoman if I choose to stay in the institutional church? I want to believe, queerly enough, that religion can help—even if the church can't. But that will take time.

The time such discernment will take will, at the very least, involves healing. In that regard, I was struck by something a colleague said to me recently: "Our body memories are the last to be healed." I interpreted this to mean that both pleasant and horrifying memories are first stored in our bodies and then in our rational brains. Because we live an embodied life, we may rationally heal and move on, but our bodies store memories and retain them for much longer periods of time, far past the time of rational healing.

This was a profound statement for me, especially as I often ponder the numerous times I have reacted viscerally to situations for which I had no rational explanation. Both my pleasant and horrifying memories of church literally follow me wherever I go. I must confront these experiences rationally and hope that the body memory healing will follow slowly as I continue to queer the spaces I enter. The uncharted space before me is open for interpretation. It is marked with complex bodies: black bodies, African bodies, married bodies, sexual bodies, dangerous bodies, male bodies, female bodies, unhealthy bodies, church bodies—too many bodies to catalogue. The space is uncharted, yes, but it also beckons with its own queerly religious energy, the energy of the nonconforming. The energy of a spirit that is not rigid but rather open to morphing with each lived experience our bodies have. I hope this queer concept can one day be embraced by the church. I wish that one day, there will be no need for women to fear living in the liminal spaces and rejecting the dichotomous lives that lead to unhealthy bodies.

Notes

1. W. E. B. Du Bois, *The Souls of Black Folk* (New York: Barnes and Noble, 2003), 137.
2. Katie Cannon, *Katie's Canon: Womanism and the Soul of the Black Community* (New York: Continuum, 1998), 29.

3. Ayana Byrd and Akiba Solomon, *Naked: Black Women Bare All about Their Skin, Hair, Hips, Lips, and Other Parts* (New York: The Penguin Group, 2005), xii.

4. Cannon, *Katie's Canon*, 31.

5. Byrd and Solomon, *Naked*, 4.

6. See chap. 8 in this present volume, Laurel Schneider, "What Race is Your Sex?"

7. *Not Easily Broken*, DVD, directed by Bill Duke (Los Angeles: Sony Pictures, 2009).

Chapter 8

What Race is Your Sex?

Laurel C. Schneider

The question "what race is your sex?" or its corollary "what sex is your race?" may seem nonsensical at first, particularly to white people. When I pose it to students, regardless of race or ethnicity their faces tend to go to a startled blank. The question seems unanswerable to many of them, like a Zen koan. Common use separates the etiology of race and sex, assuming the factors that determine race to be independent of the factors that determine sex or gender. As people of color particularly have known, race affects one's experience and even embodiment of one's gender, and gender affects one's experience and even embodiment of race, but it is difficult for everyone fully to digest the co-constitutive qualities of race, sex, and gender, or the utter dependence of one upon the others for meaning and existence. It is this co-constitutive quality of race, sex, and gender that I am interested in, primarily because of the support each construction gives in the modern West to white supremacy's tenacity.

To make the claim that sex, gender, and race all constitute each other (suggesting, for example, that whiteness itself has a gender) supposes an unseemly or even grotesque conflation of natures. In fact, correlating race and sex or gender brings into question the natural status of all three categories, implying that they could be otherwise, unmooring them from nature and thereby disrupting just about everything taken for granted in modernity. Of course, to

Reprinted from "What Race is Your Sex" by Laurel Schneider from Jennifer Harvey, Karen A. Case, and Robin Hawley Gorsline, eds., *Disrupting White Supremacy from Within: White People on What We Need to Do* (Cleveland: The Pilgrim Press, 2004). Used by permission.

make such a sweeping claim, simplistic biological definitions of race, sex, and gender cannot apply. Given the undecidability of race, gender, and sexuality on scientific or genetic grounds, however, I believe that we are justified in assuming all three to be largely other than biology.[1]

But saying that race is largely other than skin color, facial features, and hair texture, that sex is largely other than genital and libidinal formation, and that gender is largely other than hormonal deployment does not mean that the categories of race, sex, and gender become meaningless or ungrounded. Anne McClintock points out, for example, that to "dispute the notion that race is a fixed and transcendent essence, unchanged through the ages, does not mean that 'all talk of race must cease,' nor does it mean that the baroque inventions of racial difference 'had no tangible or terrible effects.'" On the contrary, she argues, "it is precisely the inventedness of historical hierarchies that renders attention to social power and violence so much more urgent."[2] The very same can be said of disputing the notion that sex and gender are fixed and transcendent essences.

It is difficult to think around the corners of the world one inhabits, or to glimpse the limits and gaps in one's own inherited view. While specific modern theorizations of racial, sexual, and gender difference began in the late eighteenth century, were increasingly scientificized in the nineteenth century, and only began to disintegrate late in the twentieth century,[3] biologistic and reductive assumptions about race, sex, and gender as divinely ordained, physically based distinctions between humans remain common. This means that in modern conceptualizations, race, sex, and gender function as more or less benign signifiers of natural (and so immutable) human difference. From this viewpoint it is what people *do* with the natural differences of race, sex, or gender that may not be so benign, but that is not the fault of nature (or God). Lately, however, as modernity shows more and more cracks, modern Western conceptions of reality and particularly of race, sex, and gender become increasingly brittle, exposing their relatively recent invention and their enmeshment in Western colonial enterprises. The idea of race, sex, and gender as meaningful signifiers of so-called natural difference is less and less persuasive, and certainly less and less benign.

I am in fact convinced that race, sex, and gender are not only constructed for particular purposes of social order but that to contemplate them in isolation from each other is to perpetuate their more insidious social and political effects and to ignore their more profound theological implications. Evelyn Brooks Higgenbotham's notion of race as a "metalanguage" rather than a stable identifier rooted in biology is helpful here in contemplating race, sex, and gender together.[4] Since the start of European colonial expansion, which, as Robert Young says so vividly, "ended in the Western occupation of nine tenths of the surface territory of the globe,"[5] Higgenbotham argues that race has served as a "global sign" or "ultimate trope[s] of difference, arbitrarily contrived to produce and maintain relations of power and subordination."[6] Taken together, I argue that race and sex co-constitute a corporate merging of meanings located in human and divine hierarchies that solidify the power and make resilient the supremacy of whites, exemplified in the white male from which all others differentiate in useful degrees of degenerate separation.

In each case, modern concepts of race, sex, and gender extrapolate an immutable nature from a few arbitrarily contrived features and each, ironically, requires constant reiteration and enforcement to remain constant or immutable. Race extrapolates nature and behavioral norms (who one is and how one should behave) from the color of skin and other geographically based, hereditary characteristics of appearance that apply regardless of other hereditary contradictions or changes. Sex extrapolates nature and behavioral norms from a few selected genetic features focused on the genitals that apply regardless of other genetic features, contradictions, or changes. And gender extrapolates nature and behavioral norms most outrageously from social claims about the nature of sex and selected behavioral patterns nominally identified as masculine or feminine, regardless of other behavioral patterns, contradictions, or changes. The result of this is a set of ideologies of race, sex, and gender rather than reliable and consistent explanations of human difference, ideologies that serve to keep individual persons in place. This dynamic would not trouble us if the places assigned to different groups based on race, sex, and gender did not so blatantly serve larger systems of privilege and power. How ideologies of race, sex, and gender intersect and produce *each other* and thereby resist change is what interests me in my own work as a white woman committed to the dogged, daily, and sometimes intimate task of subverting racism.

The issue that I plan to raise here is neither small nor is it smooth. A great deal of white evasion from racist complicity is accomplished by efforts to complicate the issue with other, attendant concerns (like sexism, heterosexism, or classism). It is not my intention to evade white complicity in racism here, but rather to search out some of the many ways that white supremacy eludes even the most seasoned, committed, and trustworthy antiracist whites when it goes incognito in the guise of unexamined sex, gender, or class ideology. While it may be clear to most that the "isms" are linked in theory, deep understandings of the ways in which modern concepts of race, sex, and gender are *co-constitutive*, meaning that they cannot meaningfully be separated *except* in support of racist and sexist goals, is much more difficult to grasp and even more difficult to practice, particularly for whites, whom the separation most effectively serves.

McClintock makes this very point when she argues that "race, gender and class are not distinct realms of experience, existing in splendid isolation from each other; nor can they be simply yoked together retrospectively like armatures of Lego. Rather, they come into existence *in and through* relation to each other—if in contradictory and conflictual ways."[7] Lorraine O'Grady puts a finer point on the inseparability and co-constitutive quality of race, sex, and gender in a quote that Evelynn Hammonds uses to begin her essay entitled "Black (W)holes and the Geometry of Black Female Sexuality":

> The female body in the West is not a unitary sign. Rather, like a coin, it has an obverse and a reverse: on the one side, it is white; on the other, not-white or, prototypically, black. The two bodies cannot be separated, nor can one body be understood in isolation from the other in the West's metaphoric construction of "woman." *White is what woman is; not-white (and the stereotypes not-white gathers in) is what she had better not be* [emphasis added].[8]

If "white is what woman is," then the co-constitutive qualities of race, sex, and gender are such that each becomes nonsensical apart from the others. This becomes especially clear when the gendering of race, or what Abdul JanMohamed calls "racialized sexuality," is more vividly limned.[9] Furthermore, one of the consequences of eighteenth- and nineteenth-century European expansion and the American slave industry is that race and gender constitute each other in such powerful and necessary ways that separating them from each other serves to mask the naturalizing functions of colonialism and so masks the pervasive tenacity of white supremacy. White supremacy in service first to European colonial expansion and American slavery and then in service to global capitalism lies at the heart of the race/sex co-constitution, a co-constitution that ultimately functions to preserve the power and privilege of white males in a symbolic and very material economy of human diversity, positioned for the maintenance of its own order and the benefit of a few.

Modernity, a period beginning roughly with the emergence of European colonialism and American slavery, denotes the rise of global industrial capitalism and its attendant obsessions with property and individualism. To say that race, sex, and gender are inventions of modernity does not mean that prior to this period meaningful concepts of race, sex, or gender did not exist. Certainly people in every culture have always found ways to distinguish between themselves in terms of sexual and reproductive practices, familial allegiances, and affectional behavior. Among others, for example, Helen Scott has argued that prior to colonial expansion, race was understood generally by Europeans to refer to familial lineages rather than to whole classes of nations and tribes. This earlier understanding materially served a feudal system of indentured servitude and class division based flexibly on individual families in ways that a modern conceptualization of race would not have done. It is only with the rise of labor-ravenous industries and agricultures in England and America that a conceptualization of race based on entire nations and continents served and took hold.[10]

Likewise, sex and gender conceptualizations follow more or less economic trajectories that, enmeshed with emergent colonial concepts of race, morphed into categories of difference that primarily served European and American colonial capitalism. While the labor of reproduction falls most heavily on females in most cultures of the world, in the European colonial enterprise, gender became racialized and classed specifically in service of creating an endless labor pool for the growing industries of the North and the growing plantations of the American South on the one hand, and in service of perpetuating and maintaining a class of white capitalist beneficiaries on the other.

Sex and Gender Co-Constituted for Supremacy

Long before the first colonial armada left port, the naturalization of gender difference and of sex had taken place in European thought, firmly establishing the legitimacy of human hierarchies in the absolute position of the male over the female in body, mind, law, and right. In the thirteenth century, Thomas Aquinas had harnessed Aristotle to consolidate and systematize a natural (meaning God-given and -established) Christian hierarchy of males over females. This meant a divinely naturalized set of gendered sexual norms in which maleness is conceived as active and dominant, while femaleness is conceived as passive and subservient. Natural gender placements thus determined natural sex and sexual practices as well. This gender and sex hierarchy was not new to the thirteenth century by any means, but Thomas's *Summa Theologica* and *Contra Gentiles* helped further to solidify and legitimize it, making masculinity and dominance co-constitutive terms that began even more explicitly to shape the meaning of Christian civilization. By the time that John Milton wrote the hugely popular *Paradise Lost* in the late seventeenth century, the idea that humans are naturally and perfectly ordered in superior and inferior categories made common sense and was understood to be divinely ordained, European in origin, and absolutely sexualized in character. All this is present in Milton's imagining of Adam and Eve before Satan has approached them:

Whence true authority in men, though both
Not equal, as their sex not equal seem'd;

For contemplation hee and valour form'd,
For softness shee and sweet attractive Grace,
Hee for God only, shee for God in him:
His fair large Front and Eye sublime declar'd
Absolute rule; and Hyacinthine Locks
Round from his parted forelock manly hung
Clust'ring, but not beneath his shoulders broad:
Shee as a veil down to the slender waist
Her unadorned golden tresses wore
Dishevell'd, but in wanton ringlets wav'd
As the Vine curls her tendrils, which impli'd
Subjection, but requir'd with gentle sway,
And by her yielded, by him best receiv'd,
Yielded with shy submission, modest pride,
And sweet reluctant amorous delay.[11]

Here the appearance of the perfect male and perfect female are gendered into dominance and submission, codified by sex and ultimately by race. How Adam's and Eve's hair look, for example, determines her wanton and subject nature on the one hand, and his "true authority" on the other. Her perfect femaleness is made evident by her appearance, an appearance codified in both sexual and racial terms familiar to any reader.

The result of such imagistic sex-gender-race conflation in the story of divine creation was deeply insidious in real life, contributing to an emergent economic and social structure based on biology. First of all, by making passivity a sign of true womanhood, no working-class or slave female could measure up to the basic definition of being a woman and survive by virtue of her class position and its requirement that she labor, although she could still theoretically submit to men. Likewise, by making dominance a sign of true manhood, no working-class or slave male could measure up to the basic definition of being a man and survive by virtue of his class position and its requirement that he submit to authority, although he could still theoretically dominate some women. In a curious and sometimes homoerotic twist, this co-constitution of gender with class and eventually with race meant (and continues to mean) that manhood is limited but not destroyed by submission to other, more powerful men. From the poorest day laborer to the Archbishop of Canterbury, submitting to more dominant males (from boss to God) is preferable to the alternative of submitting to females and so losing all claim to manhood. Shawn Copeland has observed, for example, that even in the extremes of slavery European gender hierarchies made their mark as black men were rewarded for dominating black women. Slavery, she argues, not only exploited black women's bodies and sex for labor and reproduction of labor but undermined relationships between black women and black men. "So it was that colonization and slavery, as both ideology and practice, not only sustained patriarchy but also initiated black men into, and rewarded them for, brutalizing *mimesis*."[12]

The Invention of Race for Colonial Domination

If *Paradise Lost* was the Hollywood-style image-maker of eighteenth-century England, then the divinely ordained true woman, spread across the globe through colonial expansion, was subservient, passive, soft, blonde, and slightly wanton (in need of direction and sexual supervision). Because it is this image of white femininity that defines womanhood in the colonial enterprise, both race and gender are intersecting here in a racialized sexuality. The link of sex and gender to whiteness here lies at the crux of the matter for, to echo O'Grady, "white is what woman is; not-white (and the stereotypes not-white gathers in) is what she had better not be." The only way that a statement like this makes sense is through the lens of colonialism and its attendant conflation of sex and race.

In the early and mid-nineteenth century, racial theory was a popular enterprise of European academics and politicians interested in confirming both the superiority of Europeans and the legitimacy of colonial expansion and domination over the rest of the world. The major disagreement among these theorists had to do with whether the different human races could be traced to a single source (monogenesis) or to multiple sources (polygenesis). Young points out that polygenesis had the advantage of accounting for differences between human groups on the basis of different origins, allowing Europeans to continue to affirm Enlightenment ideals of equality among men by limiting the category of man more explicitly and exclusively to those of European descent. But monogenesis had the advantage of squaring with the biblical story of Eden in Genesis 2 and tended to find more adherents despite requiring one more step to solidify white supremacy. From a monogenetic perspective, differences between human groups could be accounted for through theories of degeneration. "This meant that the pure origin of man was the white male— that universal mean and measure of all things—and that all other forms were a deterioration from this ideal, as a result of gender or geography or both."[13] The theory of degeneration also fit nicely with the European take on the biblical story of the fall from paradise. Eve, the paradigm of white womanhood, is not male and so represents already a slippage from the ideal, or at least a slippage from the universal mean and measure of all things. Her difference from Adam serves to highlight the contours of white masculinity through her deficiencies. It is to her that Satan makes his move, ensuring the further degeneration of this ideal of whiteness into the various races.

Because the modern concept of race as biology had to be invented—meaning that prior to the American slave trade and European colonial expansion there was little or no need for anyone to have a refined theory of biological or scientific differences between people—I am persuaded by the arguments that place economics at the heart of the matter. The fact that American slavery itself did not begin as a race-based institution but rather evolved out of class-based indentured servitude that failed when the demand for labor in Europe and in the Americas far exceeded both the criminal and working classes of those populations is significant.[14] At just the historical moment when Enlightenment ideals about liberty as an endowment of humanity began to be adopted and fought for in both Europe and America, the cotton and sugar economy of the American South and the concomitant textile factories of the North yawned wide for cheap, permanent labor that indentured servitude could no longer satisfy both because of the changing political idealism of democracy and the savage brutality of the work itself.

At the same time, Europeans vied for control of the world in pursuit of greater economic gain and dominance over trade. The emergence of colonial capitalism with its emphasis on private property also fueled the search for a rationale for acquiring cheaper and cheaper labor, with outright ownership of labor being the ideal. Scientific theories of race served both acquisitive goals, for the most part "substantiating convictions that preceded scientific enquiry,"[15] legitimizing and institutionalizing the already growing practice of complete ownership of human beings, their children, and the products of their labor. Doing so served the twofold purpose of making available to white colonial property owners all nonwhite peoples for exploitation without controversion of Enlightenment ideals while funneling all of the resulting wealth to themselves.

As a case in point, historians of race point to the story of legal development in the early United States to trace the evolution of theories that sought to associate all blacks incontrovertibly with slavery. For this, Scott argues, "whites had to be taught to be white and blacks taught to be black, and the two groups separated. . . . Laws against miscegenation, intermarriage and association were passed throughout the colonies in the last decade of the seventeenth and first of the eighteenth centuries [and the] former interracial coexistence among laborers was ruthlessly dismantled."[16] The invention of race as an absolute signifier of difference, a global sign, was codified in pseudo-scientific theories about biology and evolution that rested on the primacy of whiteness as the standard against which all differences were cited as degeneration and lack. Consequently, race emerged as a theory primarily of whiteness, a condition that is contradictorily evidenced in nature and necessarily achieved and maintained through practice. Facial features, skin color, bone structure, and so forth all formed a catalogue of race that, while officially disavowed by member nations after 1945 with the UNESCO statements on race, remain a part of common association and even official census and political identification throughout the world today. More subtle and so perhaps at a more powerful and tenacious level, the practices of race evidence the resilience of racism, particularly through race's co-constituting connections to sex and gender.

The Co-Constitution of Sex, Race, and Gender in Class

Because the issue of the co-constitutive quality of modern concepts of race, sex, and gender begins in colonialism, it makes sense to focus briefly on how race was gendered and sexed in support of colonial expansion and of white supremacy in particular. The evolution and naturalization of gender hierarchies parallels the evolution and naturalization of race hierarchies, but parallelism does not necessarily imply co-constitution. The fact is that race scientists made sex and gender foundational to a racial theory of white supremacy. The link was not accidental. Gendering race gave further legitimacy to both hierarchies, more firmly grounding both sex and race differentials in divinely ordained nature in such a way that the colonial enterprise could progress apace secure in the rightness of white domination of nonwhite, through the divinely preordained domination of females by males. The legitimacy for both hierarchies came from a theory of natural endowment in which the superior qualities of one group could, through a kind of trickle-down effect, improve the overall position of everyone while further cementing its own dominant position. Many slave traders and investors sought to legitimate their own practices, for example, through the notion that slavery in the land of whites was in effect an act of charity, improving the lot of otherwise free Africans mired in unhappy degeneracy. This same logic became foundational to later capitalist theory, in which the superior endowments of the wealthy would establish an unequal field of competition but insist that free mobility and deployment of these dominant resources improves the overall economic position of all players while further cementing the dominant position of the wealthy. In both equations, the contradictory and misleading motto is "everyone wins."

The gendering of whiteness as dominant, as global sign of civilization, and therefore as male (and blackness or yellowness as subordinate, as global sign of wantonness and therefore as female) has its roots deep in ancient genderings of reality. The explicit gendering of race, however, could only emerge with the invention of race as a universal concept, which occurred in the pseudo-science of race theories of the mid-nineteenth century. The degeneration of the races from original and ideal whiteness could be rationalized through the lens of sex and gender in self-referencing logic. Just as Adam needed companionship and the opportunity to fully express his perfect manhood through dominance and wise governance, making necessary the emergence of a lesser being from his own body, differentiation in the races ultimately served to provide the white race with its fullest potential for improvement through exercise of heroic dominance and wise governance over the world.

The white race is thus gendered male by virtue of its dominance, and the nonwhite races are gendered female, indicating their need for supervision. No other but gender ideology could so neatly turn a differentiation of the races into a normative hierarchy that justifies white supremacy on the one hand, and consolidates the position of upper-class males on the other hand. As Robert Young observes:

> The "natural" gender relations of European society are once again used to establish the authority of the natural laws that determine the relations between the races. Just as the white male rules at home, so he also lords it abroad. The orthodox hierarchy of gender is confirmed and reaffirmed at the level of race, which then in turn feminizes males and females alike in the black and yellow races. All hierarchies, together with their cultural values, can, it seems, be assimilated, so long as the white male remains on top.[17]

Nineteenth-century racial theorists made explicit the association between the gender dominance of males and the claims that they were attempting to establish scientifically about whiteness. This association served to bolster and clarify the dominance of the upper class within Europe by associating color and sex more and more with class position, and so bolstered whiteness as a signifier of rule throughout the world, further legitimating colonial expansion in general. Gender and race both became instruments of class by mirroring the priorities of those already in positions of power. McClintock points out, for example, that preeminent German race theorist Carl Vogt "saw similarities between the skulls of white male infants and those of the white female working class, while noticing that a mature black male shared his 'pendulous belly' with a white woman who had had many children."[18] The notoriously pendulous bellies of upper-class German males aside (and that is precisely a filter Vogt is attempting to install here), these associations served the curious task of masculinizing non-dominant females and of feminizing non-dominant males to the same end: solidifying the natural superiority of the dominant (white) male. The co-constitutive qualities of race, sex, and gender thus conceived allow them to function as stand-ins for one another, making them much more effective and, ultimately, more resilient.

The ideal of womanhood in colonial Europe (soft, subservient, passive, and preferably blonde) clarifies this point. She is also upper class because all of these qualities cannot be attained by working women. Labor invalidates passivity and softness. This means that subservience alone did not suffice to establish ideal womanhood. Indeed, the most dominated of women were also the least feminized by virtue of enforced labor (through slavery or economic necessity), and the most dominated of men were, contradictorily, the most feminized by virtue of limited power (through slavery or economic necessity). McClintock has documented the dubious gender *and race* of charwomen in Victorian England as an illustration of the gendering and racializing of class that put most women in a conflicted relationship to both womanhood and whiteness.[19]

Despite the dubious gender and race of women who were unable economically to achieve womanhood since it depended on the labor of others, marriage became an important marker of gender *and* race accomplishment, and served the progressive ideal of colonial powers. Through marriage a woman could effectively change race by improving her class position. Nineteenth-century French race theorist Joseph Gobineau strove to develop a rationale for colonial expansion through this metaphor of sex and marriage. Since the nonwhite races were female to the white race's masculinity, the white race harbors a deep attraction for the black and yellow races, literally aching for union and therefore improvement of the issue through marriage. The resistance of the black and yellow races to marriage through colonial domination is to be understood as natural, just as females tend to resist the advances of males.[20]

Gobineau's pseudo-rape fantasy of white colonial intercourse with black and yellow cultures reiterates the creed of white, upper-class supremacy, on the one hand, and addresses the growing perception of many Europeans that the upper class was becoming insipid, ingrown, and weak, on the other. The legitimation of colonial expansion through theories of racialized gender/sex and sexualized race/gender was standard intellectual practice. Virgin lands and wanton peoples were powerful sexual projections that made the fantasy of male satisfaction a metonymic for colonial expansion (or perhaps we should call it enlargement). And as Kadiatu Kanneh points out, the "feminizing of colonized territory is, of course, a trope in colonial thought."[21]

While some nineteenth-century race theorists may have worried about sexualizing race along accepted European gender hierarchies, doing so had multiple benefits for male European property owners. The gender hierarchy was a well established feature of Christian civilization, but it required reiteration and constant vigilance lest women forget their natural place. Therefore, not only did notions of sexualized race naturalize the inferiority of nonwhites, but such notions reinscribed and reaffirmed the natural inferiority of women. And for the relatively small cost of continued submission to white men, white women became willing participants and contributors to this ideology for the simple reason that they could reap a significant portion of the material benefits of sexualized race, despite the fact that doing so reinforced gender ideologies of domination and submission in order to enslave nonwhites and plunder their territories.

Another added benefit to colonial powers of sexualized race was the reinforcement of sexual placements. Joseph Gobineau, Carl Vogt, Gustav Klemm, and Carl Gustav Carus could all develop the Enlightenment thought that races have genders precisely because doing so supported the gendered heterosexual norm that authorized dominance. If, as many of them argued, the white race is masculine/dominant and the nonwhite races feminine/subordinate, colonization reiterated a heterosexual norm that supports both sexualized race and racialized sex. Heterosexual ideologies based upon a naturalization of heterosexual desire legitimated white colonization as marriage in which rape could not occur regardless of the violence of penetration. Masculinized whiteness, which equates dominance with an identity, is thereby reinforced in heterosexual terms. So the modern ideology of sex, just like ideologies of race and gender, came to reside primarily in the arithmetic of white supremacy, and colonization-as-marriage became the means of its reproduction.

As part of this arithmetic, the institution of marriage itself was usually an economic necessity for both lower- and upper-class women aspiring to some measure of class (and so race) success in Europe and the colonies. It also furthered the sex-gender-race co-constitution, making femininity and masculinity necessary sexual corollaries of one another and so necessary markers of race success, grounded in nature. The well-documented public sexual brutalization of black women in slavery and particularly the legal prohibitions against slave marriage further distanced slaves from dominant, colonial practices of sexualized gender (not to mention their own inherited gender practices), thus racializing gender all the more, in this case through prohibitions on gender practices for certain *races*. Such prohibitions served further to feminize slave men except where they could dominate slave women, and to masculinize slave women, except where they could submit to slave or free men. Most of all, such prohibitions helped to construct the natural rightness of white, upper-class sex and gender practices as paradigmatic of true and originary human ideals, thus racializing those practices and solidifying them in a class structure.[22] Enforcing limitations on all of these gendered practices to upper-class whites made evident both the whiteness of legitimacy and the legitimacy of whiteness at every level of social interaction.

The Implications

If modern concepts of race are fundamentally and ineluctably co-constituted by gender and sex ideologies, and if modern concepts of gender and sex are fundamentally and ineluctably co-constituted by race ideology, it begins to make sense that racism retains a kind of tenacity even among those who claim to be opposed to it, or that sexism and heterosexism persist among those who claim to be opposed to them. Racism is structured throughout the modern constellation of race, sex, gender, and class and can take up residence in any of these ports of meaning to weather occasional antiracist storms, only to reemerge as soon as success is proclaimed. In her argument that whiteness and nonwhiteness define each other, Vron Ware points to the tricky issue of sexualized race, suggesting that the "different elements in this system of 'race' and gender identity have no intrinsic meaning; they work only in and through differentiation."[23]

Working in and through differentiation means that the terms of whiteness and blackness (as a paradigm of not-white) and of femininity and masculinity are so interdependent that they cannot signify anything except the shape of their opposition. And in extremity, as Asian, Hispanic, Native American, and mixed race scholars have noted, those who are neither white nor black exist in ambiguity or worse, not at all. According to the vestigial colonial thinking on which race depends, however, to the extent that nonblack nonwhites can display gender, they can gravitate to a race. In an economy of oppositions, one must claim a pole or vaporize. And it is the economy of three-dimensional oppositions between race, sex, and gender that stabilizes racism, and particularly white supremacy, over time and into the present.

In other words, without femininity to define it, masculinity collapses on itself and vaporizes like Oz's wicked witch of the west. Likewise, femininity cannot hold without masculinity to define it, and whiteness collapses in on itself and vaporizes without blackness, and vice versa. But even more dramatically and to the point here, without masculinity, whiteness collapses, and without femininity, blackness collapses. Like a trick drawing that contains two different pictures that you can see only by changing what you look for, one comes into focus on the back of the other and cannot exist except in that relation. Eve Kosofsky Sedgewick has made this argument clearly in terms of sexuality when she argues that the homosexual closet is a feature of heterosexuality, not of homosexuality. The closet, or exclusion of that which exceeds

heterosexuality, limns and makes possible the heterosexual claim about itself.[24] It is for this reason that Hammonds admonishes white women to "re-
figure (white) female sexualities so that they are not theoretically dependent
upon an absent yet ever-present pathologized black female sexuality."[25]

The core of this work for whites, I believe, lies in attention to our investments in *gendered* whiteness, meaning deep-level investments in sexualized
and even eroticized assumptions of dominance and submission, authority and
passivity that make reconstruction of whiteness a deconstruction of gender,
and vice versa. To recognize whiteness masquerading as masculinity that understands itself in terms of strength, voice, leadership, vision, direction, and
authority may make some of the more tenacious and self-effacing aspects of
white supremacy emerge into the light. One of the reasons that white people have great difficulty undoing their own practices of white supremacy is
that the co-constitutive aspects of race, sex, and gender make the practices
of whiteness very difficult to perceive in oneself, particularly when they also
function as gender and sex. Gender identity is so powerfully reiterative and
self-reinforcing that even men who recognize the atrocities of masculinity
constructed as dominance tend to suffer deep anxiety over the prospect of un-
manning themselves and struggle to imagine a non-dominant or -dominating
masculinity that remains both fulfilling and satisfying. It is easier, many men
have said to me, to imagine non-submissive femininity than it is to imagine
masculinity in terms other than dominance.[26]

This is one way of looking at the stickiness of supremacy in whiteness. It
is profoundly difficult and even anxiety producing to imagine whiteness in
any other terms than dominance precisely because of its co-constitution with
a particularly deep ideology of sex and gender that comes not only from the
recent history of colonialism but from the imaginative depths of medieval and
early modern Christian theology. It is not insignificant that God stretches
out his powerfully male, languidly superior, and vividly white arm across the
vastness of the Sistene ceiling to meet the supplicating white arm of his tru-
est mirror image in Adam. There is sex, gender, and race in that construction
and it is not without allure. It is one of many moments that tie whiteness up
in masculinity and masculinity up in whiteness, for God is the original white
male and Adam is a mere first step down.

The argument that I have laid out here makes the work of antiracism much
more complicated and difficult, particularly for whites but also for nonwhites.
But I believe that without this piece of the puzzle, the work against racism
may function like a stretched rubber band. If it is not unhooked on *all* points,
it will simply rebound with a bitter bite. To put it most bluntly, can we unman
ourselves enough to begin to take the supremacy out of whiteness? What

would this look like in practical terms? What specific practices, responses, and expectations might have to change in my work and in my interactions to effect a reconstruction of whiteness that does not rest on sexualized race? This is the first question that we must ask ourselves, and we must ask it daily. Can I unman my whiteness enough to seek the guidance of nonwhites on issues unrelated to race? Can I unman my whiteness enough to listen? To accept direction and supervision? To take up what James Foreman called "janitorial research"?[27] To what lengths am I willing to go to take the gender ideology, the supremacy, out of my whiteness?

Ultimately, I suspect that whiteness has to disappear altogether, since it was created and exists solely on the basis of exclusion for colonial gain. This does not mean that as a white person I must disappear or renounce my family. It also does not relieve me of responsibility for white supremacy and its continued benefits to me and the white members of my family. I also suspect that the demise of white supremacy will take much longer than I believe it should, and so I must resign myself to small steps and build up my faith in their importance. And right there I poke a pinhole in the balloon of whiteness-as-dominance. I take up the very unwhite suggestion that Sharon Welch makes, namely, that I let go of my need for control over the results of my efforts and credit for their completion.[28]

Letting go of that need is letting go of one brick in the edifice of white supremacy that masquerades as masculinity, and of masculinity that masquerades as dominance. Welch calls this an "ethic of control" and advocates instead, based on her own study of black American women's writings, a pragmatic "ethic of risk" that does not pretend to control outcomes but keeps on anyway, believing in the value of actions that may not win wars or conquer evils, but that keep possibility open for the next generation. That much we can do, and by valuing that, letting go of such deeply ingrained needs to direct, to lead, to chair, to receive credit, to determine priorities, to win arguments, we begin to take the supremacy out of whiteness and the dominance out of masculinity.

Notes

1. See "The Human Genome," *Science* 291:5507 (February 2001): 16; For a lay discussion on the complexities of interpreting the Human Genome Project in relation to race, see Steve Olsen, "The Genetic Archaeology of Race," *Atlantic Monthly* (April 2001).
2. Anne McClintock, *Imperial Leather: Race, Gender and Sexuality in the Colonial Contest* (London and New York: Routledge, 1995), 8.

3. Robert J. C. Young, *Colonial Desire: Hybridity in Theory, Culture and Race* (London: Routledge, 1995), 91.

4. Evelyn Brooks Higgenbotham, "African-American Women's History and the Metalanguage of Race," *Signs* 17:2 (1991–1992): 251–74.

5. Young, *Colonial Desire*, 91.

6. Higgenbotham, quoted in Evelynn Hammonds, "Black (W)holes and the Geometry of Black Female Sexuality," in *Feminism Meets Queer Theory, Books from Differences*, ed. Naomi Schor and Elizabeth Weed (Bloomington: Indiana University Press, 1997), 136.

7. McClintock, *Imperial Leather*, 5.

8. Hammonds, "Black (W)holes," 136.

9. Abdul JanMohamed, "Sexuality On/Of the Racial Border: Foucault, Wright, and the Articulation of 'Racialized Sexuality,'" in *Discourses of Sexuality: From Aristotle to AIDS*, ed. Domna Stanton (Ann Arbor: University of Michigan Press, 1992), 94–116.

10. Helen Scott, "Was There a Time Before Race? Capitalist Modernity and the Origins of Racism," in *Marxism, Modernity and Post-Colonial Studies*, ed. Crystal Bartolovich and Neil Lazarus (Cambridge: Cambridge University Press, 2002), 167–82.

11. John Milton, *Paradise Lost*, Book IV, in *Paradise Lost and Paradise Regained*, ed. Christopher Ricks (New York: Signet Classic, 1968), 88, ll. 295–308.

12. M. Shawn Copeland, "Body, Representation, and Black Religious Discourse," in *Postcolonialism, Feminism and Religious Discourse*, ed. Laura E. Donaldson and Kwok Pui-lan (London and New York: Routledge, 2002), 184.

13. Young, *Colonial Desire*, 101.

14. See Scott, "Was There a Time," *passim*; also see Lerone Bennett, *The Shaping of Black America* (Chicago: Johnson, 1975).

15. Young, *Colonial Desire*, 93.

16. Scott, "Was There a Time," 174.

17. Young, *Colonial Desire*, 111.

18. McClintock, *Imperial Leather*, 55.

19. See ibid., chaps. 2 and 3.

20. Young, *Colonial Desire*, 109–11.

21. Kadiatu Kanneh, "Feminism and the Colonial Body," in *The Post-Colonial Studies Reader*, ed. Bill Ashcroft, Gareth Griffiths, and Helen Tiffin (London and New York: Routledge, 1995), 347.

22. For a relevant biblical case study in an ancient Mediterranean context of race-sex-gender co-constituitiveness, see Ken Stone, "Queering the Canaanite," in *The Sexual Theologian: Essays on Sex, God, and Politics*, ed. Marcella Althaus-Reid and Lisa Isherwood (London: T&T Clark, 2005).

23. Vron Ware, "Defining Forces: 'Race,' Gender and Memories of Empire," in *The Post-Colonial Question: Common Skies, Divided Horizons*, ed. Iain Chambers and Lidia Curti (London and New York: Routledge, 1996) 142–56.

24. Eve Kosofsky Sedgwick, *Epistemology of the Closet* (Berkeley: University of California Press, 1990).

25. Hammonds, "Black (W)holes," 141.

26. For an interesting discussion of non-dominant masculinity and satisfaction, see Scott Haledman, "Receptivity and Revelation: A Spirituality of Gay Male Sex," in *Body and Soul: Rethinking Sexuality as Justice-Love*, ed. Marvin Ellison and Sylvia Thorson-Smith (Cleveland: The Pilgrim Press, 2003), 218–31.

27. See Robert Coles, "Method," in *The Call of Service: A Witness to Idealism* (New York: Houghton-Mifflin, 1993), 9–13.

28. Sharon Welch, *A Feminist Ethic of Risk* (Minneapolis: Fortress Press, 1987), see esp. chap. 1.

Chapter 9

Toward a Queer Theology of Flourishing

Transsexual Embodiment, Subjectivity, and Moral Agency[1]

Jakob Hero

> *So God created humankind in his image,*
> *in the image of God he created them;*
> *male and female he created them.*
>
> —Gen. 1:27[2]

As biotechnology continues to progress, the possibilities for human growth, enhancement, and development increase dramatically. While many biotechnical advancements are viewed as morally neutral, others appear to carry tremendous moral weight; this is clearly the case at the convergence point of medicine and sexual identity. It is my belief that the above verse from Genesis has greatly informed an ideology—generated in Abrahamic traditions, yet permeating far beyond them—in which the sanctity of humankind's clear dimorphic sexual categories appears unquestionable and untouchable. As human beings gain more control over the functionality and appearance of our bodies, many people—particularly theologians and moral theorists—express concern that some human beings are venturing too far from the created image that God intended. As such, when the needle of a hormone-filled syringe penetrates the skin, or the surgeon's scalpel approaches breast tissue or sex organs, many will argue that there is far more at stake than changes to a person's physical embodiment of gender.

In what follows, I explore the issue of human flourishing, looking specifically at transsexuality through a bioethical and Christian theological lens. I write from the perspective of both a Christian and a transsexual. My primary interest in this work is to help trans people find wholeness in the process of transition. In doing so, I advocate a profound shift away from the ever-present soteriological notions that are the undercurrent of gendered embodiment, harkening back to the Genesis narrative above, and toward a queer notion of flourishing. This queer flourishing is not just reserved for those of us whose bodies are injected, sliced, and reshaped. It takes into account all gendered beings, offering possibilities for the performativity of holistic embodiment. Queer Christian flourishing requires that we grow beyond arguments rooted in the biblical creation accounts and move toward a theological paradigm of queer natality, through which any person, transgender or cisgender,[3] actively participates alongside of God in the lifelong project of creation. This essay is a proposal for queer subjectivity, through which trans people can flourish as moral agents, embodying integrity and human dignity on their paths to gender comfort and congruity.

Part I introduces the theological concept of flourishing and also provides a working language for deeper investigation. In Part II, I explore many of the practical issues of transitioning from one sex to another. In this section, the transsexual as moral agent and discursive subject is framed within the concepts of embodiment and integrity. In the final section, Part III, I conclude with an examination of human dignity, which supports my overall call to an understanding of flourishing for transsexuals as moral agents.

Part I: Subjectivity and Transgender Experience

Sex and Gender

The distinction between "gender" and "sex" is the foundation of much contemporary gender discourse, particularly that which emerged from the feminist milieu in the latter decades of the twentieth century. First and foremost, I must admit that establishing this binary distinction is in and of itself problematic. However, it does lend some explanation to reasons for medical transition from one sex to another, and can be a useful starting place in understanding the various processes of transition. So I ask the reader to both acknowledge this rather flawed dichotomy and to indulge me momentarily as we explore it. Gender is primarily based on self-conception and societal roles. It "refers to socially mediated expectations about an individual's role. Society divides these roles into two inflexible categories: man and woman. This strict social division is usually grounded in naturalistic assumptions that women are anatomically female and men are anatomically male."[4] Sex is a binary biological classification, into which (nearly) all people are assigned at birth; it "refers to an interlocking set of social expectations that bodies are divided and regulated into two discrete categories, male and female, which are hegemonically defined by the presence or absence of a penis and by secondary sex characteristics."[5]

Transgenderism and Transsexuality

The term "transsexual" in this essay signifies those who utilize biotechnology (whether hormone treatment, surgery, or both) to reshape or produce desired gender markers and sexual characteristics. I use the word "transgender" to name the wider range of differently gendered people including, but not limited to, transsexuals. Thus transgender is an umbrella concept under which multiple types of gender-variant embodiments and self-conceptions are found. A primary experience that distinguishes transsexuals from the rest of the transgender population is our interaction with medical professionals: endocrinologists, therapists, surgeons, speech pathologists, and the like—what medical ethicist Edmund Pellegrino would classify as "the clinical encounter."

> The clinical encounter is a confrontation, a face-to-face encounter between someone who professes to heal and someone in need of healing. Its locus is the doctor-patient, or nurse-patient, relationship. It is a phenomenon of intersubjectivity, and it is in this sense that it is a locus for the experience of human dignity and its loss.[6]

The clinical encounter is essentially the *location* of the experience of physical transformation from one sexual embodiment to another, a process called *transitioning*.

Biotechnology and Transition

The President's Council on Bioethics defines *biotechnology* as the processes and products that offer the potential to alter and, in some ways, control biology. "Overarching the processes and products it brings forth, biotechnology is also a *conceptual and ethical outlook*, informed by progressive aspirations."[7] Particularly in medicine, biotechnology refers not only to specific human-devised mechanisms of engineering and chemistry, but also to the outcomes of these technologies and the ethical—and often theological—discourse that surrounds the science and its outcomes. Biotechnology is geared toward a specific, albeit enigmatic, end: the benefit and enhancement of human lives.[8] However, because *enhancement* does not manifest uniformly in all types of human embodiment, biotechnology as a means to human flourishing can be morally complicated. Even for technologies that may themselves be conceived as morally neutral, the reasons and means of technological application can carry tremendous weight.

The biotechnological aspects of transsexual journeys rely on enhancement through endocrinology and plastic or reconstructive surgery. This is a bioethical issue, not only because of the use of medicine to shape and (re)form biology, but also because transsexuality raises important questions about ethical body manipulation. The fact that transsexual surgeries are essentially elective has led many to question whether this is an appropriate use of technology. The question of propriety is often not *how* or *what* is done to a body, but *why* it is done. Surgical procedures that are remarkably similar in application can carry very different moral implications for two different people. For instance, if a cisgendered man—meaning a genetic male, born with a penis— loses his genitalia in a tragic accident, his moral agency generally is not called into question if he chooses to have reconstructive genital surgery. In fact, the reconstruction of his penis and testicles would most likely be understood as an important step in his ability to flourish as a man and as a human being. This is not the case for a female-to-male transsexual who chooses to have genital reconstruction surgery. I believe that this indicates a hierarchy of suffering as the determinant of who should be granted access to medical technology. It points to a reductionist ideology that claims that the bodies we are born with are the ideal form of created embodiment. Opponents claim that as transsexuals we change our nature from what God intended. The assumption that the birth body is perfectly formed ignores the reality that many people are born with conditions (birth defects) for which biotechnological intervention is necessary for survival or productive functioning.

Often a person's earned right to medical intervention correlates not only with the degree of individual suffering, but also one's purported innocence in encountering that suffering. This line of reasoning is specifically problematic for transsexuals. The ideology of the innocent sufferer leads many of us toward extreme hatred for our pre-transition selves. Even those who may not be inclined to hate every aspect of their pre-transition bodies or identities find themselves pushed into the narrative of the suffering transsexual—the iconic "man trapped in a woman's body," or vice versa—because this wins our issues the status of a birth defect. Those of us who want to change our bodies would be better served by entering the process through love of self, instead of seeking hormones and surgery as treatment for self-hatred.

Justin Tanis, who transitioned from female to male while an ordained minister in the Metropolitan Community Churches, explains that it is essential for us to honor our bodies as we live in them and as we change them. This means making informed choices about what is best for our bodies.

> Honoring our bodies means learning to love our embodied selves so much that we dress ourselves as we long to dress, we shape our bodies as we want them to be shaped, and we do it from a sense of well-being. We need to proclaim the message widely in our community that you do not have to hate yourself any longer, that path to wholeness is open to every one of us. The first steps on that path are when we claim the right to our own bodies and the right to determine our own fate.[9]

Transsexual Subjectivity

The universal narrative of the suffering transsexual is a form of transsexual objectification. As a counterpart to this, the role of subjectivity and self-reflective identity claims emerges as a formative component of transgender discourse. In order to understand "transsexual subjectivity" as a unique discursive element, let us first consider—in broader context—the role of subjectivity in identity formation. Stan van Hooft develops a working usage of subjectivity as "that quality of a living thing whereby it can be said that its own existence as an individual entity is a project for it."[10] Epistemologically speaking, a *subject* owns an experience or action, while an *object* is the person or thing onto which the experience or action is directed.[11] Survival is thus a key focus of subjectivity and speaks not only to matters of life and death, but also to the survival of self-aware identities, which human beings have a vested interest in maintaining.[12]

The discursive elements of subjectivity and objectification are always already present in transgender discourse. These are constant undercurrents, whether from the viewpoint of self-identified trans people or from non-trans people, who are interpreting their external gaze in viewing, interacting with, or treating trans people. Part of the uniqueness and complication of transsexual identity is that one's own subjectivity—while internally generated—must be validated through the interpretive lens of an expert other. This is very different, for instance, from the experiences of cisgendered people who seek out cosmetic or reconstructive medical interventions for a myriad of self-defined physical problems. For the most part, Botox injections, breast augmentation or reduction, liposuction, and other medical treatments that are provided on the insistence of the patient's desire to transform his or her own body do not have a medical or psychiatric diagnosis as a prerequisite; nor does the desire for the procedure shape the boundaries of the patient's identity.[13]

From Salvation to Flourishing

Grace M. Jantzen's distinction between a language of salvation and a language of flourishing is extremely helpful in naming the necessity of the latter linguistic framework when advocating a theology of growth and wholeness over brokenness and fear.

> Fundamentally, the choice of the language of salvation rather than the language of flourishing both denotes and reinforces an anthropology of a very particular kind. If we think in terms of salvation, then the human condition must be conceptualized as a problematic state, a state in which human beings need urgent rescue, otherwise calamity or death will befall. The human situation is a negative one, from which we need to be delivered.[14]

Jantzen invites us to question what the human situation might look like if instead of salvation we turn to a model of flourishing, answering: "We could then see human beings as having a natural inner capacity and dynamic, being able to draw on inner resources and interconnection with one another in the web of life, and having the potential to develop into great fruitfulness."[15] This is a particularly useful theological paradigm for the queer community in general, and trans people in particular. "Whereas with the metaphor of salvation, God is seen as the saviour who intervenes from outside the calamitous situation to bring about a rescue, the metaphor of flourishing would lead instead to an idea of the divine source and ground, an imminent divine incarnated within us and between us."[16] While I may not be quite as eager as Jantzen to step fully away from the doctrines of the Trinity and the incarnation, I do believe that too much harm has been done—so much physical and spiritual violence has been meted out on the bodies of sexual and gender minorities in the name of Christianity—that adopting a language of flourishing is perhaps the only way to save the church from the sins of *salvation*.

It is in no way surprising that a theological anthropology that espouses an image of human beings as inherently broken, flawed, and in need of fixing is an incredible hindrance to human flourishing. In a similar fashion, it should come as no surprise that a framework that presents the pre-transition bodies of transsexuals as broken, flawed, and in need of fixing also sets up certain barriers to flourishing. All too often, the surgeons, endocrinologists, and various gatekeepers to the clinical encounter, are seen as the *saviors* to those lost souls, trapped in a pre-transition state, awaiting the much needed, urgent rescue.

I say this not to downplay the feelings of urgency in the transsexual who is awaiting access to the medical means of transitioning, but to point out the significant difference between this biotechnology-as-salvation metaphor and a model of flourishing. *Both* utilize biotechnology. The difference lies in the trans person's ability to exhibit ownership over his or her own agency in the process of transition.

The relocation of transsexuals, from objects of medical treatment and discourse to the subjects of their own unique journeys, moves us in the direction of an agent-centered, holistic approach to transsexual identity. This turn toward subjectivity need not silence the voices of non-trans people who encounter, provide care for, research, support, or love trans people. However, as those who are traditionally spoken of and spoken for, we trans people must be allowed to speak for ourselves, and these experiences and voices must be given priority in determining who we are.

Standards of Care

The World Professional Association for Transgender Health (WPATH) Standards of Care for Gender Identity Disorders[17] establish an idealized process through which trans people are permitted access to the medical technology necessary for transitioning. Although in recent years some trans-identified people have been added to the committee that produces these guidelines, for the most part it has been controlled by non-trans people.

The necessary first step of the process is official diagnosis of "Gender Identity Disorder," from the American Psychological Association's *Diagnostic and Statistical Manual of Mental Disorders*, Fourth Text Revision (DSM-IV-TR). The DSM-IV-TR offers a view of gender dysphoria that is adequate, even extremely accurate, for many transsexuals who want medical intervention. But it does not offer a description that is broad enough to include those who do not fit into certain extremely specific criteria. Although WPATH has made some great strides in widening the medical and psychiatric view of trans people and transsexual treatment, the entire process continues to be very requirement driven and goal oriented. The necessity of an expert other, who serves as gatekeeper, is still central to the process. This does not leave much room for individual diversity and the unique potential of personal discernment or agency. Those who do not meet these specific criteria have trouble gaining access to the biotechnology necessary for transition. When transsexual agency is stripped away, a power differential is created. Medical professionals function as dictators with the power to deny access to one's own desired embodiment.

Many therapists, for example, will not provide the necessary paperwork for someone to begin hormone replacement therapy unless the patient has expressed a commitment to eventually have genital surgery, which in the eyes of the medical community is the final (and some would say most important) criterion that makes one whole as a man or a woman. This produces an overly simplified policy of gender identification in which the focus of one's public image as a man or a woman is conflated with the shape of one's genitalia—an aspect of the body that few people ever see.

Califia, Tanis, and others have noted that because the diagnostic criteria of transsexualism involves a self-generated claim of transsexuality, this creates a tautology in which one's own subjective assertion as a self-identifying (and necessarily suffering) agent requires the intervention of medical professionals to enable that transgendered person (now, as object) to—in essence—*exist* as a transsexual.[18] Medical care for all people, trans or not, invokes at least some degree of vulnerability and the very real possibility that a patient will experience humiliation as an objectified *Other*. The power differential between doctor and patient is well nigh impossible to avoid. The inherent pathologization of gender dysphoria further complicates the doctor-patient relationship for trans people. The pathology of gender diversity in this way requires trans people to submit to the gaze of an (empowered) other to approve the validity of our self-knowledge as transsexuals. Our integrity as human persons becomes entangled with the external embodiment of our internal notions of selfhood. When we compromise this integrity, our agency is undermined, and we are subjected to epistemic violence and the inevitable internalization of the external objectifications of others.

The Mythical Narrative of the "True Transsexual"

I entered the first stage of my transition process as a twenty-one-year-old college student, living in Florida, with no access to a transgender community for support or guidance. I sought out a therapist who advertised as a "gender specialist." With total openness and honesty—and a fair amount of naïveté—I told the truth about my experience of gender embodiment, sexuality, and identity. Without other trans people in my life to advise me, I had no idea that telling the truth in therapy was a mistake. The truth was that although I felt extremely uncomfortable living as a woman, I was uncertain where the transition process would take me. I did not know that I was expected to express extreme revulsion at the very thought of the supposedly terrible and shameful body parts that had bestowed on me the legal category of "female." I was not sufficiently repulsed by my own genitalia. My therapist specifically asked me if having a vagina made me want to commit suicide. When I answered honestly that it did not, she frowned and wrote something on her notepad. To this day I will never understand how a therapist can look at a patient—especially someone as young as I was at the time—and find it troubling that this patient does not possess *enough* body hatred. For me, the extremely large breasts I had been carrying around since the age of fourteen, which (whether clothed or unclothed) were the most obvious markers of my femaleness, were far more problematic than what could be found between my legs. I was unaware that I should lie and say that I was already living as a man. My rather high-pitched voice and soft, feminine, facial features made attempting to live as a man prior to hormone treatment nearly impossible.[19]

I also had not known that my access to the process would be denied largely because I admitted to being sexually attracted to men. Even though at the time I had never acted on this attraction, for my therapist the notion that I would not necessarily be a heterosexual man post-transition was especially problematic.[20] This factor, compounded with the reality that my own vagina did not make me want to kill myself, and that I—in the absence of the medical technology to make this possible—was not already living as male, meant that I was denied the "true transsexual" diagnosis.[21] It is difficult to explain how strange this situation is to someone who has not lived through it. How can an outside other determine my own subjective self-identity claim?

Initially I allowed this clinical encounter to shape the way I conceptualized my own gendered self. I believed that I would never be allowed to change my body. I felt violated by this system. I hated that those who had never walked in my shoes could tell me that my own embodiment and performativity were insufficient. *These are my shoes, damn it!* And only I get to name what it means to walk in them. Although at the time, I lacked the language to name it as such, what I was missing was not only the ability to flourish, but also the framework to comprehend what true flourishing would mean. How could I even start to flourish when I did not know how to advocate for myself within the clinical encounter?

A Solution that Isn't

It was not until I met other trans people that I learned that there was still hope: I could reach my goals if I simply lied. I learned that lying was a rite of passage into the transsexual world. Armed with the manufactured narrative of a "true transsexual," I, too, could gain access to a more comfortable embodied self. But clearly this was not an unproblematic solution. I have always viewed myself as a person of integrity. Lying about who I am, especially to my therapist, was counter-intuitive. However, I found a new therapist and did exactly that. Within months I started hormone therapy, which produced near immediate masculinizing results (which more or less directly led to finding my first boyfriend and coming to accept my gay male identity). In less than a year I had undergone chest reconstruction surgery and was living unquestioned as male in all areas of my life. I was happy with the outcome but felt there was a price to pay for how I reached it. While I do not feel that my eternal soul was in danger, I do think that these lies came at an enormous cost to my psycho-social well-being.

I hate that this was the route I was forced to take. I must admit that, if I were put in the same situation, I would do it again. Yet, I believe it to have been an impediment to my overall flourishing and human dignity. I gained the freedom of embodiment I sought. I was able to access the biotechnology necessary for me to be recognized as male by others. These things came with incredible benefits, not the least of which was the feeling of amazing freedom. But before I could even begin the medical process, the joy at the idea that I can be any kind of man I wanted to be was already burdened by a lingering question. Had I already become the kind of person who gets what he wants through deception and lying?

Part II: Transsexual Flourishing in Process

Transsexual as Moral Agent and Divine Creature

The human dignity of transsexuals is highlighted and strengthened when we understand and develop our own subjectivity. We must assert our own valid-ity within self-defining categories of gender embodiment and determine for ourselves what unique combination of medical interventions are necessary to reach an acceptable level of comfort in our bodies. This does not mean that I advocate a hands-off approach in terms of medical treatment for gender conflict. I do not want to divorce transsexuality from the medical paradigm altogether. Like countless others, I benefited greatly from medically transi-tioning. Had I continued to be denied access to biotechnological intervention, my male identity would never have been fully recognizable to others—or in-deed even to myself.

Even in light of the difficulty I had with approval to enter the process, I am not willing to advocate for a system that allows unregulated and imme-diate access to these types of biotechnology for simply anyone who can af-ford it financially. The Standards of Care are a manufactured structure, not legally binding, and not actually enforced by any governing body. It is only the patients who suffer under these rules. With no official oversight process, there is no possibility of appeal if one is denied access. In the delicate balance of self-assertion and approval seeking, the transsexual entering the transition process must exercise agency and must also navigate the policies that can be used to deny us access.

I propose that transsexual subjectivity necessitates agency in two primary categories: embodiment and integrity. When the agency of the trans person is not validated by those who function as gatekeepers, we must often choose between obtaining an embodiment that makes us comfortable in our gender expression or the ability to speak freely and accurately about how we see ourselves now and in the future. A doctor or therapist who will only accept the stereotypical "true transsexual" narrative places the trans person in a moral dilemma. Which is more important—obtaining treatment or maintaining integrity? This counters the potential flourishing of transsexuals as moral agents by limiting our ability to transition without sacrificing probity.

Embodiment

Gender is an issue of embodiment for all people. It is the way in which we all, as human persons, live in uniquely sexed bodies and validate the genders of other people—whether trans or cisgendered. Although certainly connected to sexuality, the embodiment of gender is not about sexual attraction to others; it is about one's own lived experience of the individual, inner manifestations of masculinity and femininity.

Without the proper support for embodied identity formation, many transsexuals are forced into a system that claims to validate our subjective assertions of self; but this system inflicts on us specific (and largely unattainable) hegemonic ideals of maleness and femaleness. These ideals are overwhelmingly genitally focused. They emerged from writings on transsexuals by cisgendered doctors whose gaze focused mainly on body parts and lacked holistic viewpoints that considered transsexual experience. This objectification of transsexuals in terms of the genitocentric standards of non-trans bodies strikes at the very core of our embodied selves. And while genitals certainly do matter for sexual identity formation and lived gendered experience, the reality of transsexual lives—particularly the lives of female-to-male transsexuals—is that genital reconstruction is often not a viable option. The various procedures available for transsexual genital surgeries are typically cost prohibitive, and often do not produce the desired outcome for sensation or aesthetics. Yet people link maleness and femaleness to penises and vaginas, and our gender justification is often linked to whether our genitals have been surgically reshaped. A woman with a penis or a man with a vagina is seen as an affront to the ontological nature of humanity itself. In practical reality this can manifest as instant justification for meting out violence against such a "wrong" or incongruent body.[22]

A reality of transsexual subjectivity is that our unique experiences of incongruence between our gendered self-identification and our bodies—particularly genitalia—carry different weight for different individuals. How we embody our full sense of selfhood is clearly a common concern for transsexual identity formation, yet there is no singular "true transsexual" experience of embodiment. Body modification is an important piece of coming into authenticity with our selves, but we each need to come to terms with the possibilities and the limits of biotechnology. It should be pointed out that surgeons themselves are often intentionally vague or willfully dishonest about these limitations. The idea of sexual desire and fulfillment in bodies that would appear incongruent is challenging within the medical purview (and indeed the larger society within which that purview functions). Whether intentionally or as a subconscious response to an internal "ick factor," doctors have produced a narrative for transsexuals that places the importance of external appearances of genitalia above functionality. In conversations with trans people—particularly female-to-male transsexuals—I have encountered very different experiences of genital surgeries than the images presented by the medical community.[23] This is particularly the case with phalloplasty, in which a penis is constructed from tissue taken from elsewhere on the body. Every transman I have spoken to who has undergone phalloplasty complains of significant, if not total, loss of sensation. Problems with urination are also extremely common. Interestingly, despite varying levels of thwarted expectation, many of these men are extremely happy with the post-surgical results.

For many transsexuals the risks associated with genital reconstruction are worth it, for others not. What I believe matters most in terms of transsexual embodiment is not any one specific decision regarding biomedical interventions that any particular trans person makes. What matters is that trans people have the ability to make these decisions within their own subjective identity claims, which must not be reliant on an external outside other. To do this, we need frameworks and support networks that enable us to make informed decisions about our bodies. This requires a break from the philosophy behind the allopathic "fix-what's-broken" model of Western medicine, in which these biotechnological procedures are executed, but not necessarily a break from the procedures themselves. Most important, those on the outside cannot name for us the requisite amount of discomfort we are expected to feel because of our genitals or any other sexual marker. A pre-transition transsexual need not view his or her birth gender as broken embodiment that is in need of fixing. A queer theology of flourishing allows us to utilize biotechnology simply as a tool toward gender recognition. The value of this recognition cannot be overstated, yet it also must not be conflated with the ultimate end of the transsexual as a human person on the path to flourishing. As a tool, biotechnology enables trans people to live into forms of sexual embodiment that go beyond gender performativity; particularly in terms of hormone treatment, these tools are necessary for self-affirmation in gender congruence and in being recognized in one's gender by others.

Integrity

When Tanis states, "[t]hat we reflect outwardly that which is inwardly true for us is a matter of integrity,"[24] he is referring to the freedom to express our genders in dress, in behavior, and through the use of biotechnology. I propose that transsexual authenticity calls for integrity in two overlapping spheres: relationality with others and self-relationality. How we live in our gendered reality reflects integrity. However, one's ability to pass as one's internally understood gender is not the litmus test of integrity. A painful reality of transsexual embodiment is that most of us will never reach a point of total comfort in our gendered bodies. Public acceptance as the men and women we know ourselves to be is unattainable for many of us, no matter how much we change our bodies. Despite the fact that the limits of biotechnology are very real and frustrating, one's integrity can remain intact—even if she is six feet tall and balding or if he has wide hips and cannot grow a decent beard.

In her essay "On Being True to Form," Margaret Mohrmann explains the relationship of identity and integrity. "I have identity because, however much I develop over time, I am still the same created person; I have integrity because the conduct of my life is consistent with the way I was created to live."[25] While this notion of consistency with creation may seem problematic for the transsexual, Mohrmann is actually speaking of the distinction of humans from other aspects of creation—not of the distinction between types of gendered human embodiment. The differences between individual human persons do shape our identities; the human condition is universally a process of unfolding and formation. Static identity is not part of Mohrmann's integrity thesis. She traces the Greek etymology of the words "integrity" and "identity," and explains that, like the Christian notion of the *logos*, these are centered on the intentionality of human creation, which "meant that human beings were created in this way and not that; creation imparted a specific form to humans generally and to each human being in particular."[26] Mohrmann offers a twofold definition of integrity, the first part of which, *integrity as consistency*, speaks to creation. The human being's integrity is displayed "insofar as she is consistently true—physically, mentally, spiritually—both to the intentional design of her divine creation and to the trajectory of her ongoing formation toward God."[27]

The all-too-common interpretation of transsexuality is that the processes of transition fundamentally go against our intended creation. Anti-trans arguments from religious voices in the Abrahamic traditions most often look to the accounts of creation, naming a created binary gendered order as "natural" and the utilization of biotechnology as "unnatural," thus against creation. A queer theological lens allows us to see humanity not as a thing created in the past, but as an ongoing process itself. Integrity is not reliant on a static, lifelong, physical embodiment or the faithful commitment to only one performative script. Furthermore, as both process and queer theologians have taught us, the work of creation is never complete. Creation was not a onetime event that living beings simply experienced as passive recipients. Today, biotechnology presents humanity with myriad medical possibilities. These many medical advances provide evidence of our ability to participate in the ongoing processes of creation.

I propose an agent-centered transsexual subjectivity that allows us to view intentional participation in creation with a fresh understanding, not as *going against*, but as *being called to*. Tanis explains the idea of calling as a helpful way to comprehend transgender identity. He explains that a calling "is a way of being—a calling to awaken to, realize, and manifest who we are. For trans people, our calling is to a way of embodying the self that transcends the limitations [of our embodiment]."[28] The consistency of our integrity as transsexuals does not lie in our ability to fulfill gender expectation that we were born into, but to manifest a consistent integration of identity so that we "physically and literally materialize who we are on the inside and bring it to reflection on the outside."[29]

My own experience of bringing my internal understanding of my gendered self to my external embodied identity has been an exercise in integrity as consistency. God created me to be exactly who I am. My transsexual status is not a mistake of creation; it is a call to a continual process of transformation. As Mohrmann points out, "Creation is not the only way in which human beings are formed. Another, equally vital sense of formation has to do with the developments of the nascent ideal form into that of a mature adult human being."[30]

The consistency of my integrity is not dependent on my loyalty to the lifelong embodiment of the sex assigned to me at my birth. I have been formed in valuable ways from my experiences on both sides of the gender divide.

To form is not merely to cultivate or develop, but to mold, to prepare, to realize. Moreover, it is generally the case that one is formed toward something, some telos, some ideal shape or condition. It is through formation that one is helped to acquire certain dispositions or virtues and thus to become a particular kind of person progressing on the moral journey toward perfection of conduct and of humanness.[31]

My formation as an individual on the moral journey must not be conflated with my formation as an individual who is male. The end toward which I am formed, and as I am indeed continuing to be formed, is not a gendered identity at all, but rather my development of selfhood as a moral agent. Being a man who was born and raised as a girl is an important piece of my formation, but it is not the totality of my calling in this life; just being a man is not the telos of my development.

Mohrmann defines the second aspect of integrity, *integrity as oneness*, as "the 'parts' of a person—body, mind, soul, spirit—[that] comprise, in actuality, one being, a single unity and not a hierarchically ordered conglomerate."[32] Achieving a sense of wholeness of self is essential for transsexuals to embody integrity as oneness. This can be a challenge for those who have spent a lifetime feeling at odds with their own embodiment. Tanis captures this experience and its spiritual implications.

A common conception of transgendered people is that we are "women trapped in men's bodies" or "men trapped in women's bodies." . . . In my opinion, this way of looking at our bodies necessarily sets up dualisms: not only the split between female and male but also the division between body and spirit. In this view, these pairs become essentialist and oppositional and no collaboration can exist between them. In a certain sense, another being which inhabits the body must be liberated from it, rather than coming to a place of unity between body and spirit.[33]

To foster integrity as oneness, trans people must be allowed the necessary agency to make the appropriate choices about our bodies. If we enter the transition process with a self-conception of wholeness, we can transform our bodies out of love for ourselves, not by manifesting a clinically "appropriate" level of self-hatred and shame. Seeking wholeness and self-acceptance throughout the entire transition process is essential for overcoming the conceptual dualisms of selfhood that plague trans people.

It is because of this second aspect of integrity that the experience of lying to our therapists is problematic to the transsexual. As transsexuals, we must take seriously what we choose to do to our bodies surgically and hormonally; in doing so, we would benefit from considering the spiritual and psychological effects, as well as the possible physical ramifications. We must be vigilant to balance the priorities of our physical, spiritual, and emotional needs through-out the whole transition process. When I lied about my embodied experi-ences, I compromised my sense of wholeness and placed my bodily needs above my ethical beliefs about truth telling. I feel my spirit was compromised. As Mohrmann says, "The oneness of integrity forces us to take entirely se-riously things that are done to bodies as well as things that violate minds, precisely because each sort of action is done to persons, who are not body *plus* mind and soul and spirit, but are body/mind/soul/spirit: all one, non-hierarchically integrated."[34]

Part III: Human Dignity and Transgender Flourishing

The Turning Point

Let us not forget that while a trans person is going through the process of transition, he or she is also trying to handle all the other aspects of life. As my own therapy debacle was unfolding, I sought out the other source I had for guidance and support: my church. In the years prior to my decision to start the transition process, I was a very active member of a liberal, inclusive, "Open and Affirming" Christian church. The fact that they prided themselves on their acceptance of gays and lesbians, however, I quickly learned, did not mean that this church was equipped (or willing) to support a person in gender tran-sition. On the morning that I came out as transgender to my pastor, I found that the well of compassion had run dry. This story is not unique; many trans people face the loss of their church families—and far more—when they come out. But what happened next is where my story deviates from the norm. I was blessed to find a new church, after being rejected from my church home, which made all the difference. My flourishing did not come from a wholehearted ex-perience of acceptance as soon as I walked into the door of this new and un-familiar church. In fact, many people there were confused by me and did not accept me right away. But although they may not have initially recognized my gender identity in the ways I would have wanted, they always recognized me as part of God's creation. This church affirmed that I, just like everyone else, am a divine creature. This affirmation came at a time when everything in my life felt unstable. In this church I was shown that I possess a God-given human dignity that nothing and no one can take away from me—not a therapist, not a doctor, not a transphobic pastor, not even the lies I was forced to tell about myself, could erase that divine spark. With the ever-present connection to the presence of God within all of us, this church community invites its (mostly

LGBT) members to participate in a lifelong process of discernment and communion with God. A queer theology of flourishing, in which we engage in a co-creative process with God, starts with human dignity.

What is Human Dignity?

The dignity of the human person is an important and elusive element of theology and bioethics. But its enigmatic qualities need not detract from its efficacy. Ultimately, agent-centered transsexual subjectivity must be oriented toward the flourishing of the trans person if it is to have any true significance. Dignity plays an important role in identity, highlighting the common good of the human race, and the justification of a moral threshold to establish a minimum level of rights for all human beings. These are some functions of dignity, but they do not serve to define it as a concept.

Human dignity is complex and multifaceted, which is precisely what makes it useful as a concept for bioethics. The medical ethicist Holmes Rolston III defines the multiple manifestations of dignity:

> Our dignity figures in our personal identity, first at basic levels, where dignity is inalienable and common to us all, and further at developmental levels, where dignity can be achieved or lost, recognized or withheld. . . . A person's dignity resides in his or her biologically and socially constructed psychosomatic self with an ideographic proper-named identity.[35]

Historically, human dignity has often been defined in terms of the ability of an individual to think rationally. This is obviously problematic if we are to seek a universalized understanding of dignity that speaks to the reality of all human beings, some of whom live with cognitive disabilities and lack the ability of rational thought. Martha Nussbaum argues that it is not only our rationality, but also our vulnerability and many other aspects of the human condition that define human dignity.

> In general, when we select a political conception of the person we ought to choose one that does not exalt rationality as *the* single good thing and that does not denigrate forms of need and striving that are parts of our animality. . . . There is dignity not only in rationality but in human need itself and in the varied forms of striving that emerge from human need.[36]

Nussbaum's conception of dignity is rooted in what she names the "capabilities approach." In this, she argues specifically for universally, cross-culturally applied, basic minimal entitlements for all human beings. All persons access dignity through any of a list of *capabilities* that are commonly shared among human beings. The capabilities list emerged from examination into different areas of human existence, asking within each area, what ways of being, living, and acting are "minimally compatible with human dignity"?[37] We are not to define dignity in contrast to or independently of these capabilities, "but in a way intertwined with them and their definition. . . . The guiding notion therefore is not that of dignity itself, as if that could be separated from capabilities [but instead that a life worthy of human dignity] is constituted, at least in part, by having the capabilities on the list."[38]

As we come to an understanding of a basis of dignity, we are faced with the question of whether dignity is something that can, in fact, be lost. Returning to Pellegrino's use of the clinical encounter, we remember the potential loss of dignity within the vulnerable relationship of patient and practitioner. His is not only a hypothesis of loss, but also of self-reflection and understanding through relationality. He argues that relationships of intersubjectivity force human beings to assess our own dignity. "Only in the encounter with others do we gain knowledge of how we value each other and ourselves."[39] Transsexuals are all too familiar with the shame generated in a patient by an encounter with an intolerant physician. Like anyone else who seeks medical care, we must expose our vulnerable selves to the scrutiny of medical professionals, and this often feels like a threat to dignity. Pellegrino explains, "Usually, we must disrobe and expose our body to expert scrutiny with all its imperfections revealed. What we are and who we are is suppressed in the objectification of our person that a scientific appraisal of our physical state might demand."[40] The painful irony of medical transition is that in order to change our bodies we must invite people to view, touch, examine, comment on, and handle the very parts of our bodies that carry the most pain and shame for us.

Even though years have passed since my chest reconstruction surgery, when I think of that experience, I remember being prepped for surgery. I can still feel my surgeon's cold hands as he lifted and moved my breasts, marking with a pen the lines that his scalpel would soon follow. He was the first person in many years to touch, or even see, my naked breasts, and he would be the last person to ever do so. The surgery left me with considerable loss of sensation, and so this uncomfortable memory is the only connection I have to the way my nipples and the skin on my chest felt when handled by another human being. In the room along with my doctor were three nurses and my lover at the time—a man who had never, before that day, seen my chest, free of the tight binder I had used to conceal what was there. I was not even fully naked, and yet I was shamefully naked. The parts of me that had brought me so much pain and discomfort were on display. I became objectified as the bearer of these large breasts, which were sagging and exposed, now atrophied and misshapen by the effects of testosterone and years of binding. Even though everyone in that room affirmed my male identity and my decision to have this surgery, I still found it hard to hold on to my internal sense of dignity in that moment. In retrospect, I recognize that the loss of dignity in this memory is linked to my inability to access my sense of *integrity as oneness*. I had tried to reconcile with my breasts before they were gone. But, in all honesty, instead of saying good-bye, I could really only muster a slight apology that things had not worked out for us. I was terrified, being seen and touched as an object. I was also cold and very hungry. The clinical encounter reminds us that certain aspects of our dignity are fleeting.

Medical ethicist, physician, and Franciscan friar Daniel P. Sulmasy offers three categorizations of dignity that are helpful in understanding dignity as both constant and ephemeral. These categories are: attributed, intrinsic, and inflorescent. Attributed dignity is, "in a sense, created. It constitutes a conventional form of value."[41] Intrinsic dignity is the "worth or value that people have simply because they are human, not by virtue of any social standing, ability to evoke admiration, or any particular set of talents, skills, or powers."[42] In the clinical encounter I just described, my intrinsic dignity was never at stake. My membership in the human race was never questioned. The sense of lost dignity that any human being feels when exposed and naked in front of the clinical gaze of medical professionals threatens attributed dignity; that is what I encountered. Sulmasy's final category, *inflorescent dignity*, brings the most relevant understanding of dignity to the question of flourishing of moral agents—a key concept, we recall, in the notion of agent-centered transsexual subjectivity. Inflorescent dignity refers to individuals who flourish "as human beings—living lives that are consistent with and expressive of the intrinsic dignity of the human."[43]

Returning to Tanis's hypothesis that gender is a calling, we see that ultimately—despite the discomfort and vulnerability of preparing for surgery, and the physical pain that came after—the clinical encounter of my chest surgery affirmed my inflorescent dignity. It allowed me access to the life I knew I was called to live. It also, in a mundane way, connected me to dignity through the reality of a shared sense of human embodiment. Instead of just viewing the clinical encounter as a potential for lost dignity, I would like to offer another view, one in which even the cost to attributed dignity ultimately leads to the overarching goal of flourishing, namely, through the experience of vulnerability.

As Nussbaum points out, vulnerability is one of the key ways that we encounter dignity. The vulnerability I experienced helped to form me as an individual oriented toward connection with God. While transsexual surgery is certainly not a typical path to inflorescent dignity, through living in a space of vulnerability as a human being, facing my fears, and fully accepting what I had to do in order to achieve an authentic embodiment of integrity, my dignity was upheld and affirmed. The experience of lost attributed dignity also aided my growth toward inflorescence, through my own self-relationality and in my spiritual connection to other vulnerable human beings. While my specific circumstances were relatively rare, this clinical encounter connects me to all other people whose own unique medical circumstances have left them scared, cold, exposed, and even hungry as they awaited surgery. Although I could have understood these things in a theoretical way prior to that experience, I could not fully conceptualize them when I was an outsider to this kind of clinical encounter. By extension, the potential loss of attributed dignity can lead to flourishing, when the moral agent allows that vulnerability to transform personal suffering into solidarity with others. Ideally, the trans person who feels cold, terrified, naked, and hungry before surgery can experience flourishing, even in that moment, through connection to the rest of creation—not only to the pain of others receiving medical treatment, but also to broader tragedies of terror, pain, helplessness, and want.

The affirmation of my inflorescent dignity in my transition experience points me toward an understanding of human dignity, but it does not mean that I have achieved my ideal embodied self, or that I am finished in my task of personal formation toward God. The affronts to my attributed dignity throughout my time of gender transition have left psychological scars as real as those physical reminders that stretch across my chest. I have offered this analysis of my own experience, not because it carries any unique moral weight, but rather because it is only the details that separate it from any other narrative of an individual who seeks to flourish. When the transsexual is no longer the object of another's gaze, but embodies the necessary subjectivity for moral agency, he or she is open to the potential for human flourishing. Our pain links us to the suffering of all sentient beings, and perhaps a call to ease that pain, whether or not it resembles our own.

The paths one takes through the processes of transition are often mistakenly seen as salvific. Although it is a secular manifestation, this reflects a familiar theological trope. A broken being, made monstrous in a disgustingly flawed embodiment, is freed from bondage. In this view, who functions as the sanctified savior? The surgeons with their scalpels and the endocrinologists with their prescription pads hold the power to allow or deny access to salvation—the correction of gender incongruence. By shifting from a language of salvation to a language of flourishing we open up new possibilities for the entire field of transsexual health care. But beyond that, a queer theological notion of flourishing allows us to envision all of creation as a continual process of cooperation in God's work. As such, all human persons gain responsibility to one another through solidarity. It thus becomes clear that the issue is not, and never has been, gender embodiment and performativity, but rather a totality of wholeness and transcendence. Queer theology and transsexual bodies can teach all of us something very valuable about flourishing. The natality of queer culture comes not in the reproduction of living beings, but in the continual creation of solidarity and community. The final outcome is never final; the process of flourishing, like the process of creation itself, is always ongoing.

Notes

1. I would like to thank Karen Lebacqz for her help and support in writing this essay, particularly in steering me toward human dignity as a lens through which to consider the significance of biotechnology.
2. All biblical references appear from the New Revised Standard Version, unless otherwise noted.
3. "Cisgender" is a term used to signify non-trans people, those whose bodies and identities are congruent with the sex they were assigned at birth.
4. Henry Rubin, *Self-Made Men: Identity and Embodiment among Transsexual Men* (Nashville: Vanderbilt University Press, 2003), 19.
5. Ibid.
6. Edmund Pellegrino, "The Lived Experience of Human Dignity," in *Human Dignity and Bioethics* (Washington, DC: The President's Council on Bioethics, 2008), 522.
7. The President's Council on Bioethics, *Beyond Therapy: Biotechnology and the Pursuit of Happiness* (New York: Regan Books, 2003), 2.
8. Ibid.
9. Justin Tanis, *Transgendered: Theology, Ministry, and Communities of Faith* (Cleveland: The Pilgrim Press, 2003), 174.
10. Stan van Hooft, *Life, Death, and Subjectivity* (Amsterdam and New York: Rodopi Press, 2004), 30.
11. Ibid., 29.
12. Ibid., 30.
13. For example, one does not become a Botoxist, after receiving Botox. It is important to note that many of the procedures mentioned here may seem significantly less drastic than sex-reassignment, in terms of both physical risk and significant shift in appearance. However, this is not the cause of the discrepancy in the stated requirements of identity justification. Perhaps a more analogous medical procedure to consider is gastric bypass surgery. Much like the process of gender transition, the patient seeking gastric bypass must undergo an extensive counseling and approval process. However, they are not expected to argue for a

psychiatric diagnosis of dysphoria and do not have to have their own subjective notion of selfhood affirmed by the objective criteria of the psychiatric and medical communities.

14. Grace M. Jantzen, *Becoming Divine: Towards a Feminist Philosophy of Religion* (Manchester: Manchester University Press, 1998), 161.

15. Ibid.

16. Ibid.

17. WPATH Standards of Care, formerly known as the Harry Benjamin Standards of Care, are available for download at http://www.wpath.org/publications_standards.cfm.

18. Patrick Califia, *Sex Changes: Transgender Politics*, 2nd ed. (San Francisco: Cleis Press, 2003), 59. See also Tanis, *Transgendered*; Rubin, *Self-Made Men*; and Bernice Hausman, *Changing Sex: Transsexualism, Technology, and the Idea of Gender* (Durham, NC, and London: Duke University Press, 1995). Note that not all of these writers conceptualize the right of transsexual self-identification in the same way; for instance, Hausman can hardly be called an advocate for transsexual subjectivity.

19. The Standards of Care dictate specific periods of time that one must attempt to live in one's preferred gender before he or she can start the medical process of transition.

20. This is an example of a requirement of transition that is at the discretion of the therapist. WPATH does not consider this a requirement and it is not found in the current Standards of Care. However, the original Standards of Care (1979) did list the absence of "heterosexual" attraction (i.e., opposite sex attraction to birth sex) as necessary for "true transsexual" status, and thus access to the medical processes of transition.

21. Ironically, my health insurance refused to pay for the therapy because it dealt with my "Gender Identity Disorder," despite the therapist's refusal to give me the "true transsexual" diagnosis; the GID diagnosis meant even my therapy could be considered "elective."

22. As an example, consider the case of Tyra Hunter, a woman who died from lack of immediate medical care after paramedics in Washington, D.C., cut off her pants (to treat her injuries following a car accident) and discovered that she had a penis. Witnesses later testified that the paramedics pointed, laughed, and ridiculed Hunter, while she lay helpless in a state of semi-consciousness. See Califia, *Sex Changes*, 232–34.

23. On numerous occasions in the course of my trans activist work, I have found myself in de facto FTM-only spaces, in which I have experienced a different level of transsexual discourse. While I can offer this only as anecdotal evidence, I do so with the explanation that this is knowledge that perhaps can only come from the safety of discussions in the context of those key elements of shared embodiment that must be given primacy in the validation of transsexual subjectivity. What I have learned in these shared spaces of transmasculinity is unique to

those times and places of relationality. Cisgendered people can take for granted the experience of shared gender camaraderie that happens in everyday life; being in transmale-only space is for most of us a rather rare event—thus I give it a voice in this essay, despite the trickiness of citation.

24. Tanis, *Transgendered*, 173.
25. Margaret E. Mohrmann, "On Being True to Form," in *Health and Human Flourishing: Religion, Medicine, and Moral Anthropology*, ed. Carol R. Taylor and Roberto Dell'Oro (Washington, DC: Georgetown University Press, 2006), 92.
26. Ibid.
27. Ibid., 90.
28. Tanis, *Transgendered*, 147.
29. Ibid.
30. Mohrmann, "On Being True," 92.
31. Ibid., 93.
32. Ibid., 90.
33. Tanis, *Transgendered*, 161.
34. Mohrmann, "On Being True," 99.
35. Holmes Rolston III, "Human Uniqueness and Human Dignity: Persons in Nature and the Nature of Persons," in *Human Dignity and Bioethics*, 129.
36. Martha Nussbaum, "Human Dignity and Political Entitlements," in *Human Dignity and Bioethics*, 363.
37. Martha Nussbaum, *Frontiers of Justice: Disability, Nationality, and Species Membership* (London: Belknap Press, 2006), 161–62.
38. Ibid., 162.
39. Pellegrino, "Lived Experience," 521.
40. Ibid., 524.
41. Daniel P. Sulmasy, O.F.M., "Dignity and Bioethics: History, Theory, and Selected Applications" in *Human Dignity and Bioethics*, 473.
42. Ibid.
43. Ibid.

Chapter 10

The *Baklâ*

Gendered Religious Performance in Filipino Cultural Spaces

Michael Sepidoza Campos

In the 1970s, a Tagalog film captured Filipino popular imagination for its in-your-face take on the *baklâ*, the effeminate gay man who personifies Filipino popular conceptualizations of homosexuality. The story line was banal and predictable and, for the most part, perpetuated shallow stereotypes of homosexuality. But one comical confrontation between a macho father and his ridiculously effeminate teenage son left many in stitches and me with much to think about.[1]

The scene opens with a father dragging his son to a barrel filled with water. Rumormongers have just outed the boy to his family, and so the father is determined to force the truth out of his son (even though the boy is already swathed in a flowing psychedelic blouse!). With each dunk of his son's head, the father barks: *Walanghiya kang anak: Ano ka, babáe o lalake* (You shameless son: What are you, woman or man)?! And with each gasp for air, the son exclaims, *Babáe, po* (A woman, sir)! So even more furiously, the father pushes his son underwater, insistent that he assert his manhood. But each time, the boy insists piteously: *Babáe ako* (I am a woman)! Finally, in dramatic flourish, the father dunks his son even deeper into the barrel, practically drowning the "woman" out of the boy. And he succeeds. Near death, weakly clutching at his throat, the son finally relents: *Hindi po ako babáe* (I am not a woman). But before the father manages a triumphant smirk, the son sputters: . . . *dahil sirena ako* (because I'm actually a mermaid)!

As a young boy, I remember painfully guffawing along with the rest of the audience. I clearly appreciated the juxtaposition of truth and unveiling, power and abuse; the metaphor levied upon water as both a space of drowning and—as asserted by the self-proclaimed mermaid—life. There prevailed the recognition that being *baklâ* assumed a lifelong wrangling for air. Just as its etymology melds *babáe* (woman) and *lalake* (man) into an awkward verbal utterance, the *baklâ* embodies conceptual ambiguities in gender and identity. Within a culture that imposes clean distinctions between *lalake*/man and *babáe*/woman, to be *baklâ* implies participation in the undulating terrain of gender in-between-ness. The space for the *baklâ* exists in flux.

By engaging different voices in popular Filipino gay culture, I hope to map and define the social spaces marked for/by the *baklâ*.[2] I depend heavily on the research of Filipino anthropologist Martin F. Manalansán IV and literary scholar J. Neil C. García. Incorporated into their studies are informal narratives that I hope will both validate the *baklâ's* voice and so nuance the ways in which he configures both his space as well as those allotted for the *babáe* and the *lalake*.

Since identity emerges out of a network of relationships, I claim that the *baklâ* is as much a community's articulation of gender as the fruit of an individual's unfolding. Forging an essentialized femininity upon the male body, the *baklâ* can be said to accomplish two apparently contradictory things at the same time: acquiesce to the prevailing *lalake*/*babáe* binary and thereby expose the limitations of a two-gendered conceptualization of human sexuality. I would argue that this double-gesture surfaces a genuinely queer space. While acquiescence emerges as an initial and necessary tactic for survival, it *unveils* the complexities of assumed gender categories that augur a potentially transformative articulation of gender fluidity.

The dynamic of coming out serves as the conceptual locus from which I hope to illustrate *how* the *baklâ* maneuvers through the hazy boundaries of private and public spheres. The simple choice to live truthfully, as assumed in any decision to come out, does not easily translate in a social matrix that sometimes values the community above the individual. Thus, the dichotomy between the choice to be public about one's sexuality (that may very well lead to social expulsion) and to remain in the closet (that may well secure one's social respectability) is imaginary. Most *baklâ* find that their initial struggle to come out leads *not* to banishment, but to the gradual occupation of a social niche that has long been allotted *for* them.

Yet as clearly illustrated in the film, social integration does not come easily or naturally. Concessions are made, sometimes under duress. Here I hope to illumine ways through which the *baklâ* transgresses spaces designated for his ilk, juxtaposing the scandal of his public performance with the *disente* (decent) performativity of the *lalake* and the *babáe*.[3] Judith Butler's claim of gender

performativity as social fabrications that have been naturalized through repetition resonates deeply with my position. I argue that at certain moments in his
performance, the *baklâ* exposes hierarchies of power that justify his marginalization. So long as he occupies and contours a specific epistemological space,
the *baklâ* acts, chooses, and breathes in ways that both validate and critique
the *lalake/babáe* binary. Indeed, Butler acknowledges that although "parody
by itself is not subversive . . . there [is] a way to understand what makes certain
kinds of parodic repetitions effectively disruptive, truly troubling, and which
repetitions become domesticated and recirculated as instruments of cultural
hegemony."[4] If this should be the case, I assert that the *baklâ* wields a similar
potential to discern, and so undermine, the abusive hegemonies that have long
framed his identity.

In his ethnographic study of a gay Santacruzan in New York, Martin F.
Manalansán reveals the fecundity of religious symbols for the *baklâ*'s meaning-
making mechanism.[5] I argue that if the *baklâ* were to ever find space in which
to parody, subvert, and transform gender norms, it would be through religious
discourse. Grounded upon five hundred years of colonial subjugation, Filipino
culture is religious, indelibly Catholic.[6] Hence, Christian themes structure
the Filipino's symbolic, mythical, and epistemological framework. Just as religion configures the *baklâ*'s social space, it also serves as the vehicle through
which transgression takes place.[7] The anomalous *baklâ* unravels neat sexual
categories. To be *baklâ* is to be *bastos*, crass, rude—overtly *sexual* in a prudish culture.[8] The late Argentine theologian Marcella Althaus-Reid endorses
the potency of this tactic in contexts where religious language sanctions the
separation of body and spirit, divine and profane. Such spaces, she observes,
propagate a heterosexist hegemony that privileges masculinity and so renders
inferior other ways of being:

> It is difficult for people to see the sacred in their lives outside heterosexual
> parodies, repeated endlessly in the authoritarian structures of Latin American
> governments and societal patterns. The Virgin Mary was a girl, the angel was
> a boy and God the father, a father. The role of sexual stories in theology has
> been to repeat and reinforce (hetero)sexual imaginations beyond naturaliza-
> tion processes by divinizing them, but also by concealing the questioning of
> reality and obstructing the creative imagination to find alternative ways of life.[9]

By sexualizing God-talk, therefore, one reveals the indecencies of a dogmatic
system that hide beneath a façade of purity, holiness, and righteousness.

The *baklâ*, as the curious love child of the *lalake* and the *babáe*—indeed,
as the feminized and thus impotent *lalake*—renders indecent the gender assumptions and role of sexual desire in Filipino social dynamics. When he

affects feminine speech to flirt with men, dresses like the Virgin Mary during religious processions, and revels in the campy glamour of beauty pageants, the *baklâ* discloses both polyvalent identities and the potency of desire. He unveils the very religious framework that regulates Filipino sexual mores. And so, the *baklâ* becomes a conduit for scandal. Ultimately, I hope this kind of project will trace the paths through which the *baklâ* destabilizes the decent expectations of Filipino gender identities and so enable a glimpse of the possibilities of transformation for himself and the community/ies he calls home.

The Effeminate Man: Mapping the *Baklâ*'s Social Domain

Is the *baklâ* gay? This question delineates, for the most part, the frontiers of public discourse concerning the *baklâ* in Filipino culture. In contemporary urban societies, including Manila, concepts of gayness presuppose an identity that is defined by the object of desire and the subsequent choice of sexual partner. Regardless of one's comportment (to a certain extent), it is the person with whom one sleeps that determines sexual orientation. Eve Kosofsky Sedgwick wisely notes that while this may be the case today, it has not always been so:

> It is a rather amazing fact that, of the very many dimensions along which the genital activity of one person can be differentiated from that of another (dimensions that include preference for certain acts, certain zones or sensations, certain physical types, a certain frequency, certain symbolic investments, certain relations of age or power, a certain species, a certain number of participants, etc. etc. etc.), precisely one, the gender of object choice, emerged from the turn of the century, and has remained, as *the* dimension denoted by the now ubiquitous category of "sexual orientation."[10]

As a gender marker, "*baklâ*" transcends contemporary insinuations of desire. Even García, who tends to equate gayness with *baklâ*, nuances his position by alluding to *behavior* as the defining public face of the *baklâ*:

> Gays who are not engaged in identifiably *baklâ* occupations, who are not irreducibly *baklâ* in appearance and comportment . . . are precisely the "invisible" gays who have escaped from the more coercive effects of homophobic domination.[11]

In so claiming, García distinguishes the overtly effeminate gay man—who is *baklâ*—from the more covert, "invisible" variety—who may *not* be *baklâ*. The *baklâ* is thus defined as much by public comportment as by the assumed object of his sexual desire. Profession, speech, accent, and fashion sense define the *baklâ*. More pointedly, it is the *baklâ*, not the straight-acting, "invisible" gay man who suffers the brunt of homophobia.

Within the Filipino cultural matrix, the *baklâ* signifies a man with an ex-aggerated feminine persona. Hence, a child could be called *baklâ* for being passive and self-effacing. He may or may not be drawn to men sexually, but an artistic teenager who relishes poetry over basketball has inevitably warranted the condescending label. Conversely, the professional executive who maintains a respectable family life while discreetly engaging in sex with men evades the accusation so long as he maintains public significations of masculinity.

Straddling the feminine-masculine binary, the *baklâ* not only blurs the clean delineation between the *babáe* and the *lalake*, but also *reinforces* the boundaries of differentiation that separate the *babáe* from the *lalake* from the *baklâ*. Pierre Bourdieu describes this dynamic of role anticipation and regu-lated improvisations as the *habitus*, where individual agents apprehend and perpetuate socially sanctioned behavior. Within the *habitus*, cultural mores emerge not from any clear sense of agency but from a preexisting modus ope-randi through which individuals forge meaning.[12] By melding the social roles allotted for both the *babáe* and the *lalake*, the *baklâ* serves as a conduit for self-location: the *babáe* and the *lalake* recognize who they are (and are *not*) through the *baklâ*'s parody of femininity and rejection of masculinity. Cor-respondingly, the *baklâ* grounds his own meaning upon this very binary that leaves him bereft of category, at least superficially.

For the *baklâ* to "exist," he must occupy spaces of the *babáe*. This is poi-gnantly manifest in his self-perception as a *real woman* who must engender sexual partnerships with *real men*. British anthropologist Fennella Cannell highlights this in her ethnographic study of everyday life in a small town in the Bicol region of the Philippines:

> It is significant that although *baklâ* sometimes call themselves "gays," using the English word, they entirely reject the Western understanding of gay sexuality, that is, that gay men are those who desire other gay men. Most *baklâ* I knew had never heard of this definition of being gay, and they vehemently deny either that they would ever be attracted to each other, or that their boyfriends are gay in any sense. *Baklâ* say they are men "with women's hearts" who therefore love men, and love to dress in women's clothing and perform female roles.[13]

But a glaring fact remains: *baklâ* is not *babáe*. His relegation to women's spaces requires specific navigational skills. One cannot simply act *baklâ* and be embraced as a woman. The *baklâ* caricatures femininity; his performance of womanhood is seen as paradoxical. García notes that among the *baklâ* "the sense that they have male bodies, and that they are men, is never lost to them. Instead, it becomes heightened, albeit in a renewed and more subversive form, by the very act of putting on the clothes of women."[14]

Cannell's study of the relational economy between the *baklâ* and his sexual partners further distances the *babáe*'s and the *baklâ*'s social spaces:

> Their ability to keep a boyfriend will always be threatened by the fact that they have no womb and cannot bear a child. . . . Because of this, they often look for younger boyfriends, to whom they become a kind of financial sponsor, paying for their education or to set them up in business, while nevertheless casting themselves in the role of housewife and emotional dependent.[15]

Economic and social participation is thus key to a *baklâ*'s identity maneuverings. He is considered, for the most part, a breadwinner. The *baklâ* is expected to funnel a good portion of his earnings to his lover and to the family's upkeep. Devoid of familial responsibilities, the *baklâ* is called upon to provide emotional support, to nurse and care for ailing family members. Rarely the absentee uncle, the *baklâ* assumes parental surrogacy in the care of his siblings' children.

Among the *baklâ* I know, social relationships contour the spaces and moments in which they wield an overtly *baklâ* self. When asked to elaborate upon the nature of his familial relationships, the openly flamboyant Jay asserts that "I am smart, I am creative, I am funny, I am caring, I am a good son, I am an industrious student, I do not bring problems or shame to the family—who cares if I'm gay?"[16] While refreshingly unapologetic, Jay's claim exposes a key layer to the *baklâ*'s public performance: the role of shame in the construction of a social identity. A *baklâ* bears unspoken responsibilities that leave him beholden to higher standards of success and/or virtue. He is embraced if he brings respectability to the family, disdained if his proclivities warrant them shame. Social integration comes at a price. Carefully crafted reputations and the exchange of money secure the *baklâ*'s place in community. The *baklâ* who turns his back on his family is *walanghiya* (shameless, *sin vergüenza*), devoid of symbolic capital.[17] Meanwhile, the *baklâ*'s unassuming sexual partner— indifferent, affectively remote, on the receiving end of the *baklâ*'s financial largesse—remains tenaciously *lalake*. Indeed, García observes that since being *baklâ* assumes both feminine comportment and interiority,

> A man who commits same-sex acts with another man remains "heterosexual" (that is, not-homosexual) so long as he does not act effeminately, dress up like a woman (or become fussy about his clothes), and so long as he is "emotionally detached" from his *baklâ* partner. Inner identity, or *kaloóban*, and not external action, largely determines sexuality.[18]

People know they share the same bed, deriving pleasure from each other's bodies. But the "boyfriend" only does it for the money, not love (supposedly);

he's the top, the one who penetrates (so he claims). The "boyfriend" stands little to lose, the feminization of his *baklâ* partner having long secured his public masculinity.

Passive and relentless, breadwinner and nurturer, mother and uncle: the *baklâ* elicits a breadth of identities that ebb and fluctuate.[19] More than likely he is gay, but in comportment, he is obstinately *babáe*. Beyond the confines of femininity, however, the *baklâ* must also perform the traditional roles of the *lalake*. In this regard, Cannell is right: the *baklâ* can never be *truly babáe* because his effeminacy does not absolve him from the accompanying duty to provide for his family, to be breadwinner, to be *lalake*. Thus for Manalansán, the *baklâ's* capacity to bridge gender categories demands "a sense of self entrenched in the process of transformation."[20] The *baklâ* must evolve, change, and accommodate. Femininity forges for him a place within the *lalake/babáe* binary only to the extent that it affords him space to survive. Unlike the mimicry of female impersonators, the *baklâ's* "public performance" is intimately grounded upon an interiority that affirms his womanhood. He acts as woman because he believes himself to be one. Tragically, he is also not blind to the even more painful reality that he is not.

Unfurling the Cape: Blurring the Private and Public Spaces

In the late 1990s, the word *rampa* (fashion ramp) assumed a visual and conceptual significance among my *baklâ* friends in Boston. Long employed in *swardspeak*, the *rampa* image refers to the catwalk on which fashion models peddle beauty and desirability.[21] We use the expression *rarampa ako* (I will go "ramping") to articulate an imagined space at which we flaunted our desirability, difference, and beauty. To *rampa* is to put one's self out there, performing as it were, an idealization of who we would like to become (or are).

In a sense, the *baklâ* is clearly conscious of performance when he goes ramping. One does not *rampa* on a whim but does so in front of an audience. Unlike the quotidian performances described by Cannell, going on "*rampa* mode" is *intentional*, not the sanctioned mimicry of femininity that defines the *baklâ's* habitus. To *rampa* is to draw attention, not blend in. Here, the *baklâ* glories in difference, clearly aware of his transgression.[22] The intentionality of ramping thus blurs the distinction between a *baklâ's* expected public comportment and his *self-definition*. In choosing to *rampa*, the *baklâ* acknowledges volition in his becoming. He *chooses* to come out with flair!

While most *baklâ* use the contemporary phrase "coming out" to describe their public emergence, there are gradations in the level at which one chooses to make this declaration implicit or explicit. Often these levels of openness mirror the nature of one's relationships. Coming out to friends and new acquaintances is easier; family dynamics necessitate more subtle negotiations. When asked to differentiate his coming out to family and friends, Jay asserts that while it was important for him to affirm his sexuality in professional settings, he found no such imperative among family members. In fact, he saw no need to define his sexual orientation against his daily interaction with the family:

> You have to be "in" to come "out." This is a transformative action: from hiding inside the closet to coming out of it, from not knowing or being in denial to acknowledgement. If you are what you are all the time, not needing to hide anything, and there are no new self-realizations, I guess coming "out" would be unnecessary.[23]

Emile, another informant, nuances this interplay by alluding to the complexities of an "implicit outing" among close family members. Like Jay, Emile assumes that his family knows of his sexuality and of his relationships with men. He too has not made a public declaration of his identity, choosing instead to render the implicit obvious:

> Not all my family knows. If they do know, it's a matter of "don't ask don't tell" though I do want them to ask so I can tell. For the family (members) I did come out too, it was harder than with friends—for all except my sister where it was just assumed.[24]

And so Emile and Jay exemplify the quandary of gay Filipinos who must weave familial and professional webs that constitute the fabric of their identities. Although their coming out may not reflect the in-your-face boldness of ramping, intentionality still prevails in their decision to remain both *in* and *out* of the closet. Both continue to ramp, preen, and parody the expected gender roles to which they are relegated, but within limits of acceptability. *Bahala na sila* (Let them think what they want) is often the *baklâ*'s rejoinder when cautioned against subverting social propriety.[25]

In popular North American idiom, to come out assumes a hidden identity that is revealed for all to see. Exposure of the hidden self results in the formation of new narratives; old language is reconfigured to acknowledge a new epistemology. Often, coming out is imaged as the point at which silence is banished, speech retrieved. Sedgwick, however, finds this assumption both myopic and diminishing of efforts to subvert prevailing gender categories. By identifying closetedness as "a performance initiated . . . by the speech act of silence," Sedgwick confers potency upon silence as an *act* of speech. One does not *articulate speech* upon coming out. Rather, the forced silence of the closet *speaks as much of*—and so dispels—the illusory power of heteronormativity.

In or out of the closet, silence bears its own accusatory gaze. Thus, Sedgwick argues against clear delineations between life within the closet and life beyond it as such claims ignore the multi-layered strategies that individuals employ to foster belonging and meaning.[26]

Sedgwick's refusal to succumb to the in/out binary resonates deeply with the *baklâ*'s ambivalent dance in public and private spaces. Indeed, Manalansán mirrors this stance in his analysis of a colloquial phrase that reflects the cultural specificity of the *baklâ*'s social exposure:

> The term "coming out" has been translated in *swardspeak* as *pagladlad ng kapa* or "unfurling the cape." . . . The *swardspeak* term reveals the performative element of the *baklâ*. Many Filipinos, including scholars, believe that the clothes the *baklâ* wears are external signs of the inner core, of essential qualities of feminine sensibility and emotion. . . . Therefore, the act of "unfurling" does not actually reveal a secret self but rather an unfelt or unapprehended presence.[27]

Sedgwick and Manalansán thus both assert that to come out—indeed, to *rampa*—is to unfurl a reality that is *already known*. For the *baklâ*, this is a conscious act of becoming, one that embraces *fidelity* to cultural and familial ties (for better or for worse). Instead of situating self away from others, the *baklâ* forges new relationships in an already familiar space. This is especially so because in the act of unfurling, one retrieves, not creates, an unspoken reality that has long been felt by family members. In effect, there prevails a blurring of sorts between the *baklâ*'s private and public lives. Ted's coming out to his parents illustrates this ambiguity well:

> I came out first to my father when I was 23 years old, who took it quite well. I learned to never underestimate your parents, they are not dense. My father mentioned he knew it all along, and was wondering why it was significant for me to make it known to him formally. I mentioned it was more for me, really. He took it upon himself to mention it to my mother and cautioned me against telling her formally. He mentioned that he will do that for me in due time. I often wonder if he ever really did mention this to my mother. I followed his advice. My mother to this day is in a fog of denial, hoping that I would change my "choice." I have (since) stopped behaving differently in front of my mother or my father.[28]

Arising from a close-knit, extremely religious, and politically prominent family, Ted's coming out necessitated a reconfiguration of the public spaces that he inhabited. By claiming the space of the *baklâ*, Ted forced his father to restructure the family's public façade. They too, had to come out. Thus, his father's insistence on silence signified not the rejection of his son, but the fear of having to reorient one's *public* significations.

On the other hand, Ted's mother's decision to remain "closeted" not only demonstrates the power of shame in Filipino culture, but also emphasizes Sedgwick's point that "ignorance is as potent . . . as knowledge."[29] In choosing not to acknowledge her son's homosexuality, Ted's mother abdicates from any responsibility of having to configure her own public space. She shields herself with intentional naïveté, thus leaving Ted with the burden of accommodation. Ted, not his mother, must tiptoe around the unspoken truth. And Ted, not his mother, must pander to the illusory comfort of silence. Luckily, Ted had enough self-possession to subvert this abusive dynamic in choosing to stop "behaving differently" in front of his parents. Implicit or otherwise, Ted, the *baklâ*, unfurled his cape and rendered obvious that which had long been known. But like other *baklâ*, he remains firmly enmeshed in the family web, bound to both new and old social obligations.[30]

The process of unfurling is thus neither seamless nor predictable. Yet Jay's, Emile's, and Ted's narratives also reveal set patterns of disclosure in the *baklâ*'s unfurling. One cannot simply "unfurl and leave," as it were. There prevail boundaries to which one is held accountable as a member of a specific community. I remember all too clearly how these unspoken rules configured my own navigation in the weeks leading to our senior prom. At the time, our class officers had determined that only students with dates could attend the senior banquet. The only exceptions were our *baklâ* classmates; they could attend as singletons. At the private, all-boys Catholic school I attended, this accommodation signaled a spirit of openness that up to that time seemed unimaginable. I was impressed. But the elation soon dissipated when I realized that straight students without dates could *not* attend the prom. Neither overtly effeminate nor out at the time, I cringed at the idea of having to perform the role of the "perfect boyfriend" for a night. Thus I found myself in gender limbo, neither enough of a *baklâ* or a *lalake* to attend! The celebration had room only for the *lalake* (who preened about with dates draped on their arms) and the *baklâ* (who were actually relegated to spaces of asexuality!). There was no space for those who trumped the social pressure to date. In effect, the policy signaled our automatic expulsion from the ritual.

While the event could be said to exemplify tolerance toward the *baklâ*, I claim that the space allotted for the *baklâ* that evening was actually sustained by discriminatory attitudes toward effeminate boys who were further emasculated by the no-date policy and the date-less others who embodied gender ambiguity by default. Categorized as the "co-ed (feminized) classmate"—and therefore the complementary opposite of the school's lionized jock—the *baklâ* was denied the right to express his sexuality in ways that transgressed heteronormative values. To bring a date—especially a boy from another school—would have been tantamount to an unfurling of sorts, a revelation that the *baklâ* were *sexual* beings whose public demonstration of desire would have undermined these jocks' very masculinity as peers who shared the same social space with the *baklâ*.[31] This threat alone warranted the *baklâ*'s forced asexuality for the night. In retrospect, what frustrated me most about the prom was our easy acquiescence to these unspoken rules and our accompanying inability to recognize injustice.[32] Thus, we participated in a collusion of marginalization by failing to expose subtle acts of exclusion. Furthermore, its context as a coming-of-age ritual rendered these discriminatory actions—and our complicity—even more potent, perhaps traumatic.[33]

Because the lines that divide private and public spheres are, at best, suggestive, the *baklâ*'s social navigations offer no clear logic of progression toward transformation. This is why I argue for the importance of *agency* in one's coming out. If taken seriously, unfurling one's cape usurps the oppressive silence that suffocates life within the closet. But the effects of this silence are pervasive and extend well beyond the closet. Once a new social space is mapped out, relationships must change. To live within socially sanctioned spaces, while momentarily sufficient, emerges as essentially dehumanizing in the long run. And so, integrity necessitates a dying of sorts. Sometimes, one must risk the loss of relationships. This involves choice, a decision to live honestly.

Within a stratified society like Manila, reconfiguring fidelity to familial and social ties entails possible loss of resources, social networks, and opportunities for upward mobility. One must grapple with existing relationships while forging new ties that affirm one's participation in the public sphere. By claiming speech and so refusing to participate in a dance where "ignorance and opacity collude or compete with knowledge in mobilizing the flows of energy, desire, goods, meanings, persons," the *baklâ* bears the potential to challenge the complicity of the *lalake* and the *babáe*.[34] To intentionally come out is to reconsider the ways through which one enlivens desire, attraction, friendship, boundaries, and identity.

And so while unfurling one's cape may imply but a process of *re-entry* into common social spaces, I argue that any act of re-entry necessitates a disjuncture of knowing, the banishment of the silence that sustains the domination of heteronormativity. In unfurling his cape, the *baklâ* exposes the hypocrisy of the gender dance that limits one's capacity to flourish, even to flame as necessary.

Prancing in the Sanctuary: Ambivalent Performances

In Catholic Philippines, religious processions and patronal feasts punctuate the life cycle of a village community. Births, deaths, and life transitions are circumscribed by religious symbolism, forging identities that are grounded as much upon pragmatic need as a shared metaphysical hope. While Bourdieu posits the importance of ritual in the formation of community identity, he also asserts that "rites take place because and only because they find their *raison d'etre* in the conditions of existence and dispositions of agents who cannot afford the luxury of logical speculation, mystical effusions, or metaphysical anxiety."[35] Thus, while religious celebrations may exhibit the deeper "metaphysical anxieties" of faithful Filipinos, these processions respond to ordinary needs—from the affective to the economic—that cultivate opportunities for community consolidation.[36]

As a child, I participated in religious celebrations with a mix of enthusiasm and curiosity. Such events were loud, festive, gaudy, and dramatic. Permission was granted, at least by my family, to cross boundaries of propriety, gender, and class. We could mingle in the town square freely, to reconnect with distant relatives and occasional acquaintances. Imagery comprised the day's narrative, words rendered lyrical through song and prose. Performances piqued at one's intuition and affect, not logic. During the Holy Week leading up to Easter, in particular, our town would host a procession of religious images portraying Jesus' suffering and death. Given the brutal circumstances of the crucifixion, life-size statues of Jesus, the disciples, Roman soldiers, and the Virgin Mary would be awash in sorrow, darkened by blood and the twisted anguish of body and spirit. Yet, these sorrowful *santos* (saint figures) would be dressed up magnificently, veiled with rich, expensive cloaks, aglow beneath bejeweled coronets and celestial accoutrements.[37] The *carrosas* (carriages) on which these statues were displayed would be as majestically outfitted. For a few hours, the provincial simplicity of my hometown would be immersed in glamour seen but twice a year (the feast of the town's patron saint being the other hallowed event). Indeed, the entire procession evoked the ambience of a highly competitive pageant that pit one radiant *santo* against the other.

Years later, I learned that many of these *santos*, particularly those renowned for their beauty, were actually maintained by wealthy *baklâ* patrons. If they belonged to society matrons, such images would often be placed in the care of a talented *baklâ* celebrated for his taste. Clearly, these *santos* occupied a place of prominence within the *baklâ*'s social domain. It is an interesting place of contrasts: divine imagery juxtaposed with the earthy, almost gaudy aesthetics of the *baklâ*. For a brief moment in the town's collective spirituality, it is the *baklâ* who acts as priest, who dresses the *santo* and so re-images God before the people. The antiseptic worship of institutional liturgy is usurped by glamour, beauty, exaggeration, femininity, earthy humor, and camp.

The potency of religious symbol cannot be exaggerated in a culture that has endured more than five hundred years of Spanish (Catholic) and American (Protestant) colonization.[38] Religious language serves as the cultural framework upon which Filipinos, the *baklâ* included, configure social location. Manalansán illustrates this through his analysis of the clever social navigations that took place at a Santacruzan (Holy Cross) procession hosted by a Filipino-American gay society in Manhattan. In his study, Manalansán defines the Santacruzan as a

> response to the radical changes caused by Spanish colonization. . . . Celebrated every May, the Santacruzan has been appropriately called the "Queen of All Filipino Fiestas." The procession is a symbolic reenactment of the discovery of Christ's cross by Queen Helena, or Reyna Elena, the mother of Emperor Constantine of the Holy Roman Empire. . . . The procession includes a series of *sagalas* (muses). These *sagalas* are a constantly changing coterie of personages, which makes it possible to adapt the ritual to changing historical and cultural contexts.[39]

The series of muses who accompany Queen Helena in her search for the true cross embody biblical and historical personages (like Judith, Constantine, and Helena) and classical virtues that reflect community aesthetics (like Justice, Truth, and Hope). All are feminine personifications. Thus, with the exception of Constantine, who is often portrayed by a child, feminine imagery dominates the religious pageantry.

In Manalansán's ethnography, the gay society that hosted the Manhattan event took liberty in adding their twist to the religious display. Such localized innovations are typical. What renders the Manhattan event unique is the intentional use of symbols that expose the many contradictions and amalgamations that defined the *baklâ*'s life in diaspora. And so, the Queen of Justice emerged in S&M garb, while Judith, the victorious warrior and savior of her people, stomped onstage bearing the severed head not of Holofernes, but of recently elected George H. W. Bush.[40] The progression of religious images parodied political, religious, and social discourse, trumping spaces of propriety, peddling alternative realities and contexts.

In profound ways, Manalansán's observations unveiled the ambivalent—and perhaps reactionary—relationship of the *baklâ* to social and religious institutions. Located within a specific cultural matrix, the *baklâ* wielded the symbolic tools of his context to both affirm and critique the values of his cultural patrimony. And so, the *baklâ*'s commemoration of the Santacruzan served as much a *reaction* to as a proactive *remembering* of his roots. As Manalansán asserted, only the most prominent muse, the Reyna Elena, emerged unscathed from the panoply of camp:

> The finale of the show returned to tradition as Reyna Elena and Emperatriz (the empress) came out dressed in traditional gowns and tiaras. Reyna Elena carried flowers and an antique cross as all Reyna Elenas have done in the

past. There was no attempt at camp; rather, there was an insistence on, to use the word from vogueing, or house culture, "femme realness" in deference to tradition.[41]

At the end of the day, the *baklâ* remained rooted in the values of his culture, society, and gender.[42] The prestige attached to one's selection as Reyna Elena was palpable. Extravagant sums were spent on costume, with the *baklâ* Reyna Elena having invested hours of practice to ensure a near-perfect mimicking of the "real" Reyna Elena's feminine regality. This was not the time for camp. There was reverence assumed in his performance.

This interplay of alienation, camp, and acquiescence to religious discourse exemplifies how religion configures all aspects of the *baklâ*'s daily existence. For the most part, such negotiations are tedious at best, and dehumanizing at worst. Most of my informants have spent a lifetime contending with religious values that have long relegated them to spaces of silence. Having been educated in Catholic institutions, these men have learned to tiptoe around the social and ecclesial biases that came with their becoming gay men.[43] For some, guilt served as the typifying category of one's relationship with the church.[44] Emile underwent various forms of counseling, all exacerbating his guilt, before coming out. He describes his experience as a

> constant struggle, depending on the religious influences in my life. In high school, my Jesuit spiritual director did not necessarily make me feel guilty, though that came quite naturally. My college chaplain and counselor helped reverse the guilt. The guilt returned by my joining a conservative prayer group, which I tolerated for 5 years before finally leaving due to their request for me not to bring my partner at the time.[45]

One the other hand, Joe, a nonprofit worker, asserts that in

> the university, one of my theology professors gave my class a lecture on the various theological views on homosexuality. . . . He said that the homosexuality has been condemned because of the impossibility of procreation but that such view of procreation is limited. He said that some theologians view the growth of individuals in a loving relationship (homosexual or not) as procreation in itself—it's like a new life is created. . . . That theology class helped me in the process of coming out.[46]

Joe and Emile demonstrate in their ordinary relationships the performative ambivalence of Manalansán's Santacruzan *sagalas*. There is a clear sense of otherness when faith is brought to bear upon one's space in community. Emile's seeming need to be "validated"—as exhibited in his repetitive adherence to religious authority—is not entirely unique to his experience. Joe certainly grappled with this relationship as well. However, his capacity to transcend the limited discourse of his religious upbringing was also borne out of positive encounters with teachers and authority figures who permitted him to be *baklâ*.

Bourdieu notes that in the configuration of any social space, there are "rules of honor" that are observed by community members. Honor assumes the existence of hierarchies, authorities, and obligations. While unspoken rules of conduct ensure the harmonious existence of the community, spaces of allowance also exist for contradictory values and comportment. Quoting Karl Marx, Bourdieu insists that individuals must maintain "unceasing vigilance" so as to be "carried along by the game, without being carried away beyond the game."[47] A community is comprised therefore of individual agents who negotiate shared sets of values. To claim that a *baklâ*, by virtue of his ambiguity, acts transgressively is an oversimplification of a more complex web of relationships to which he is accountable. He cannot merely come out and abandon the homophobia of his context. There are responsibilities to be assumed. And the fulfillment of his obligations constitutes as much his honor as that of his family. The *baklâ* must therefore play the game in ways that both forge his belonging while allowing space for contradiction. Manalansán illustrates this well by articulating that "selfhood and self-making is primarily about locating oneself in a circle of social relationships and obligations."[48] For the *baklâ* to abandon social obligations is to take on shamelessness. This deprives one of honor and, by extension, an allotted space of existence.

The *baklâ*'s negotiation around religion evokes a complex social navigation because religious language frames Filipino cultural discourse. Certainly, it would have been logical for Emile to dispense with religious authorities after having endured the unwarranted guilt heaped on his *baklâ* shoulders. But he persisted to find other religious voices that would give credence to his *kabaklaán* (*baklâ*-ness). Queerly enough, religion validates as much as it critiques. The *baklâ* knows this and so chooses to engage his religio-cultural worlds in pious language long familiar to both. But like many before him, the *baklâ* does not merely don the veil of silent obeisance. Rather, he prances upon the altar and so redecorates the sanctuary to affirm his God-given aesthetic. In so doing, the *baklâ* lays claim to his right to exist.

Beyond Siren to Reyna Elena: Imagining Transformation

I began this essay with a story of abuse, suffocation, defiance, and a grasping for air. The intent was to illustrate the parodies performed by and for the *baklâ* within a definitively macho and heterosexist Filipino culture. I argued that the *baklâ* clearly occupied an allotted social space in which he is able to foster relationships that are both meaningful and life giving. However, I was also careful to qualify that accessing such spaces required tedious machinations within a *lalake/babáe* binary that forces effeminacy upon the *baklâ*. To be *baklâ*, to be gay, and to be recognized as such in the Philippines implied a certain level of feminine performativity. Effeminacy thus served as one's ticket to social inclusion. But as illustrated in my discussion on coming out, effeminacy also reflected a deeper misogyny that marginalizes both the *babáe* and the *baklâ*. However the *baklâ* chose to define himself over and against dominant Filipino culture, he would not be able to avoid the two-step dance of acquiescence and resistance. Damned if you do, damned if you don't.

In so claiming, I resonate with Butler's notion that "acts and gestures, articulated and enacted desires create the illusion of an interior and organizing gender core, maintained for the purposes of the regulation of sexuality within the obligatory frame of reproductive heterosexuality."[49] By parroting the *babáe*, the *baklâ* upholds the performative hegemony of the *babáe/lalake* heterosexist binary. The fact that he has to fight his way to claim the space of effeminacy allotted for him exposes the latent heteronormativity of Filipino discourse. Although I am sympathetic to García's claim that for the *baklâ*, the parody of the feminine belies a deeper correspondence to a female interiority, I tend to see this interior/exterior binary as indicative of the *baklâ's* even deeper oppression. So beholden is he to women's spaces that the *baklâ* finds it impossible to imagine himself as anything *but* woman. And so, in the *baklâ's* public comportment, Butler is right to demand that "there must be a way to understand what makes certain kinds of parodic repetitions effectively disruptive, truly troubling."[50] When the nearly drowned teenage boy in my opening narrative embraced the identity of the mermaid—the wondrously feminine sea creature who thrived at the margins of human imagination—he parodied the tragedy of women's subjugation. Forced to drown away his effeminacy, the boy reincarnated his feminization upon a phantasmic water siren that embedded him more deeply into the *baklâ's* spaces! A part of me wished to interpret his defiance as a direct confrontation to his father's abuse; yet I also saw this as a metaphor for the *baklâ's* painful social negotiations. Having long been forced to contend with the *babáe/lalake* binary, the *baklâ* (in the body of the teenage boy) could no longer imagine himself outside the locus of the feminine. I think this is why for many *baklâ*, who they are constituted an essential claim upon womanhood. And I further argue that this explains in part the nature of the *baklâ's* deeper oppression: he sees himself as someone that he could never be.

Eve Sedgwick wisely observes that gender binaries—in which the *baklâ* himself is deeply entrapped—grounds the many other hegemonies that comprise broader cultural discontent:

I'll argue that the now chronic modern crisis of homo/heterosexual definition has affected our culture through its ineffaceable marking particularly of the categories secrecy/disclosure, knowledge/ignorance, private/public, masculine/feminine, majority/minority, innocence/initiation, natural/artificial, new/old, discipline/terrorism, canonic/noncanonic, wholeness/decadence, urbane/provincial, domestic/foreign, health/illness, same/different, active/passive, in/out, cognition/paranoia, art/kitsch, utopia/apocalypse, sincerity/sentimentality, and voluntary/addiction.[51]

In so claiming, Sedgwick broadens the implications of gender categorization to all aspects of the human condition. Being a man or woman defines one's place in community. It is about the spaces to which one is relegated, obligations that must be fulfilled. Intentionally abdicating from one's location endangers the integrity of the larger hegemony that keeps things in place (and thus secures the power of certain people). And so, when the *baklâ* cannot but *see* himself as *babáe*, he perpetuates systems of oppression that relegate to the margins women and many others who stand in opposition to the heterosexual male. In his "forced" parody of femininity, the *baklâ* deepens further the wound of misogyny. The oppression of one becomes the diminishment of all.

In order to avoid this cyclical mayhem, the *baklâ* must discern avenues through which he can both subvert the limitations of his social location *and* exemplify liberative agency to the broader community. This may not be difficult to do. Distinguished largely by gender signification, the *baklâ* already lays bare the *babáe/lalake* binary that frames Filipino culture. And unlike "*babáe*" and "*lalake*," the label "*baklâ*" already assumes an overt sexuality that could very well undermine Filipino moral systems. Manalansán's analysis of *swardspeak* and the numerous sexual innuendoes assumed in it clearly implicates the *baklâ* as both overtly sexualized and, so, morally ambiguous.[52] Thus, the *baklâ* embodies a prostituted self who offers a shocking alternative to the hypocrisies of Filipino social politesse.

Althaus-Reid asserts that in highly religious contexts—like the Philippines perhaps—moral values that privilege pure, hyper-spiritualized imaginations of the Divine cement a heteronormative bias, leaving women, the poor, and sexual minorities silenced, bereft of space. In order to prevent the further imprisonment of such voices, there prevails the need to counter religious antisepticism by rendering theology (or God-talk) *indecent*. She claims that

Indecent Theology is a theology which problematizes and undresses the mythical layers of multiple oppression in Latin America, a theology which, finding its point of departure at the crossroads of Liberation Theology and Queer Thinking, will reflect on economic and theological oppression with passion and imprudence.[53]

Simply put, Althaus-Reid prescribes a way to break out of the suffocating grasp of gendered binaries through the *sexualization* of theological—and, by extension, popular—discourse. And so here lies the *baklâ*'s potential to both subvert and transform. Already marked as a gender anomaly, he does not have to pander to the *disente* niceties to which the *lalake* and the *babáe* (especially the *babáe*!) are bound. This lends transformative potency to the *baklâ*'s speech and comportment. Manalansán's study of the Santacruzan illustrates this opportunity well. By camping familiar imagery—religious icons that stand close to the Filipino Catholic's heart—the Manhattan *baklâ* succeeds in trumping not only the *babáe/lalake* binary but also the very spaces that they themselves occupy. In parodying the Queen of Justice in S&M garb and the biblical Judith as the executor of political revenge, the Santacruzan *baklâ* exposes the folly of religious language and unveils the structure that keeps *babáe*, *lalake*, and *baklâ* in their appropriate places.

Althaus-Reid's prescription leaves the *baklâ* with a simple challenge to revel in the life-potential of his anomaly. Yet this remains a formidable task as well, especially for those who have found ways to flourish within their home communities. Indeed, how does one critique a system that has long given one tools to speak, maneuver, and so live? Manalansán highlights this tension when he observed how the Manhattan Santacruzan induced mixed sentiments from the predominantly Filipino gay audience. Some found the images *too* shocking, *too* American, not at all reflective of traditional *baklâ* Santacruzans in the Philippines where the *baklâ* took their femininity seriously. While Manalansán accounts for such reactions as indicative of transient identities in diaspora, I would strongly add that it was the very *foreignness* of the diaspora that allowed these *baklâ* to transgress given cultural cues and so open avenues to challenge Filipino cultural hegemonies.[54] Perhaps the crux of the *baklâ*'s transformative potential lies in his exile. Perhaps there is much to be said about retrieving—instead of dispelling—spaces of marginalization. Perhaps only when the *baklâ* learns to acknowledge his difference as good, not as an object of apology or justification, can he broaden imaginings of transformation.

Unfurling the *Baklâ*: Free to Be

The *baklâ* precariously walks the tightrope of transgression and social acquiescence. It is easy for him to fall back to form and perpetuate systems that have silenced him. Sedgwick cautions precisely against superficial attempts at change and usurpation:

> Even though the space of cultural malleability is the only conceivable theatre for our effective politics, every step of this constructivist nature/culture

The Baklâ 185

argument holds danger: it is so difficult to intervene in the seemingly natural trajectory that begins by identifying a place of cultural malleability; continues by inventing an ethical or therapeutic mandate for cultural manipulation; and ends in the overarching, hygienic Western fantasy of a world without any more homosexuals in it.[55]

Indeed, the pitfall of any subversive effort is the danger of merely replacing one form of hegemony for another. To avoid this, the *baklâ* must appropriate his exile into a place of intentionality and belonging, a locus where his difference can expose the fragile configuration of the heterosexist binary. Filipino poet Jaime An Lin conveys a paradigm of agency that I find helpful in this act of appropriation. Included in a larger anthology of Filipino gay/*baklâ* literature, Lin's poem "Short Time" embodies the tension between subversion and acquiescence in his poetic imaginings of the *baklâ*'s erotic epiphany of Jesus. Dreaming of past lovers in empty rooms, Lin imagines perhaps the "true" love of Christ: "O Christ, were I loving you / Drinking your blood, eating your flesh!"

In a few verses, Lin unveils the *baklâ*'s complex navigation between self, God, love, and others. He plays with stereotypes, pandering to popular sentiments about the *baklâ*'s sexual proclivities. By entitling his piece "Short Time," Lin accentuates the immorality of the prostitute-haranguing, motel-frequenting *baklâ* who thrives in the furtive shadows of Manila's moral universe.[56] And yet, it is the *baklâ* who encounters Jesus; he who drinks of God's essence (in the sacred blood, the semen?); he who eats of God's flesh (the divine penis?). To speak loosely of this is shocking. But to describe such surreptitious encounters in defiantly sacramental terms transgresses levels of decency that sustain Filipino religious and cultural propriety. Ultimately, what lends poignancy to this poem is the fact that it ends with the *baklâ* lying alone in his bed, naked, devoid of any cultural significations that validate his existence. He no longer needs to grasp at femininity to exist; he no longer needs to claim a mermaid-like self to breathe. Even the God with whom he shared the bed was gone. The *baklâ* stands alone with his shadows, free at last to be himself.

Lin's words of subversion exemplify the *baklâ*'s compelling capacity to cull the artificiality of moral norms. While rendering Christ indecent offers its own value, it is his simple articulation of desire *bereft* of guilt, remorse, and sin that reveals a more textured understanding of the *baklâ*'s power to undermine assumed cultural markers. By advocating guilt-free sex, Lin dismantles an ethical economy obsessed with right conduct, where to pay for sex is okay so long as one acknowledged its inappropriate implications; to sin alright so long as one sought forgiveness. When Lin exposes the pleasurable contours of sex (and, sometimes, its accompanying losses), he not only affirms its goodness but also re-enfleshes all forms of human encounter. He disengages the profane/mundane binary that has long imprisoned Filipino moral systems and so blurs the defining gender lines that dull the *baklâ*'s capacity to transform. By subscribing to an immoral stance, Lin unveils the untenability of certain religious claims. He leaves vulnerable a moral system that depends upon the subservience and acquiescence of the *baklâ*, *babáe*, and the *lalake*.

The substance of Manalansán's Santacruzan and Lin's poem rests upon their irreverent juxtaposition of the mundane with the divine. When one parodies religious talk, one challenges both cultural values and a cosmological worldview that frames a people's concept of reality. When a *baklâ* mimics femininity, he is tolerated because he does what is expected of him. But when he sullies religious discourse through the earthiness of his desire, he risks shame and the painful reconsideration of his community's epistemology. Perhaps this may not be a bad thing after all.

We are born in specific cultures, weaned upon particular worldviews, and so forge realities that repeat the contexts from which we emerge. The heart of the *baklâ*'s prerogative rests not upon his ability to differentiate self and so escape the pains of marginalization; instead, he is called, by virtue of his membership in community, to expose oppressive hegemonies that silence many like him. In so doing, the *baklâ* embodies Sedgwick's eloquent claim that "[i]t's only by being shameless about risking the obvious that we happen into the vicinity of the transformative."[57] This is where his potency lies.

From the early chapters of his work, García pushes the *baklâ* to come out, an ironic exhortation given the *baklâ*'s already in-your-face personality in Filipino popular culture. But what he truly argues for is rendering obvious the *baklâ*'s *difference* as a reality that must be taken seriously. The hope behind this challenge extends beyond the *baklâ*'s immediate benefit. It bears an all-encompassing implication to the way we understand self, community, difference, and God. I affirm García by arguing that the *baklâ*'s status as a "gender anomaly" lends him a *privileged moment* for transformation—a queerly religious space. Hence, to the same degree that Althaus-Reid pushes us to eroticize God-language, the *baklâ* ought to glean subversive opportunities beyond his marginal spaces in order to broaden the limitations of his cultural and religious universe. He needs to rightly sexualize his space. Expose his desire. Mimic *babáe*. Parody *lalake*. Come out. And be.

Notes

1. In my futile attempt to locate the film's title and year of release, I found a slew of websites that alluded to this confrontation. In fact, one site dedicated to transsexual issues in the Philippines (TransLifeInManila.blogspot.com) featured a

text of these lines in its opening page. Apparently, the infamous father-son exchange has since passed into popular lore, reincarnated as a joke that exemplifies the *baklâ*'s navigations in Philippine macho society.

2. Since *baklâ* signifies an effeminate male in Filipino popular discourse, I will focus here on the navigations of feminized men in public space. While I could claim a converse reference to masculinized women (who most often signal same-sex desire in the same cultural space), I choose to limit my focus on the *baklâ* as a marker for gender transformation.

3. *Disente* (n., Tagalog rendering of the English word *decent*). In contemporary Tagalog, *disente* describes not only social decency, but also an idealized quality to which all are held accountable. It assumes proper breeding, comportment, and acceptance of location. A *baklâ*'s *disente*-ness gradates from one of total lack, as in the case of the extremely flamboyant *baklâ*, to one of social propriety, as in the case of a successful professional who upholds respectable gender signs in the public domain. One of the worst reprimands a parent can exact upon a child is to label her or him as *walanghiya* (shameless, bereft of decency). I return to this below.

4. Judith Butler, *Gender Trouble* (London and New York: Routledge, 1999), 176–77.

5. Santacruzan literally means "holy cross" (from the Spanish, *santa*, "holy," and *cruz*, "cross"). Held each May, this Catholic procession commemorates St. Helena's discovery of the "true cross." While its origins are clearly Spanish, the Philippine version of the Santacruzan emphasizes the figure and prominence of St. Helena over that of her son, the Emperor Constantine, who is credited with the legalization of Christianity in the Roman Empire upon the Edict of Milan in 313 CE.

6. I make this claim fully aware that diverse religious traditions and histories intertwine to constitute even what is popularly perceived to be a peculiar brand of "Filipino Catholicism." Chinese, Indian, and Muslim influences—some predating the arrival of the Spanish *conquistadores* in the early sixteenth century—pervade Filipino religious sensibility. These do not even include the multiple native religious practices that have "survived" centuries of colonization. In a sense, what is considered "Filipino Catholic" is itself an amalgamation of cultural and religious practices, a syncretistic phenomenon that evokes multiplicity rather than a cohesive religious identity. For a general overview of these diverse historical threads, see Teodoro A. Agoncillo, *History of the Filipino People*, 8th ed. (Quezon City, Philippines: Garotech Publishing, 1990). Agoncillo's text has long occupied a privileged position in Philippine secondary and higher education curricula.

7. Martin F. Manalansán IV, *Global Divas: Filipino Gay Men in the Diaspora* (Durham, NC: Duke University Press, 2003), 127–36.

8. In the central Philippine Cebuano language, the word *bastos* (Spanish) refers, in part, to the jagged edges of a broken glass. Hence, one who is *bastos* is "rough around the edges," unrefined.

9. Marcella Althaus-Reid, *Indecent Theology: Theological Perversions in Sex, Gender and Politics* (London and New York: Routledge, 2000), 126.

10. Eve Kosofsky Sedgwick, *Epistemology of the Closet* (Berkeley: University of California Press, 1991), 8.

11. J. Neil C. García, *Philippine Gay Culture* (Quezon City, Philippines: University of the Philippines Press, 1996), xiv; see also Manalansán's observation: "In other allegedly antecedent forms such as those in Latin American and Asian countries, participation in same-sex acts is not the crucial standard for being labeled homosexual or identifying as gay; rather, gender performance (acting masculine or feminine) and/or one's role in the sex act (e.g., being anal inserter vs. insertee) form the standard." Manalansán, *Global Divas*, 23; Norwegian sociologist Annick Prieur undertakes a similar study of male effeminacy in Mexico City that echoes Manalansán's assertions. See Annick Prieur, *Mema's House, Mexico City: On Transvestites, Queens, and Machos* (Chicago: University of Chicago Press, 1998).

12. Pierre Bourdieu, *Outline of a Theory of Practice* (Cambridge: Cambridge University Press, 1977), 78–79.

13. Fennella Cannell, "The Power of Appearances: Beauty, Mimicry, and Transformation in Bicol," in *Discrepant Histories: Translocal Essays on Filipino Cultures*, ed. Vicente L. Rafael (Philadelphia: Temple University Press, 1995), 241.

14. García, *Philippine Gay Culture*, 215–16.

15. Cannell, "Power of Appearances," 241.

16. Jay, email interview, November 12, 2006. Having responded in English, Jay loosely translated "*baklâ*" to "gay." As I continue to illustrate, the two are not necessarily congruent.

17. Bourdieu's discussion of symbolic capital resonates deeply with the dynamics involved in the *baklâ's* social navigation. By equating his worth to economic generativity, the *baklâ* enters into a relationship that commodifies his gifts in exchange for social acceptance: "Economic power lies not in wealth but in the relationship between wealth and a field of economic relations, the constitution of which is inseparable from the development of a *body of specialized agents*, with specific interests; it is in this relationship that wealth is constituted." See Bourdieu, *Outline*, 184.

18. García, *Philippine Gay Culture*, 205.

19. It is interesting to note that as more *baklâ* migrate to the United States, many find themselves situated in spaces where their social navigational skills prove inadequate, archaic. The hyper-masculinity of gay men's culture in the United States forces many *baklâ* to conform. Nonetheless, Manalansán observes that even in diaspora, the word "*baklâ*" does not lose significance. It is modified, however. It serves as a cultural marker for one's ethnicity, racial otherness: "The majority of my informants did not cross-dress, but they drew on the *baklâ* as a social category and as a pool of meanings in analyzing every event in terms of the intersection of race, gender, and sexuality. In some situations, *baklâ* symbolized Filipino queerness while gay symbolized white queerness" (Manalansán, *Global Divas*, 24).

20. Ibid., ix.
21. *Swardspeak* refers to a uniquely gay lingo popular among the *baklâ*. Manalansán locates *swardspeak* in the Filipino language Cebuano (*sward*, which in upper-class Cebuano urban talk means sissy). It is a fluid argot that changes as swiftly as popular culture, signifying mechanisms of social navigations for the urban *baklâ*. Manalansán elaborates: "I argue that Filipino gay men use *swardspeak* to enact ideas, transact experiences, and perform identities that showcase their abject relationship to the nation" (ibid., 46).
22. When I came out during my years as a graduate student in Boston, I relished every opportunity to set my difference out there for all to see. My friends called this the "*bagong ladlad* (newly unfurled) syndrome." There were times when on a whim, and right in the middle of a busy city street, my friends and I would sashay and mimic the exaggerated gait of Christy Turlington. We would strike catwalk poses, vogue, and shriek. To this day, I chuckle at the expressions of many who shook their heads in dismay at the three flaming *baklâs* who made *rampa* on the hallowed pathways of the Boston Commons.
23. Jay, email interview, November 16, 2006.
24. Emile, email interview, November 20, 2006.
25. *Bahala na* literally means, "whatever will be, will be." Sometimes, its etymology is traced to a pre-colonial name for God/Creator, that is, *Bathala* (thus resulting to a translation that alludes to "letting God's will be done"). For the most part, this common phrase employs a fatalistic surrender to a cosmological logic that frames human existence.
26. Sedgwick, *Epistemology*, 3–4.
27. Manalansán, *Global Divas*, 27–28.
28. Ted, email interview, November 12, 2006.
29. Sedgwick, *Epistemology*, 4.
30. During a passing conversation years ago, Ted mentioned that being the only son, he still feels pressured to somehow produce an heir to the family's political legacy. Acknowledging the impossibility of marriage, his religious parents have thus abandoned traditional paths. Now, they jokingly push him to give them a grandson, regardless of reproductive method.
31. At one point, the high number of *baklâ* in my high school led to our pejorative labeling as an "all-gay school."
32. This is a presumption, obviously. I would think that there were other members of my class who found the situation immediately appalling.
33. Bourdieu uses Edmund Husserl to describe the dynamic of oppositions that define a ritual practice. In the case of my high school prom, the acquiescence of the *baklâ* (and the date-less) classmates to the date-only policy required for prom attendance exposes the problematic—and artificial—construction of the prom ritual. But it was a construction that nonetheless strengthened the hegemony of the day. Bourdieu, *Outline*, 106–7.
34. Sedgwick, *Epistemology*, 4.

35. Bourdieu, *Outline*, 115.
36. During a stint as a Catholic seminarian in my parish, I came to know that town fiestas were staged as much for civil and ecclesiastical income as for religious commemoration.
37. I recall one image of Jesus whose corpus was bound to a pillar, scourged to near-death by Roman foot soldiers. Instead of a brutal representation of the event, however, the Jesus-image elegantly leaned against a pillar laden with local blossoms. The crown of thorns that signaled his humiliation sat precariously on his perfectly curled—and blond—tresses. He was so beautifully coiffed that we took to calling him the *parlorang Kristo*. The word *parlora* is derived from the English word "parlor," in reference to the stereotypical *baklâ* profession of hairdressing. In essence, we called Jesus *baklâ*.
38. I am referring largely to the history of central and northern Philippines. Islamic presence in the south goes back at least seven hundred years. I argue that while there persists unique expressions of homosexuality and/or effeminacy in Muslim Philippines, these need to be nuanced and so differentiated from the social spaces of the *baklâ*.
39. Manalansán, *Global Divas*, 128–29.
40. Manalansán observed that the careful selection of popular imagery to emphasize the Santacruzan theme of that year reflected the critical interplay of sexuality, politics, race, gender, and colonial critique in the Manhattan community. See ibid., 132–36.
41. Ibid., 132.
42. I assert that Manalansán's reading of the *baklâ* Santacruzan exposes the cultural performativity implicit in the constitution of Filipino-American life. Manalansán's subjects "hint" at Filipino-American selves fluent in multiple cultural, economic, political, and religious languages. They become recognizable to *both* Filipino and American contexts because they hold both categories—or locations?—in tension with the other.

    The notion that identities, genders, and cultures are made *real* through ritual encounter elucidates the formidable genderfuck that Manalansán's informants deploy in their parody of Santacruzan. There is an ambivalence in the Santacruzan's ritual subversion because in their very critique of Filipino religiocultural values, the *baklâ* participants herald an accompanying *commitment* to home. Their parody of the Philippine and U.S. political landscapes only makes sense when they themselves are recognized as Filipino *and* American. In a later essay, I elucidate further the postcolonial implications of the *baklâ* space and identity in diaspora.
43. It is important to note that while all my informants self-identify as gay (and so, are loosely categorized as *baklâ*), they do not all perform the effeminacy expected of the *baklâ*. Thus, their coming out is further complicated by an attempt to fit into masculinized spaces that assume heterosexuality. This seems to be the ambivalence that Filipino author Danton Remoto awkwardly describes by claiming

that, "In the Philippine context, to be homosexual means to be '*baklâ*,' an effeminate gay who wears makeup and dyes his hair peroxide blond. It also means to be
a straight-acting man who is attracted to another man. This attraction can take
the form of affection and sexual relations. Some gays have slept with girls; some
still do, and they're called bisexuals. Some people slide on the sexual spectrum
with the grace of butterflies. There are also gays who choose to live a double life
and they're called closet queens." See Danton Remoto, *Gaydar Essays* (Pasig City,
Philippines: Anvil Publishing, 2002), 161.

44. Since *baklâ* is loosely interchanged with gay/homosexuality in the Philippines,
church teachings concerning homosexuality are automatically extended to the
baklâ. Effeminacy becomes a marker for gender and, so, moral transgression.
45. Emile, email interview, November 23, 2006.
46. Joe, email interview, November 16, 2006.
47. Bourdieu, *Outline*, 10.
48. Manalansán, *Global Divas*, 41.
49. Butler, *Gender Trouble*, 173.
50. Ibid., 176–77.
51. Sedgwick, *Epistemology*, 11.
52. Manalansán, *Global Divas*, 51–53.
53. Althaus-Reid, *Indecent Theology*, 2.
54. Manalansán, *Global Divas*, 138–39.
55. Sedgwick, *Epistemology*, 42.
56. In Manila street talk, *short time* refers to the length of time that one spends in a
motel with a prostitute. Since motels charges by the hour, the amount of pleasure
one derives from the encounter depends both upon the availability of cash and
the desirability of one's partner.
57. Sedgwick's "vicinity of the transformative" articulates eloquently my own vision
for the *baklâ* as a transformative agent. I do not exact the burden of social transformation upon the *baklâ* alone. But his social (and personal) liminality certainly
forges for him opportunities for birthing. See Sedgwick, *Epistemology*, 22.

Chapter 11

Of Bodily Anamnesis

Postcolonial, Queer, Religious Analysis[1]

Heike Peckruhn

> *In that sense we must remember that the starting point of our theologies are bodies, but the rebellious bodies: . . . the body "as is" before theology starts to draw demonic and divine inscriptions in it.*[2]

Postcolonialism as a discursive field encompasses a wide variety of theories, methodologies, and perspectives, and broadly is concerned with representations, knowledge, and power differences at work in colonialism and its aftermath. Leela Gandhi describes postcolonialism as an interdisciplinary project of revisiting, remembering, and interrogating the colonial past, and asserts that it is best described as the theoretical resistance to the amnesia of the colonial aftermath—anamnesis.[3] Anamnesis means "loss of forgetfulness," recollection, and in Platonic philosophy is what constitutes learning. This demanded my attention. My late grandmother, who had suffered from Alzheimer's disease, passed away as I began writing this essay. We had always lived together in a multigenerational, multicultural, multiconflictual household. Over the course of twelve years, Alzheimer's not only caused my grandmother to forget a multitude of things, but images of her body and memories crumbling burned into my memory, erasing my memories of our happier and healthier days together. At least that's how I like to remember those days of living together. Yet with her passing, more recent memories began being remembered with older ones, recollecting her full embodied presence over her lifetime—anamnesis. As I remember her, I am intensely aware of the intentionality with which I am able to include (and exclude) memories of her and us at will. There are always moments in which unpleasant memories emerge, and I am tempted to force them back into amnesia. But that would dis-member her/us again, now, wouldn't it?

Anamnesis suggests agency in the acts of memory and remembering, be it in textual, oral, or unvoiced embodied practices. Postcolonial discourse aims at recollecting the seductions of colonial power and preserving knowledge and agency produced in response to the particular colonial encounters. Postcolonialism then is the discourse and conceptualization of the cultural and political identities of colonized subjects, an intense discursive and conceptual activity that theoretically makes sense of colonial encounters and their effects.[4] The subject remembers the formation of colonized others, and the memories of experienced pasts, presents, and envisioned futures are captured in discursive productions.

Religion, gender, and colonialism represent some of the influential forces in our world today. In this essay, I make a case for a triple analysis—postcolonial, queer, religious—which, I argue, parallels postcolonial projects of anamnesis, only it is not always clear (nor does it have to be) which area of colonization (religious, sexual, racial, economic) steps into the foreground in the remembering and re-membering, and subsequently, the entanglements of memories might induce anamnesis vertigo. What am I looking for in staging this project of remembering postcolonial and queer religious memories? Whose memories should we seek to recover, renarrate, and reconfigure and for what purposes? Who are the colonized, queer bodies performing religious practices that are qualified to remember and what qualifies them? What of those re-membering/ed bodies who display an awareness of postcolonial criticism but still come from a background of supporting and/or benefiting from the conquest of and hegemonic rule over other parts of the world not their own? How do embodied realities show us how forgetting and remembering takes place through colonization and other violent and intimate relationships? Early critics already recognized the double inscriptions of colonialism on both colonizer and colonized, constructing the colonized other in order to uphold and affirm an image of the Western subject.[5] Colonization and subsequent efforts of decolonization affected the colonial metropolis as much as the colonies.[6] Decolonization and postcolonial conditions therefore affect the colonized and the colonizers; both need to struggle to disengage from the epistemological[7] and political hegemonies imposed. Just as it is not obvious to distinguish oppressed from oppressors,[8] it is not simple to determine who is colonizing, colonized, or positioned in postcolonial conditions. In a postcolonial world in which local relationships are always simultaneously caught in a global web of capital, international markets, social structures, and cultural exchanges, no bodies are exempted from the work of anamnesis, and neither are any memories off limits for reconstellation or re-membering.

As hinted at above, I am referring to "postcolonial" here not in a chronological sense, implying that postcolonial scholars necessarily need to stem from formerly colonized, now independent nation-states who transcended colonialism politically. I follow Stuart Hall in his affirmation of "postcolonial" as a functional referent when it serves as a descriptive and reinscriptive term referring to processes of disengagement from colonialism and its particular effects. Postcolonial efforts reinscribe colonization as a transnational and transcultural global process, producing decentered and diasporic rewritings of the nation-centered imperial grand narratives. This acknowledges that the colonial is not dead, but lives on in aftereffects and still plays out its hegemonic reach in complex restagings of its colonizing project in postcolonial contexts.[9] Postcolonial discourse brings with it an obligation to negotiate its own contradictions, signified in the "post" of postcolonialism: it follows and therefore derives from colonialism, not just chronologically, but also politically, and yet the "post" also signals a cultural obligation to imagine and execute a departure from colonialism.[10] Epistemologically, this implies that one can geographically inhabit a space impacted by colonization and thoroughly display "colonization of the mind," the internalization of imposed racial and cultural hierarchies.[11] Noteworthy is also the criticism launched against postcolonial theory as a product of Third World diasporic elites, who established a place for themselves in Western academic circles, only to reinscribe colonial power by adding new remembered knowledges to privileged discourses.[12]

In my discussion, I make use of projects from writers who display all of these concerns with the social, cultural, political, economic, and sexual impact of colonialism, particularly those who investigate religious and theological issues. Not all of these would call themselves "postcolonial," and might prefer "anti-colonial" or "de-colonial" as descriptors for their projects in an effort to emphasize the continued colonization of land and peoples. While I will respect those acts of self-definition, I also seek to present a multiplicity of voices and remembered experiences, aiming for a postcolonial and queer anamnesis as heterogeneous dialogue to reflect particular and local experiences of colonialism, racism, heterosexism, and Christian imperialism.

The intersections of disciplines investigating the different discourses around issues such as racialized, genderized, sexualized, and hereticized others comprise complementary and contradictory theories and methodologies. Some studies analyze the entanglement of religious doctrines and ideologies with the colonial conquest of the Americas;[13] some investigate relational and reciprocal construction of race, class, and gender in the context of imperialist

colonial expansion;[14] still others highlight the influences of colonial enterprises in the disciplines of biblical interpretation[15] or religious studies.[16] Yet
few works have undertaken an intersectional analysis that seeks to employ an
analytical lens incorporating the three fields of religious studies, queer theory,
and postcolonial analysis. The aforementioned types of study are important
investigations, yet adding religion to the colonial constructions of race, class,
and gender or analyzing sexual constructions in the colonial imposition of
biblical hermeneutics would expand the critical analyses offered. In this essay,
I highlight a postcolonial anamnesis that queers colonial and Eurocentric conceptions of "religion," followed by an introduction to postcolonial discourse. I
will then point to postcolonial and queer intersections before formulating the
obligation of a postcolonial, queer religious analysis to remember the three
focal points of queer religious identities, colonized difference, and heteronor-
matized sexualities. By featuring the work of the late Marcella Althaus-Reid,
I present an example of how a triple analysis can help to remember repressed
memories.

Religious Anamnesis: Remembering of Queer Religious Identities

For those particularly engaged in queering religious discourse, postcolonial
theorizing offers invaluable tools in re-membering and recollecting not just
religious practices, but the practices of religious studies themselves. Queering
religion can indicate projects that seek to make religious doctrines, practices,
and spaces more inclusive to queer persons. But boundaries of "religion" can
be blurred as well. A lucid act of queering what has come to be known as "religion" has been provided by Talal Asad, who demonstrates that "religion" is
a constructed concept of and imposed by European modernity and its global
reach.[17] To understand the cultural hegemony of the West, we must then remember that "religion" was created as a category based on the Western Christian configurations coming out of the Protestant Reformation in Europe,
which rendered other cultures local and ahistorical, and thereby "religious"
over against rational, secular (though Christian) Europe.[18]

The late Vine Deloria Jr. recollects how Native American religions ultimately differ from Christian theologies, as the former are based on space/land
in their construction of reality, and the latter using time (specifically linear
time) to construct universal history and theology. In *God Is Red*,[19] Deloria
not only elaborates on the implications of being primarily oriented in space
(versus in time), he also demonstrates how Christian cognitive structures imposed religion as primarily a belief rather than a practice. Conceptualizing

religions primarily as orthodoxies continues to foster racial, environmental, and cultural violence, as everyday rituals connected to land and its people might at best be considered religious, but movable, and at worst be discounted as superstitious and indefensible. This forgetting of religion as that which orients us in this world[20] might be composed of not only different components, but even very different worldviews that do not dismember body, mind, and soul. So when Winona LaDuke, an indigenous American environmental activist, describes Native American environmental struggles, it is a not simply a political struggle.[21] Anamnesis of religion will help re-membering that religion is not a separate entity; in fact, in some contexts, it is indistinguishable from politics, culture, economics, ethics, or any other aspects of life.

Laura Perez works from a similarly queered religious anamnesis when she discusses the politicized spiritual aspects of Chicana life in Chicana art.[22] She asserts that by bringing material and spiritual realities together, Chicana artists function as *curanderas* (healers), healing the violently separated being of the colonized, pointing to a new hybrid identity in which spirituality is integral to social justice.[23] She points to the existence of a socially and materially embodied s/Spirit that is evident in Chicana reality and artwork, a spiritual reality that requires an active response just as other social issues do, such as race, gender, sexuality, and class.[24] Perez recollects cultural and spiritual identities against the amnesia of the symbolic imposed by hegemonic culture by privileging the re-membering of the embodied in-between reality that makes indigenous consciousness and knowledge. Re-membering and re-imagining the past in Chicana artists' work then creates a new imagination of social realities, identities, and spirituality, which is an inherently political act.[25] Perez thus allows for a queering of religion by reading what has been confined in the boxes of art, aesthetics, or politics as religious practices and performances.

Chicano religious scholar Luís León describes religious performances and narratives of marginalized people in the U.S.-Mexican borderlands. While certain acts or expressions might mimic established religion and its institutions, they need to be understood as mimicking subversions, resisting institutionalized religious power, and bringing it back into the hands of the marginalized.[26] Changing the meaning and interpretation of religious symbols, therefore, is not only religious, but cultural and political practice.[27] Incorporating various religious practices is not necessarily understood to be a syncretism of clearly defined different "religions," but as a recollection of embodied practices, rituals, and knowledges out of the overlapping spheres of life that European Enlightenment and modernity separated.

These kinds of examples of queering religion remind us that we often forget to begin looking at religious practices and the embodied memories when investigating religion as thought systems. And it reminds us of the genealogy of religion as it emerged in relation to European, Christian modernity and its violent underside—colonial conquest.

Staging Postcolonial/Queer Anamnesis

Reverberations of difference and identity have already appeared in the discussion above, echoes of themes that have occupied many discussions within postcolonial and queer discourses. Critical investigations into difference and identity are partly inherited through postcolonial and queer appropriations of poststructuralism and its rejection of humanism's universalizing, normative concepts of humanity and rationality. Michel Foucault, in his characterization of epistemic shifts in Western European thought, highlights the "order of things" as based in conceptualizations of sameness and difference, and he articulates marginalized, subjected knowledges as disturbances and resistances in a hegemonic system.[28] Notions of difference become inscribed on models of identity, which, as Judith Butler (building on Foucault) asserts, are not the fixed and consolidated differences attached to a subject, but systems of power/knowledge constituting and regulating the sexual field and producing specific binary sexual identities for specific heteronormative aims.[29] The agency of a subject for Butler is always within the cultural inscriptions of identity, or in performances of identity that are intelligible within social constructions. Reinscriptions, or subversions of cultural norms, still manifest only as they are comprehensible performances within constraints and processes of iterability[30] or, as we might call them here, intelligible memories.

Jacques Derrida, who is widely appropriated by postcolonial theorists, also critiques Western rationality. But rather than focusing on resistance in different knowing and thinking, he proposes deconstruction as a way to attend to corrosion already inherent in metaphysical structures. In other words, he understands the overarching systems that house our memories as inherently decaying from the inside. Deconstruction aims to first reverse the binary hierarchy by revaluing the devalued, and then, importantly, to displace the binary through locating the subordinate in the heart of the dominant. A deconstruction of fixed binary identities then allows for an exposure of co-constitution and interdependency of that which is supposedly oppositional. The different is always an internal component of the self.[31]

To stay with our imagery, our stories of who we are depend on constructing our memories regarding who we are *not*, and deconstruction is anamnesis of the omitted parts in our stories that we have dumped into the memory files of others. Marxism as another basis for postcolonial analysis and politics allows for recollection of the material conditions of colonial, neo-colonial, and post-colonial existence, but it also adds yet another uneasy theoretical partner in the discursive mix.

Postcolonial and queer theory share the Western intellectual inheritances noted above. Both disciplines appropriate Foucault's argument of power constituting the texture of social relations, and power constituting and naturalizing what comes to be "truth."[32] Yet Foucault has been critiqued for forgetting imperialism[33] and mis-remembering religion. Postcolonial discourse appropriates and re-members Foucault and his methodologies to analyze colonialism and its power/knowledge systems and to contest Eurocentric configurations of the non-West. And it takes up Derrida's deconstructive practice, which challenges and undermines essentialist and oppositional positions.[34] Where queer theory challenges naturalized heterosexuality and its oppositional binary, homosexuality, and instead highlights the instability and the mutual constitution of both, postcolonial inquiries challenge Western epistemology and its claims of universals (particularly the universal validity and supremacy of its culture) and the rationalization of colonial discourse through oppositions (West/East, civilization/barbarism, human/savage).[35]

For postcolonial critics working out of Marxist economic analysis, the pro- and anti-humanism inheritances in the anamnesis tool kit make for difficult navigations in regards to ethics and politics, since Marxism has been unable to theorize colonialism as exploitative West-Others relationship, and Marxist humanists consider possible universal conceptualizations of a humane social order through rational and universal consensus.[36] Queer theory is also informed and challenged by Marxist analysis, and recent works have begun to formulate radical queer politics responding to economic and sexual exchanges and injustices in hegemonic global capitalism.[37]

The discursive recollection in postcolonial studies brings with it an obligation for continuous self-assessments. Postcolonial analysis needs to remember that it was the internal Western self-critiques that provided theories and methodologies useful for analyzing the West from the outside, and postcolonial discourse remembers being a product of the structures and discourses it seeks to resist and deconstruct. As Edward Antonio asserts, it would be naïve to expect postcolonial discourse to be free of the ambiguities that come with the appropriation of different theories and methods, particularly since the realities that postcolonialism recollects and explains are constituted by these very ambiguities.[38] And without critical remembering and awareness of the constituting internal ambiguities and conflicts, postcolonialism runs the danger of rendering non-Western knowledge and theories still as Other in relation to the West.[39]

Postcolonialism as an intellectual discipline of deconstruction is a process of double anamnesis that dismantles particular (colonial, neo-colonial, and even postcolonial) structures of thought in order to reveal their underlying assumptions and power relations foreclosed from memory. It exposes colonial amnesia to create new possibilities that open a passage for remembering otherwise.

Postcolonial discourse, as a theoretically and methodologically complex blend of contradictions, ambiguities, negotiations, antinomies, compromises, and acts of resistance, shares with queer theory a focus on recollecting, re-membering, and reformulating questions of difference and identity. As previously mentioned, this can be traced back to the shared opposition to universalized notions of Enlightenment humanism and epistemology. The fixed and consolidated difference of the colonized Other refuses to remain as the constituting outside of the Western subject and is slipping back in to disturb from inside, just like the homosexual Other resists remaining the constituting boundary of the heterosexual subject, and makes its way in to queer stabilized notions of natural sexuality.

Yet in regards to these projects, Hall reminds us of Foucault's warning that the dismantling and deconstruction of core concepts in "post" discourses does not lead to their disappearance, but to their proliferation, though now from decentered positions.[40] In other words, once we attempt to recollect and remember the elephant in the room, we end up finding, seeing, and talking about elephants everywhere.

Postcolonial resistance from in-between spaces[41] of identity and culture against violent cultural, political, and economic impositions, reinscribing the social imaginaries of dominant power/knowledge systems, these aims ring familiar to those engaging queer theory. Yet despite these mutual concerns and common methodologies, one field does not render the other obsolete. In recent years, the discursive encounters between queer and postcolonial studies have investigated the mutual and overlapping concerns in the respective fields.[42] Yet given the continued unease of non-Western critics and charges of Western imperialism within queer studies and indictments of heterosexism within postcolonial studies, the conversations or potential collaborations between the two are not staged easily. Concerned with normative representations of Otherness, both queer and postcolonial studies find themselves challenged to investigate their own forgetting of complicities in normative projects.

Western gay cultures defined models of homosexuality as well as political agendas for sexual liberation, and in doing so often imposed interpretative frameworks on non-Western societies and bodies, forcing forgetting of different sexual expressions and politics. Sexual desires and expressions in "other" countries might not fit into Western conceptualizations of LGBT or queer expressions, yet might have to articulate themselves within Western frameworks and thus find themselves as the Other in a queerness binary of the West and the Rest. Aiming to be indeterminate and to be after the ambiguous and transgressive,[43] queer theory seeks to criticize normative projects, yet also runs the danger of normalizing marginal sexualities by stabilizing its critical position outside a Western definition of hetero/homo binaries.

Recent postcolonial feminist critiques address issues in anticolonial and postcolonial struggles that resorted to patriarchal and heterosexist models of nation building.[44] Issues of citizenship, cultural representation, and globalization merge with concerns of sexuality, and scholarship dedicated to researching sexual and gender expressions in the postcolonial world contributes to the postcolonial studies field by queering the conceptualizations race, class, and gender.[45] Still postcolonial analyses often neglect to investigate (though they might briefly touch on) same-sex desires and homoeroticism in colonial and postcolonial contexts when they recount memories of sexual ambivalences and anxieties in imperial endeavors.

Colonial Anamnesis—Remembering Colonized Differences

One of the inaugural figures of postcolonial discourse, Edward Said, advances in *Orientalism*[46] that Western knowledge about Oriental societies is inextricably linked to the Western colonization thereof and to the inherent belief in the supremacy of the Western civilization and religion of the colonizer. Said follows Foucault in the tracing of knowledge as power and shows how the academic disciplines of history, literature, linguistics, philosophy, and religion created, presented, and disseminated "true" knowledge about the Orient.[47] Orientalist knowledge as productive power not only affirms control over the Orient and produces advantageous positions for the Orientalist, but effectively creates the Oriental subject's identity. What deceptively passed as objective facts about the Orient were representations and creations of difference that enabled colonization, exploitation, and domination of the Oriental other.[48]

These representations are in no small part the creation and constitution of the West itself, enabling forgetting of heterogeneous, fluid identities on either side. Said's anamnesis recollects and re-envisions the irreversible intermixing and cultures and ideas of colonial relationships in an optimistic, humanist fashion in order to leave behind a rhetoric of blame within binary oppositions and prescribes multicultural education to treat the amnesia of the colonizer/d.[49]

The questions of imposing memories[50] and re-membering traces of self-definition defined to a large extent the early articulations of postcolonial criticism and the projects following their trajectories. Said has been harshly criticized by feminist scholars for his negation and erasure of gender. Meyda Yeğenoğlu's *Colonial Fantasies*[51] builds on Said's work and expands it by intersecting feminist theory with analysis of Orientalism: focusing on veiled women of the Orient, she investigates how representations of cultural differences and representations of sexual difference are linked and constitute each other. Yeğenoğlu theorizes how the veil serves as a site of fantastical inscriptions of nationalistic ideologies and discourses of gender identity, and it is the trope through which fantasies of penetration into mysteries of the Orient and access into the interiority of other are achieved.[52] Yeğenoğlu re-members articulations of the historical with the fantasy, the cultural with the sexual, desire with power.[53] Mapping cultural and sexual difference onto each other, the Orient is theorized and understood as fantasy built on sexual difference. The presumption of a hidden essence and truth behind the veil is the means by which both Western/colonial *and* the masculine subject constitute their own identity.[54]

Gayatri Chakravorty Spivak, our second inaugural figure in postcolonial discourse, argues in *A Critique of Postcolonial Reason: Toward a History of the Vanishing Present*[55] that history and its subjects have been constructed as a colonial undertaking, and all Eurocentric cultural productions (philosophy, literature, history, and culture) produce and reify imperialist discourses. Any deconstruction needs to attend to the margins of the constructed norm. But one must not simply attend to the (post)colonial subject/native informant/ethnic minority. The subaltern[56] is not simply a person that is located outside of the hegemonic, hierarchical system of production. Subalterity is a space of difference that has no access to the system—the subaltern cannot speak in a way that is audible to those who might want to speak for them.

Spivak also stresses the gendered-ness and heterogeneity of the subaltern; in the conceptualization of subaltern history and memory, the male remains dominant as subject and thus female subaltern memories are doubly eradicated.[57] She problematizes subaltern studies and argues that any attempt to make audible the voice of subalterns is the subjection of the latter to epistemic violence: granting the subaltern a collective voice by intellectually expressing solidarity homogenizes the irretrievable heterogeneity of subaltern subjects, and establishes a dependence on intellectuals situated in the West to speak for the subaltern rather than creating condition of audibility.

Spivak problematizes Third World scholars joining the Western elite academic circles by articulating that double negative: imperialist hegemonies are spaces one *cannot not want* to inhabit, but is nevertheless obligated to critique and change from within.[58] Culture regulates what one knows, and one's knowledge always needs to be situated within one's place in a capitalist, imperialist global economy.[59] Postcolonial critics, in their attempts to recover subaltern voices and consciousness, need to examine their complicity in colonial and neo-colonial political domination and exploitation. Given the complex situation Spivak articulates—attempts to deconstruct Western hegemonies from within while appropriating theories and methods that have been tools in colonization, highlighting different knowledges as a non-Westerner while also resisting the West/Rest oppositionality—Spivak conceptualized "strategic essentialism." This refers to a temporary agreement to present oneself (as an individual or group) in a certain homogenized, essentialized way in order to allow for solidarities and coalitions to advance social causes.[60] Spivak complicates anamnesis in postcolonial, queer, and/or religious studies, demonstrating that any recollection of memories is always complicit in advancing or producing amnesia. Differently said, you have to be able to express your memories a certain way for others to remember with you, which always unfailingly alters the memory itself. In other words, don't forget that you'll always forget while you remember.

Homi Bhabha completes our re-membering of the postcolonial inaugural trinity. His most cited contribution to postcolonial discourse is his articulation of performative politics of resistance in *The Location of Culture*.[61] Culture is a crucial component in Bhabha's notion of resistance. It is the space of aesthetic practices, performance of self-defense, an engagement with the social world through writing and politics. Culture is a space of creativity that comes out of the fracture created by injury, alienation, nostalgia, and split desires within the colonial relationship.[62] The performances of the colonized of excessive submissiveness, exaggerated deference, and enthusiastic appreciation of the colonizer's power constitute what Bhabha terms "mimicry"—a performance that is resemblance and menace.[63] Ambivalence and mimicry then constitute the third space outside of the binary of colonizer and colonized—hybridity.

A hybrid is the incalculable colonized subject, which is not a combination or synthesis of two or more entities that are reflected partially, but a liminal space that is neither.[64] Because the translation or encounter between different cultural forms occurs where both spaces are already preoccupied, liminality here articulates the space that belies any attempts at settled assumptions about identity because of inherent contradictions and instabilities that often come to haunt the subject.[65] Hybridity as a space of identity (individual, communal, national) is the third space that is itself productive and aesthetic, produces new cultural formations, and consists of doubts, split selves, and ambivalence just like the colonial encounter itself that produced it.[66]

Bhabha articulates the condition of cultural displacement and social discrimination as the location of agency and empowerment.[67] Yet Bhabha is skeptical about the ability to transcend the injuries of colonial violence and to overcome the alienation of self, and he conceptualizes the "interstice," the in-between space of identity designations, as an ever-unsettled oscillation of polarities, and as such Bhabha's cultural hybridity entertains possibilities of differences without assumed hierarchy/ies.[68] Bhabha's postcolonial hybrid signifies cultures of postcolonial resistance contra modernity: contingent, discontinuous, contentious, resistant of/to modernity, employing their borderline condition to translate and reinscribe the social imaginary of the modern center from a space of endless recurrences of impossible negotiations.[69]

Vitor Westhelle appropriates Bhabha's concepts in *After Heresy*,[70] and argues that the fundamental mechanism for emergence of postcolonial religious consciousness is hybridity, the third space of transmutations, dissimulation, mimicry, disguised intrusion. The context of postcolonial religious scholarship is the emergence of this consciousness, which arises when postcolonial subalterns no longer accept hegemonic rule and imposed representation of themselves. Yet it is also marked by colonial impositions, such as demands for coherent political and cultural identities,[71] or demands for an indigenous originality that is still measured by Western categories.[72] Religious or theological resistance can be in the form of mimicry, camouflage, or dissembling and may not be recognized as such.[73]

Sexual Anamnesis—Remembering Heteronormatized Sexualities

The chapters in this anthology already cover the impositions of heteronormativity and queer resistances in relation to religious expressions and practices. I hope it will suffice at this point to remind ourselves only briefly of the ways in which queer theory and the queering of religious/theological studies have recollected bodies and voices to remind postcolonial discourse of its own amnesias.

Judith Butler destabilizes binary constructions of gender or other sexual identities (i.e., gay/lesbian) and articulates sexual constructions through her conceptualization of performativity. She also challenges feminist theory by asserting that sex is not clearly distinguishable from gender, and that there are no fixed or authentic gender identities behind which it is safe to rally. Gender is what one does, not who one is. Butler's groundbreaking articulations and their ethical implications have been applied in the field of religious studies,[74] investigating the performances of religion, sexuality, gender, and nationality.

Applying queer theory to Christian theology appears to limit its remembering to a queering of Western, often white theological discourses, and while remembering sexism, patriarchy, and (perhaps) disability and race, imperialism and the colonial export of Christianity's sexual constructions are often still forgotten, as are the various intersections of the different oppressions mentioned.[75] Postcolonial discourse can remind religious and theological projects of queering of the entanglements of sexual, colonial, religious, and racial genealogies. Applying Foucault and Butler in religious/theological queer anamnesis projects might perpetuate the forgetting of race and colonialism evident in Foucault's and Butler's methodologies and concepts.[76]

Anchoring Postcolonial, Queer, Religious Anamnesis in Bodies

One of the scholars employing a triple analysis of postcolonial, queer, and religious analysis is the late Marcella Althaus-Reid.[77] She deploys methodologies from poststructuralism, Marxism, post-Marxism, queer theory, and postcolonialism while always positioning herself as a feminist liberation theologian. Althaus-Reid investigates different symbolic orders and their expansion through capitalist Christian (neo)colonialism, and aims to articulate liberation from a postcolonial queer and queer postcolonial perspective. She displaces and exploits tensions in the posited different dual identities of queer/religious, postcolonial/queer, religion/postcoloniality. Considering sexuality critically, she displaces religious discourse and explores and exhausts creative tensions in postcolonial analysis of religious and sexual materialities, ideologies, and hegemonies.

In *Indecent Theology*,[78] Althaus-Reid attends to the postcolonial, queer, religious triad by challenging binary oppositional gender constructions and heterosexist normatizations in liberationist theologies that aim for economic decolonization. And she challenges queer theology for constructing a binary of sexuality and political economies, attaching queered sexualities to the cultural and political interests of Western, white, middle-class subjects. Connecting sexualities, politics, economics, and religious practices and structures, she argues that postcolonial resistance needs to remember that constructions of sexualities are as much enmeshed in the violent maintenance of colonial hegemonies as economics, politics, and religious imperialism. Althaus-Reid is able to address the deceptions of hegemonic structures, without inducing dizziness in her spinning around the foci of the colonial, the sexual, and the religious. She does so by remembering to allow for bodies to begin inducing anamnesis.

Althaus-Reid points out that theological discourses have domesticated bodies, excluding challenges from different perspectives, particularly those perspectives that seek to hold together the intersections of sexual identity with racial and political constructions.[79] The way human beings are understood is directly related to the way God or divine principles are conceptualized. Accordingly, the way colonization and religious and sexual hegemonies manifest on bodies reveals truths about human existence.[80] Emphasizing the immanence of God in all bodily experiences,[81] she particularly focuses on uncovering that which has been denied as sites of divine revelation by the disciplining discourse of heterosexual, patriarchal colonialism.

Methodologically, Althaus-Reid then develops her hermeneutical practices out of bodily practices—sexual, colonial, religious. Focusing on the construction of human beings, their bodies and conceptualizations through a triple lens of postcolonialism, queer theory, and religion is Althaus-Reid's method to deconstruct and reimagine identities—human or divine. She calls this a scandalous position of hermeneutical perversion, the transgression of taboo subjects in theology.

In *The Queer God*, Althaus-Reid's description of a queer hermeneutics is an event more than a method. It is queer, as she proposes, as it is a "deliberate questioning of heterosexual experience and thinking . . . which requires us to come clean about our experiences, which in some way or other always seem destined to fall outside the normative sexual ideology of theology."[82] It is postcolonial as it investigates indigenous religiosities, sexualities, and economies that have been and are marginalized by heterosexual, Western, Christian hegemonies. And it queers religious discourse as she moves fluidly between exclusive boundary markers of "this" or "that" religion, investigating the religious fragments and mixings on the margins.

Yet because her approach never loses sight of the three foci, she re-members connections between desires that are material, economic, sexual, religious. And in focusing on the existence of bodies themselves, Althaus-Reid can weave hermeneutical circles that are not moving, however obscurely, toward a telos. Instead, her hermeneutical circles move in, through, and around bodies, the existence of which is the locus and focus of her theological thinking. Binaries do not exist in bodies, and to disengage from binaries religiously/theologically, moving toward intentional instability, is possible through attention to the queerness of bodies.[83] She seeks to enter religious discourses without remaining bound within disciplinary ways of analysis, and attempts to envision new hermeneutical circles and sources from the forgotten and indecent memories. She circumvents theologizing about individualized bodies by investigating the sites of interrelation, exchanges of intimacy, sexual identities, physical and emotional desires, and politics.[84]

Althaus-Reid understands queer sexual practices as always inherently religious, and vice versa, and as such they provide her with hermeneutical templates to approach her constellation of bodies. She describes her approach to hermeneutics as a staging of bodies in multiple and infinitely small series of variations, to keep seeing and re-creating, to be in an obsessive pursuit of variety. Instead of focusing on core concepts or symbols to deconstruct, Althaus-Reid theologically reads the scene for the multiple bodies present, and attempts to look for their multiple combinations, transgressing traditional, approved sites of discourses and dislocating discourses from their naturalized loci.[85] The fluidity she displays is that of permanently introducing "unsuitable" new partners in theology.[86] She attempts "combinative reduction," to reach corporeal meanings through multiple combinations of relationships, and when the staged combination of bodies and relationships is saturated, the scene is dissolved and the dissolution gives way to another scene.[87] The task is to do a materialist, concrete theology that aims to scandalize, that is, to force remembering to take place in the intersections of theology with other discourses on sexuality, race, and class.[88]

For example, she uses voyeurism to explore the theological and moral gaze, the flow of guilt and desires, the exercise of power and identities, and explores different angles and relationships within a variety of human-god-human constellations. She wonders if God's identity might depend on our relationships, our befriending, loving acts, and thinking about God from a "voyeur's epistemology [that] favors mutuality in the construction of God's identity. God is then here not the big eye which follows us . . . but a dialogical God, whose identity is dependent somehow on people's own loving relationships."[89] Althaus-Reid explores colonizing theologies in alliance with heterosexual nation-states in the creative religious practices of marginalized bodies. By anchoring her anamnesis in bisexual bodily constellations, she explores challenges to ideological orders within the relationships and spiritualities of trialogical configurations.[90] She asks about who/what is behind the political power of constructing non-consensual covenants and what sorts of mechanisms are found to tell us of an attempt at consensuality. Or she finds subversions in theologically engaging the poor, raced transvestite who seeks to survive marginalization and oppression by prostituting in a nightclub. She resists essentializing "the poor" as well as their desires, and complicates religion, citizenship, and notions of justice through her theological readings of sexual practices and embodiments.[91] Althaus-Reid deconstructs, remembers, and reconfigures bodily practices in a hermeneutical circle—and then simply moves on to remember something else without fixing theological memories into myth.

This epistemological mode is open to different practices of dialoguing and reflecting that are communal and localized; it is reflecting on body-filled locations, spaces made of embodied inter/actions and events. It is the existence of bodies that encourages, sometimes forces, anamnesis.

Anamnesis on the Go

In this essay, I hoped to show that a postcolonial, queer, religious anamnesis is a process of learning to remember through and with our bodies and bodily practices. Remaining focused on bodies will allow us to recollect the theories and methods of intersecting and overlapping discourses without becoming attached to them. Remembering the different projects presented here, it might be tempting to attempt a construction of a best practices analysis, an overarching discourse in which we can find refuge from accusations of exclusions and amnesias. Here we need to remind ourselves in a postcolonial and queer fashion that our memories as such are never objective and their recollection cannot be exhausted. Memories are not a telos, no matter how attached we are to some versions. The bodily anamnesis I proposed here therefore is a method, one that I hope is fluid enough to be able to incorporate other discourses and bodily experiences as they are presented to us.[92] Giving bodies center stage in anamnesis, bodies that will encroach our knowledge with surplus memories, will allow us to make use of overlapping and contradictory methods without forgetting what we are actually trying to do.

Remember to learn about living together.

As I'd like to call to mind right now, that's what Grandma used to say.

Notes

1. I am grateful for the help of Dr. Deborah Creamer, Brooke Fawley, and Roshan Kalantar, whose encouragement, insightful comments, and critiques have informed and greatly improved this essay. Thank you.
2. Marcella Althaus-Reid, "'Pussy, Queen of Pirates': Acker, Isherwood and the Debate on the Body in Feminist Theology," *Feminist Theology* 12:2 (2004): 158.
3. Leela Gandhi, *Postcolonial Theory* (New York: Columbia University Press, 1998).
4. Ibid., 4–5.
5. I am thinking, e.g., of Aimée Césaire, Frantz Fanon, or Albert Memmi.
6. Stuart Hall, "When Was the 'Post-Colonial'? Thinking at the Limit," in *The Postcolonial Question: Common Skies, Divided Horizons*, ed. Iain Chambers and Lidia Curti (New York: Routledge, 1996), 246.
7. Epistemology refers to the study of knowledge: How do we know? How do we achieve knowledge? What is it?
8. See, e.g., the elaboration on a matrix of domination in Patricia Hill Collins, *Black Feminist Thought: Knowledge, Consciousness and the Politics of Empowerment* (New York: Routledge, 2009).

9. Economic development and growth of indigenous capital in former colonies often remains dependent on neo-colonial capitalist structures, wherein local elites manage a postcolonial nation-state in a web of globalized imperialism. See, e.g., Achille Mbembe, *On the Postcolony* (Berkeley: University of California Press, 2001).

10. Gandhi, *Postcolonial Theory*, 6.

11. Find early articulations of this notion in Ashis Nandy, *The Intimate Enemy: Loss and Recovery of Self under Colonialism* (Delhi: Oxford University Press, 1983).

12. This criticism has been presented by Gayatri Chakravorty Spivak. See further discussion of her work below.

13. George E. (Tink) Tinker, *Missionary Conquest: The Gospel and Native American Cultural Genocide* (Minneapolis: Augsburg Fortress, 1993).

14. Anne McClintock, *Imperial Leather: Race, Gender and Sexuality in the Colonial Contest* (New York: Routledge, 1995).

15. R. S. Sugirtharajah, *The Bible and Empire: Postcolonial Explorations* (Cambridge: Cambridge University Press, 2005).

16. Richard King, *Orientalism and Religion: Postcolonial Theory, India and the "Mythical East"* (Oxford: Oxford University Press, 1999).

17. Talal Asad, *Genealogies of Religion: Discipline and Reasons of Power in Christianity and Islam* (Baltimore: Johns Hopkins University Press, 1993).

18. Similar articulations and arguments are made, e.g., by Arvind Mandair, "The Global Fiduciary: Mediating the Violence of Religion," in *Religion and Violence in South Asia: Theory and Practice*, ed. John R. Hinnells and Richard King (New York: Routledge, 2007); and Richard King, "The Association of 'Religion' with Violence: Reflections on a Modern Trope," in *Religion and Violence in South Asia: Theory and Practice*, ed. John R. Hinnells and Richard King (New York: Routledge, 2007).

19. Vine Deloria Jr., *God Is Red: A Native View of Religion*, 3rd ed. (New York: The Putnam Publishing Group, 2003).

20. This definition comes from Charles H. Long, *Significations: Signs, Symbols, and Images in the Interpretation of Religion* (Philadelphia: Fortress Press, 1986), 7.

21. Winona LaDuke, *All Our Relations: Native Struggles for Land and Life* (Cambridge, MA: South End Press, 1999).

22. Laura E. Perez, *Chicana Art: The Politics of Spiritual and Aesthetic Altarities* (Durham, NC: Duke University Press, 2007).

23. Ibid., 20.

24. Ibid., 25.

25. Ibid., 23.

26. Luís León, *La Llorona's Children: Religion, Life, and Death in the U.S.-Mexican Borderlands* (Berkeley: University of California Press, 2004), 199.

27. Ibid., 4–5.

28. Michel Foucault, *The Order of Things: An Archaeology of the Human Sciences* (New York: Pantheon, 1970). Philosophically, Foucault undertakes a subversion of Immanuel Kant, who inquired into the normative limits of knowledge

and established the rational subject as the center of philosophy. Where Kant theorizes universal mental structures in the human subject (time and space) that constitute and limit our knowledge, Foucault takes his analysis into the impossibilities of knowing, inquiring about the conditions of knowledge, *how* it becomes possible to think one way and *im*possible to think another way. See also Foucault, *The Archaeology of Knowledge*, 2nd, rev. ed., trans. Alan Sheridan (New York: Routledge, 2002). For a discussion of Foucault's influence on queer theory, see John Blevin's "Becoming Undone and Becoming Human: Sexual and Religious Selves in the Thought of Michel Foucault and Judith Butler" in this volume.

29. Judith Butler, *Gender Trouble: Feminism and the Subversion of Identity* (New York: Routledge, 1990). For a discussion of Judith Butler's influence on queer theory, see John Blevin's "Becoming Undone and Becoming Human: Sexual and Religious Selves in the Thought of Michel Foucault and Judith Butler" in this volume.

30. See Judith Butler, *Bodies That Matter: On the Discursive Limits of "Sex"* (New York: Routledge, 1993). Butler builds here on Derrida's concept of iterability, which is based on the contestation of authenticity. What can be recognized can be repeated, but as such can be copied, which prevents the tracing of an original. Butler uses this to argue that gender is such a repetition of recognizable performances, though the latter always just refers back to previous performances made intelligible through repetition rather than original authentic expressions. More on Derrida below.

31. See Jacques Derrida, *Disseminations*, trans. Barbara Johnson (New York: Continuum Books, 1981); see also *Margins of Philosophy*, trans. Alan Bass (Chicago: University of Chicago Press, 1982). Where Foucault subverts Kant, Derrida engages G. W. F. Hegel. Thus, another argument central to Derrida's philosophy is the *différance* that language exposes as language represents an absence: it always negates what it claims to affirm, as the use of metaphors always distorts and inscribes associations and thus presents unequivocal meanings that are not present in the thing described. In his elaboration on metaphors, Derrida also traces how the control and dissemination of metaphors can never be fully controlled, as there will always be at least one that evades the control of meaning. Deconstruction also plays out in Butler's articulation of performativity where gender performances are shown to implicate and co-constitute what is considered binary.

32. See Michel Foucault, *Power/Knowledge: Selected Interviews and Other Writings, 1972–1977* (New York: Pantheon, 1980). For a discussion of Foucault's influence on queer theory, see John Blevin's "Becoming Undone and Becoming Human: Sexual and Religious Selves in the Thought of Michel Foucault and Judith Butler" in this volume.

33. Said and Spivak criticize Foucault's increasingly narrow focus on individuals and neglecting larger imperial social webs and structures, rendering imperialism irrelevant in Western analysis. See Edward W. Said, *Culture and Imperialism* (New York: Vintage Books, 1993), 41; Gayatri Chakravorty Spivak, *A Critique*

of Postcolonial Reason: Toward a History of the Vanishing Present (Cambridge, MA: Harvard University Press, 1999), 279.

34. This is in no small part due to Gayatri Chakravorty Spivak's contributions in her translation of Derrida's *Of Grammatology* to which she wrote a lengthy introduction, establishing her reputation in academic circles.

35. Gandhi, *Postcolonial Theory*, 25, 32.

36. Ibid., 24–28. Questions complicating postcolonial Marxist analysis are: Do postcolonial politics and ethics require consensus? But is consensus always already under imperial dominance? These questions imply certain acts of forgetting necessary when employing Marxism without critically investigating its universalizing theoretical reach.

37. See, e.g., Martin Manalansan and Arnaldo Cruz-Malave, eds., *Queer Globalizations: Citizenship and the Afterlife of Colonialism* (New York: New York University Press, 2002).

38. Edward P. Antonio, "Introduction: Inculturation and Postcolonial Discourse," in *Inculturation and Postcolonial Discourse in African Theology*, ed. Edward P. Antonio (New York: Peter Lang, 2006), 3–4.

39. Gandhi, *Postcolonial Theory*, ix.

40. Hall, "When Was the 'Post-Colonial'?" 248.

41. The "in-between" spaces here refer to Homi Bhabha's conceptualization of the interstitial. See my discussion of Bhabha below.

42. See, e.g., John C. Hawley, ed., *Postcolonial, Queer: Theoretical Intersections*, SUNY Series Explorations in Postcolonial Studies (New York: State University of New York Press, 2001); see also *Postcolonial and Queer Theories: Intersections and Essays*, ed. Emmanuel S. Nelson, vol. 101, Contributions to the Study of World Literature (Westport, CT: Greenwood Press, 2001).

43. Annamarie Jagose, *Queer Theory: An Introduction* (New York: New York University Press, 1996), 96–97.

44. See, e.g., a discussion of the veil as trope in colonial and postcolonial social constructions of identity and agency in Meyda Yeğenoğlu, *Colonial Fantasies: Towards a Feminist Reading of Orientalism* (Cambridge and New York: Cambridge University Press, 1998). For a history of the nation and contemporary political global order, see Michael Hardt and Antonio Negri, *Empire* (Cambridge, MA: Harvard University Press, 2000).

45. See, e.g., McClintock, *Imperial Leather*.

46. Edward W. Said, *Orientalism* (New York: Vintage Books, 1979).

47. Ibid., 27–28.

48. Ibid., 200–204.

49. Said, *Culture and Imperialism*, 18.

50. Albert Memmi articulated this imposition of colonial memory and history as "usurpation." See Albert Memmi, *The Colonizer and the Colonized* (Boston: Beacon Press, 1991), 8–9, 52–53.

51. Yeğenoğlu, *Colonial Fantasies*.

52. Ibid., 39.

53. Ibid., 26.

54. Ibid., 37–38.

55. Spivak, *Critique of Postcolonial Reason.*

56. This term has been made popular in postcolonial discourse by the subaltern studies group, a project led by Ranajit Guha that reappropriated Gramsci's term "subaltern" (literally, someone of inferior rank, used in the sense of economically dispossessed) and used to indicate "the people"—not the elite of a society, but the landless, the peasants, the lower castes. Guha, in Marxian fashion, attributes a political consciousness to the subaltern, which needs to be retrieved, understood, and harnessed. See Gandhi, *Postcolonial Theory*, 1–3.

57. Gayatri Chakravorty Spivak, "Can the Subaltern Speak?" in *Colonial Discourse and Postcolonial Theory*, ed. Patrick Williams and Laura Chrisman (New York: Columbia University Press, 1994).

58. Gayatri Chakravorty Spivak, *Outside in the Teaching Machine* (New York: Routledge, 1993), 64.

59. Spivak, *Critique of Postcolonial Reason*, 356.

60. Gayatri Chakravorty Spivak, Donna Landry, and Gerald MacLean, eds., *The Spivak Reader: Selected Works of Gayatri Chakravorty Spivak* (New York: Routledge, 1996), 141–47.

61. Homi K. Bhabha, *The Location of Culture* (New York: Routledge, 1994).

62. Ibid., 62–64, 313.

63. Ibid., 126–32.

64. Ibid., 49–51.

65. Ibid., 234–35.

66. Ibid., 160.

67. Ibid., 12.

68. Ibid., 5.

69. Ibid., 9, 120.

70. Vitor Westhelle, *After Heresy: Colonial Practices and Post-Colonial Theologies* (Eugene, OR: Cascade Books, 2010).

71. Ibid., 57.

72. Ibid., 60.

73. For an example of Bhabha employed in postcolonial theology, see Wonhee Anne Joh, *Heart of the Cross: A Postcolonial Christology* (Louisville: Westminster John Knox, 2006).

74. See, e.g., Saba Mahmood, *Politics of Piety: The Islamic Revival and the Feminist Subject* (Princeton, NJ: Princeton University Press, 2005); see also Ellen T. Armour and Susan M. St. Ville, eds., *Bodily Citations: Religion and Judith Butler* (New York: Columbia University Press, 2006).

75. See, e.g., Gerard Loughling, ed., *Queer Theology: Rethinking the Western Body* (Malden, MA: Blackwell Publishing, Ltd., 2007). While this anthology seeks to rethink the Western body, as the title infers, the essays seem to neglect the

colonial and/or neo-colonial impositions of Western Christianity on the rest of the world. Queering the body of Western theology needs to attend to the implications in (neo)colonization of the theological sources attended to, lest it exports its queer theological liberation as a colonial amnesia into other contexts who might engage in queering Western theologians, albeit from different embodied contexts and with different memories informing their anamnesis. Another example of the forgetting of race and colonialism is Robert Goss, *Queering Christ: Beyond Jesus Acted Up* (Cleveland: The Pilgrim Press, 2002). While Goss cites nonwhite contributions, he nevertheless displays racial and colonial amnesia in his theological constructions.

76. Examples of insightful and articulate scholarship applying Foucault and Butler in the investigation of colonialism, sexuality, and race are McClintock, *Imperial Leather*; Ann Laura Stoler, *Carnal Knowledge and Imperial Power: Race and the Intimate in Colonial Rule* (Berkeley: University of California Press, 2002). Though neither one attends to religion more than in passing.

77. For a good description of Althaus-Reid's theological project as well as criticisms of it, see Angela Pears's discussion in Angela Pears, *Feminist Christian Encounters: The Methods and Strategies of Feminist Informed Christian Theologies* (Burlington, VT: Ashgate Publishing Company, 2004).

78. Marcella M. Althaus-Reid, *Indecent Theology: Theological Perversions in Sex, Gender and Politics* (New York: Routledge, 2000).

79. Marcella Althaus-Reid, *The Queer God* (New York: Routledge, 2003), 8. Althaus-Reid points out that even theologies considered liberationist can hold such a theology stance.

80. See the introduction to Lisa Isherwood and Marcella Althaus-Reid, eds., *The Sexual Theologian: Essays on Sex, God and Politics* (London: T&T Clark International, 2004), 7–9.

81. Emphasizing bodies as starting point for theology, Althaus-Reid moves away from reason as the privileged mode of theological reflection, which as one method has been a trope to define decency, excluding from theological reflection that which is not presentable.

82. Althaus-Reid, *Queer God*, 2.

83. Ibid., 27.

84. Ibid., 34.

85. Ibid., 27–29.

86. Ibid., 17.

87. Ibid., 29.

88. Ibid., 34–35.

89. Ibid., 43.

90. Ibid., 114–20.

91. Althaus-Reid, *Indecent Theology*, 32–33, 85–86, 112–14, 36–37.

92. I wonder what a quadruple or quintuple analysis might yield, incorporating anamnesis regarding ableism or anthropocentrism, for example.

Chapter 12

God, Sex, and Popular Culture

*The Evil Demon of Images
and the Precession of Lady Gaga*

Richard Lindsay

This essay is about religion, images, God, and Lady Gaga. If you're reading this several years from now, you may find the pop star reference quaint. You, reader of the future, may know Lady Gaga as a still-relevant, continually re-invented performer and cultural icon, or you may know her as nothing more than a trivia question from early twenty-first-century Internet culture. But regardless of her staying power as a music star, chances are you know someone *like* Lady Gaga. You know a performer, we'll call this person the Post-Gaga, who has captured the media zeitgeist, has continually reinvented herself or himself in a never-ending quest for attention, and has found a way to court controversy, probably through a mix of sex and religion. The Post-Gaga has stolen Lady Gaga's act and made it her or his own, to the point that the "origi-nal" is forgotten. The Post-Gaga is her or his "simulacrum."

The following of Lady Gaga onto the cultural stage by an emulator, usurper, or clone is as predictable as your new computer being obsolete within three years. In a hyper-real, hyper-media hyper-culture, moving at hyper-speed, performers, cultural moments, snippets of songs, and videos buzzing around the world on the Internet form themselves into a never-ending collage of col-lective consciousness. Images, symbols, and signs become untraceable as one replaces the other in rapid succession. This is the essence of the simulacrum—the simulation of a simulation for which the original has been forgotten.

In such an environment, can anything as seemingly permanent as God hold any meaning? What is to be made of the inevitable crisis of meaning brought about by systems of images drowning out traditional religious imagery? What happens when religious symbols *themselves* become appropriated as part of mass culture? Does this kind of queering of symbolism represent the next phase of religious meaning or spell its doom?

I propose that even though God can no longer be *represented* in the never-ending simulacrum of images, God is present *in* the never-ending simulacrum of images, and the human creativity that constructs them. This itself is a queer insight. I don't mean that this is a lesbian, gay, bisexual, or transgender insight, per se, but that our understanding of the system of representation, the classic Platonic exchange of symbol for ideal, must be queered if religious symbolism is to survive the onslaught of images.

Although God is transcendent, God is immanently present in the process of human civilization—there is a *panentheism* in popular culture. In this essay, I take up the challenge to a postmodern conception of God presented by Jean Baudrillard in his essays on the destruction of the "real" by the precession of images, using the perspective of process theologian Charles Hartshorne. I conclude that seemingly opposed concepts of material culture and spiritual meaning are not unlike the contested relationship between sex and religion, and it is often those who approach the rift from a queer perspective who begin to see possibilities for synthesis. In the end, the categorical distinctions that Western religious sensibility has demanded—between the religious symbol and God, between the sacred and the secular, between spirituality and sexual spectacle—dissolve in pop culture's prodigal use of symbolism. Artists like Lady Gaga . . . or the Post-Gaga . . . or whatever comes next . . . queer these traditional distinctions by turning themselves into a never-ending series of graven images.

For a moment, let us return to the turn of the century—eons ago in the breakneck evolution of media and the Internet.

Lady Gaga and the Post-MTV Music Video

After the late 1990s, when MTV stopped playing music videos, there was no longer an incentive for labels to invest millions in their production. Music videos, rather than being an art form unto themselves, reverted to their former function as relatively cheap advertisements for music. As the recording industry began an implosion brought on by the collapse of local radio and the MP3 download, even this commercial function became questionable. The result was less funding, lower production values, bored music stars and directors, and thousands of static shots of people in fashionable clothes shouting at a fisheye lens on a stationary camera.

Enter Lady Gaga (ca. 2008), an artist with an unparalleled knack for self-promotion in the Internet age. Transforming the music video into a viral advertisement not just for her songs but for a slew of product placements—everything from high-end electronics to mayonnaise—she brought the economic incentive back to the genre, and the resources needed to reset the bar for quality. With Gaga, the music video witnessed the return of lengthy narratives full of pageantry, passion, and choreography unseen since the days when artists like Madonna, Michael and Janet Jackson, and Prince competed to outdo each other with ever more elaborate productions.

In June 2010, Gaga released the video to the song "Alejandro" from her second album, *Fame Monster*. A sexual fantasy full of symbolism associated with religion, the moral guardians of culture wasted no time objecting to the video, thereby playing their prescribed role in its promotion.

One of the loudest and most interesting reactions came from William Donohue, president of the Catholic League for Religious and Civil Rights. In a press release under the headline "Lady Gaga Mimics Madonna," he denounces her as "squirming around half-naked with a bunch of half-naked guys, abusing Catholic symbols." He refers to her as a "Madonna copy cat" and a "Madonna wannabe." Donahue concludes, "She has now become the new poster girl for American decadence and Catholic bashing, *sans* the looks and talent of her role model."[1] The objection to Gaga's use of "Catholic symbols" was to be expected from this organization, which polices what it sees as anti-Catholic bias rampant in modern culture. What was not expected was the suggestion that Madonna was the *original* "poster girl for American decadence and Catholic bashing," and that she, unlike Gaga, possessed beauty and talent. Donohue seems almost nostalgic for Madonna's brand of sacrilege.

Actually, there are any number of symbols, images, and narratives that Gaga exploits in "Alejandro."[2] The video, filmed by fashion photographer Steven Klein, features Gaga as a steampunk Queen Elizabeth, catwalk-strutting models dressed like fascists, and Gaga participating in an S&M grope-fest with shirtless male dancers in black high heels and, inexplicably, Three Stooges haircuts. Washing over the viewer are essences of David Bowie, Annie Lennox, and Janet Jackson; references to *The Passion of Joan of Arc*, *The Devils*, *Triumph of the Will*, *Rocky Horror Picture Show*, *Cabaret*, and *Metropolis*; and, of course, the life opus of Madonna. Viewing the video, I'm reminded of *Evita*, the *Sex* book, "Erotica," "Vogue," "La Isla Bonita," and "Like a Prayer." Gaga even takes Madonna's famous "cone bra" a step further, by wearing a bra bedecked with two machine gun barrels. This cornucopia of pop culture is used or abused *alongside* of cross images, a frozen, gelatinous Sacred Heart, and a rosary Gaga swallows in reverse motion—while dressed in what appears to be a red latex nun costume.

In addition to this "religious" symbolism, the video functions as a camp tribute to gay male culture. The dancers, dressed in leather Nazi drag, strut and flounce with flamboyantly exaggerated motions. Shirtless, machine gun–toting models doze in fishnet tights. In one shot, male dancers throw their partners to the ground face-first, straddling them in an act of simulated sex and/or domination.

On a *Larry King Live* interview on June 1, 2010, before the video was released, Gaga confirmed that the video was to have a "homoerotic military theme," and said, "It is a celebration of my love and appreciation for the gay community, my admiration of their bravery, their love for one another and their courage in their relationships."[3] In the same interview, Gaga claimed to be bisexual. This places her in a long line of outré pop performers, including David Bowie, Lou Reed, Iggy Pop, Madonna, Grace Jones, and Mick Jagger, who used perceptions of sexual fluidity as part of their stage personas. Regardless of who she makes her bed with, anyone who wears a dress made out of meat, as Gaga did at the 2010 MTV Video Music Awards, is undoubtedly queer.

Furthermore, Gaga, who was raised Catholic, characterized herself in the Larry King interview as "very religious": "I believe in Jesus, I believe in God, I'm very spiritual, I pray very much." In addition to her personal devotion, however, Gaga expressed her frustration with the intolerance of religious institutions. "There is no one religion that doesn't hate, or speak against, or be prejudiced against another racial group, or religious group, or sexual group, and for that, I think religion is also bogus." The combination of passionate performance, transcendent, even spiritual spectacle, and a message of tolerance and self-actualization (all of which have particular resonance with queer communities) might be called the Gospel according to Gaga. In another memorable appearance at the Video Music Awards, this time in 2009, in which she came to accept an award dressed in red lace that covered her from head to knees, she threw off her veil, lifted her trophy into the air, and shouted, "This is for God and for the gays!"[4]

Whatever the religious or sexual influences on "Alejandro," a closer look reveals that the entire video is built on instability of symbolism. At the opening of the video, male dancers appear to be carrying religious symbols, particularly a Star of David, made of wood or metal, in a kind of militaristic procession. But the props have been constructed with extra parts and pieces so they don't *quite* match religious symbols. Likewise, in one take, Gaga sings in front of what appears to be a wooden cross. But the "cross" has two diagonal supporting beams underneath its arms, making it possible that it's just a piece of stage equipment.

The uncertainty extends to the sexual performances in the video, as well. The dancers' moves suggest stereotypical homosexuality, and yet several of them participate in simulated sex acts with the barely dressed Gaga. One of Gaga's costumes, with a white latex hood and an upside-down red cross over the crotch, suggests a kind of lewd Joan of Arc, especially with a projection screen behind her showing crackling flames. But who's to say, as her male dancers toss Gaga as the "Joan" figure around in some kind of orgiastic ritual, what exactly the outfit "represents"? And what about the behavior of these strange bowl-headed dancers? Are they fascists or fashionistas? Are they goose-stepping or catwalking? Are they Nazis or leather daddies? And really, what's the difference?

The queering of cultural and religious cues in the video offers a significant challenge to William Donohue's objection to the "abuse" of "Catholic symbols." But Donohue undermines his own argument in his naming of Gaga as a poor substitute for the more "authentic" blasphemer Madonna. In decrying Gaga's mimicry of Madonna, Donohue acknowledges that "religious" symbolism already has an autonomous, secular system of meaning in popular culture. When Madonna wore crucifixes against her nearly naked skin during the 1980s, she poached the symbol, draining the cross of its traditional meaning and filling it with her own meaning as a statement of sexual freedom. Since Madonna's time in the media spotlight, we are several cultural cycles removed from the idea that traditional religious imagery points directly and unambiguously to the divine.

Madonna's entire career has been based on breaking taboos around sexuality and religious symbolism. In the video for "Like a Prayer," she dances in front of burning crosses with a black gospel chorus singing in the background, challenging the use of the burning cross as a racist image. In the same video, she kisses a black saint figure (thought to be St. Martin de Porres), suggesting erotic connection and spiritual transcendence as a means of overcoming racial difference. In her documentary *Truth or Dare*, shot during her "Blonde Ambition" tour in the early 1990s, Madonna constantly pushes the boundaries of spiritual and sexual imagery—for example, "masturbating" a thurible carried by a dancer dressed as a priest.[5] The film shows Madonna acting as an all-accepting mother figure (a Madonna, really) to her gaggle of gay dancers.

The confusion in the film between Madonna as rock star and the Mother of Sorrows becomes even more pronounced when Madonna receives a visit from a high school friend, Moira MacDonald. Moira tells her she is pregnant and asks Madonna to bless the child in her womb so it will be a girl and she can name her Madonna. The singer obliges, placing her hands on the expectant mother and offering an ironic blessing. Finally, just as Madonna is leaving, Moira gives her an abstract painting she has made of the singer, which she calls "Madonna and Child."

After the singer has left, Moira tells the camera, "I remember praying to Madonna," and after her interaction with the music star, in which the line between pop icon and religious icon has been so blurred, the viewer wonders what she means. Did she pray to *the* Madonna or to Madonna the singer? And which one is *the* Madonna anyway? Moira quickly clears this up (more or less): "to her mother, Madonna, because it was the closest thing to God." And so we find out that Madonna is not just named for the Virgin Mary, but for her mother, Madonna.

The Confusion of Images and "the Desert of the Real Itself"

This confusion of images is the subject of several important pieces by the some-time bad boy of postmodern philosophy, Jean Baudrillard. In his book *Simulacres et Simulation (Simulacra and Simulation)* and his essay "The Evil Demon of Images and the Precession of Simulacra," he suggests that with the modern proliferation of images through mass media, there is a crisis of the real, what Baudrillard calls "the desert of the real itself."[6] "The mad pursuit of images" has led to the point where images no longer represent anything other than other images or previously stated ideas.[7] Society is lost in a world of pure simulacra, simulation that has been repeated to the point that we no longer have contact with the simulation's original meaning. "The real is produced from miniaturized cells, matrices, and memory banks, models of control—and it can be reproduced an indefinite number of times. It no longer needs to be rational, because it no longer measures itself against either a real or negative instance."[8]

He spells out the order of the creation of simulacra as follows, the successive phases of the image:

+ It is the reflection of a basic reality.
+ It masks and perverts a basic reality.
+ It masks the absence of a basic reality.
+ It bears no relation to any reality whatever: it is its own pure simulacrum.[9]

As Baudrillard explains, "In the first case, the image is a good appearance— the representation is of the order of sacrament. In the second, it is an evil appearance—of the order of maléfice. In the third, it plays at being an appearance—it is of the order of sorcery. In the fourth it is no longer in the order of appearance at all, but of simulation."[10]

An example might come from the image of the Madonna herself. The first order simulacrum is the figure of Mary the mother of Jesus, as portrayed in the Bible. Mary as a biblical character is a reflection of the "basic reality" of a figure that existed in history, however accurate the scriptural accounts of her may be. The second order, in which the basic reality becomes perverted, might be the Madonna of Marian cults and holy cards, "masking or perverting" the basic figure of Mary with a layer of sentimentality and the idealization of the perfect woman. The third order of simulacrum would be the singer Madonna, who uses her baptismal name as a springboard to pop blasphemy. The Ever-Virgin becomes "Like a Virgin" ("touched for the very first time"); the Rosary prayer becomes "Like a Prayer" ("I'm down on my knees; I wanna take you there"); the Immaculate Conception becomes the "Immaculate Collection"—Madonna's greatest hits album. The fourth-order simulacrum is Lady Gaga's "Alejandro," where the character or historical figure of Mary has been forgotten completely, as the video emulates not *the* Madonna, but Madonna. The video is pure simulacrum.

Baudrillard's use of the term "sacrament" to describe the first-order simulacrum is instructive, because he believes the deception of simulacra has implications for the Divine self:

All of Western faith and good faith was engaged in this wager on representation: that a sign could refer to the depth of meaning, that a sign could exchange for meaning, and that something could guarantee this exchange—God, of course. But what if God himself can be simulated, that is to say, reduced to the signs which attest his existence. Then the whole system becomes weightless, it is no longer anything but a gigantic simulacrum—not unreal, but a simulacrum, never again exchanging for what is real, but exchanging in itself, in an uninterrupted circuit without reference or circumference.[11]

He refers to the Christian conflicts over iconography as illustrating the problem of God. "Thus perhaps at stake has always been the murderous capacity of images, murderers of the real, murderers of their own model as the Byzantine icons could murder the divine identity."[12] According to Baudrillard, the iconoclasts understood the "demonic" power of repeated images, that the images of God in iconography would soon become metonymy for God's self, and therefore lead to atheism. In Baudrillard's appraisal, atheism was always the truth to begin with.

This is precisely because they [the Iconoclasts] predicted this omnipotence of simulacra, the faculty simulacra have of effacing God from the conscience of man, and the destructive, annihilating truth that they allow to appear—that deep down God never existed, that only the simulacrum ever existed, even that God himself was never anything but his own simulacrum—from this came their urge to destroy the images.[13]

In their repetition, religious symbols, images, and iconography become flattened and lose any sense of meaning, like an MP3 player in the shape of a cross that can be filled with gospel music or death metal. In the postmodern image-based world of information, even the term "icon" no longer means what it once did. A Web engine search under the word "icon" will produce six pages of smiley faces, corporate logos, and faux file cabinets for use on a computer desktop before *one image* of Jesus Christ and the saints from sixteenth-century Russia appears. Certainly Madonna or Lady Gaga could come up under a search for "icon" as well.

But it is not only "secular" culture that has exploited symbolism for its own purposes. An entire Christian material culture has grown up alongside conventional popular culture. This includes the evangelical tendency to appropriate popular culture through such products as Christian pop music and Christian fashion, a religious bait and switch in which culture is drained of its secular meaning and refilled with an unsatisfying slurry of fossilized theology and unconvincing hipness. Christian products like "skinny girl jeans" with a Bible quote placed just above the waistband and T-shirts from the "Not of this World" line that appropriate symbolism from hip-hop and skater subcultures send the message that the meanings ascribed to cultural elements can be poached and changed according to one's use.[14] But in making crosses and Bible verses part of a fashion statement, the poaching goes the other way too. These religious symbols take on the language of lifestyle branding developed by the advertising world and, thus, simply become another brand.

It is this draining of meaning from symbolism that Baudrillard addresses when he writes:

> The transition from signs which dissimulate something to signs which dissimulate that there is nothing marks the decisive turning point. The first implies a theology of truth and secrecy. . . . The second inaugurates an age of simulacra and simulation, in which there is no longer any God to recognize his own, nor any last judgment to separate true from false, the real from its artificial resurrection, since everything is already dead and risen in advance.[15]

"Dead and risen in advance" would be a good summary of any theology that can be summarized on a T-shirt. At that point, the cross or the Bible as *symbols* have ceased to point to anything more mysterious than their own self-reference as cultural products. There is no God remaining to be offended in the symbolism of Christianity as appropriated by popular culture.

Baudrillard would question the very idea of looking for any reference to God or even any *meaning* in popular culture, since it is all based on a never-ending circle of simulacra. But for those of us who continue to hope to search for meaning, the question remains: Is religion even possible in an image-dominated society?

It may not be if we assume, as perhaps Baudrillard does, a radical separation between the Divine and the human. Orthodox theology often assumes that the Divine is "wholly other" than the human, and humans can make little sense of God outside the revelation of scripture or tradition because "God's ways are not our ways." This high doctrine of God preserves God's majesty but does little for human attempts at meaning making through culture.

But what if God exists in our continual obsession with creating images? What if God exists in the very pixels of our simulacra, the "miniaturized cells, matrices, and memory banks, models of control"? What if God is transcendent and all-surpassing, but also immanent and indeed intimate to the world?

Panentheism: The "Supremely-Relative God"

David H. Nikkel describes "panentheism" as the concept that "non-divine individuals are included in God, are fully within the divine life."[16] This view of God holds itself against doctrines in which God is "wholly other," a being apart from all creation. It is a median position between deism, which says that God is completely aloof except in the act of creation, and pantheism, which says the material world, itself and alone, is the divine being.[17]

In considering the qualities of what makes God divine, theologians have come up with different standards, including omnipotence, immutability, omniscience, and perfect righteousness. Charles Hartshorne tries to get at what the supreme quality of God would be, based on human need, and his idea is "supremely-relative," or "surrelative."[18] Relationality to human beings, that is to say, relational love, would be the essential quality of God. "A personal God is one who has social relations, really has them, and thus is constituted by relationships and hence is relative—in a sense not provided for by the traditional doctrine of a divine Substance wholly nonrelative toward the world."[19] This is not to say the summation of God's character is in this relationality. Hartshorne distinguishes between God's "concrete" quality of divine relativity and the "abstract" quality of absolute transcendence, at least insofar as it is logically possible to be transcendent without being non-relational.[20] But despite God's surpassing nature, God is really *affected* by God's relationships with creation. It would be impossible to say that God "loves" creation in any sensible understanding of the term if God is not in some way affected or even changed by that loving relationship. "God orders the universe, according to panentheism, by taking into his own life all the currents of feeling and existence."[21]

Considering the history of Christianity, it seems strange that this idea of divine relationality is considered at best a minority report on God, or at worst complete heresy. Christianity is built on the basis of a Jewish tradition (the apostle Paul would say "grafted" onto this tradition: Rom. 11:24) in which noted figures questioned God's morality (Job); wrestled a blessing away from God (Jacob in Gen. 32:26); bargained with God over the terms of the destruction of a city (Abraham in Gen. 18:23–33); and changed God's mind about destroying the Israelites (Moses in Exod. 32:14). The principal belief of Christianity is that God went through the messy and imperfect human processes of conception, birth, growth, suffering, and death (not to mention resurrection). Yet we are supposed to believe God was *unaffected* by this history? As Hartshorne writes, "Unless, then, it is possible to be 'in relation' without in any way becoming 'relative,' without the relations qualifying the terms of these relations, there can, it seems, be no intelligible treatment of either relativity or absoluteness."[22]

Put another way, as queer theologians Marcella Althaus-Reed and Lisa Isherwood write, "That God is in the flesh changes everything. . . . Theology that has incarnation at its heart is queer indeed. What else so fundamentally challenges the nature of the divine and human identity? That the divine immersed itself in flesh, and that flesh is now divine, is queer theology at its peak. There can be no sanitization here, or something of the divine essence will be lost."[23] What this suggests then, is that Christ is not so much an exception to the divine-human relationship—a special example never to be duplicated— but a revelation of the reality of the divine-human relationship. The divine really does exist in the finite existence of human persons and bodies, including human creativity, the human desire to manufacture images, and the sensual spectacle of human sexuality. What Christ represents is the perfect realization of the human potential to embody the divine.

This concept of God brings the divine to a level of intimacy not possible if God is "wholly other." It is a paradoxical combination of magnificence and humility, an idea that should be fully compatible with a Creator who created both supernovas and cells, planets and protozoa. The grandeur of God can be considered in the grooves of our fingers. This idea that God may not *just* be "out there," but also presently "right here," brings the possibility of authenticity even in a world of simulacra. If God is really present in the material being of the universe, there is no need to despair of the loss of an image's "signification."

Gaga is Good

That queer theologians and pop music stars with a queer sensibility have figured this out is no surprise. Queer people have always taken dominant symbolisms and structures of meaning and used it for our own purposes. Faced as we are in modern Western culture with binary gender construction and the literally sacrosanct (according to the church) model of the monogamous heterosexual relationship, we've created our own variations on gender and sexual practice. We've expressed our gendered and sexual selves as drag queens, sissies, butch and femme lesbians, tranny boys and girls, leather daddies, bears, and twinks. We've created varied relationship structures, including the queer celibacy practiced by many in religious orders, the bed hopping of lifelong single sexual adventurers, monogamous same-sex couples, faithful couples with "arrangements" for sex with other people, and polyamory.

We've created our own rituals, including coming out, Pride processionals, and reclaiming the spiritual ecstasy of dance in the club and circuit party. We've created our own symbols that take on iconic and religious qualities, like the rainbow flag (originally made with eight stripes, framed by the colors hot pink, symbolizing sexuality, and violet, symbolizing spirit);[24] the AIDS quilt—a massive community tapestry of mourning; and the pink triangle, which, like the Christian cross, started as a symbol of annihilation and became a symbol of liberation. We've created our own system of saints and martyrs, including Judy Garland, Harvey Milk, and Matthew Sheppard.

When institutional religions would not take us in, we created our own religions, from Goddess worship to Radical Fairies—and even stranger than these, subcultures of queer Presbyterians, Lutherans, Episcopalians, and Roman Catholics. Through churches like the Metropolitan Community Church, we exposed the innate queerness of evangelical, charismatic, and Pentecostal practices.

These are all examples of exploring the malleability of symbolism and structures of meaning. But they also represent something deeper—not the Platonic exchange between symbol and referent, but the diversity of forms, symbols, and relationships that God's image takes on when refracted through the endless creativity of the human spirit. God is there as we construct and deconstruct our identities, and as we forge our icons, idols, and graven images—not inhabiting the product of our art, but inhabiting the soul of the artist collaborating with the Creator. This is the true implication of being made in the "image and likeness of God" (Gen 1:26). If there is no spark of the Divine in us, in our very cells, in our very being, then *we* are mere simulacra—images, copies, no more. In an age of infinite replication, this becomes a frightening proposition, as it becomes more and more difficult to distinguish between ourselves and our work personas, family personas, screen personas, and avatars.

As a queer performer, Lady Gaga has an innate understanding of the malleability of symbols, and the malleability of self. She has taken the pop star process of continual reinvention and ramped it up to Internet speed. She has reinvigorated the moribund art form of the music video with her outrageous sense of style and spectacle. Like her precursor, Madonna, and like the LGBT community she revels in, she has blurred the boundaries between the erotic

and the spiritual, the sacred and the profane, in ways that force Western institutional religion to confront the queerness of its own project of relating finite
humanity to an infinite God. For these reasons if nothing else, Gaga is good.

Notes

1. William Donahue, "Lady Gaga Mimics Madonna," June 9, 2010, http://www
.catholicleague.org/release.php?id=1881 (accessed November 6, 2010).
2. "Alejandro," June 8, 2010, *Lady Gaga Vevo Channel*, http://www.youtube.com/
user/LadyGagaVEVO (accessed January 20, 2011).
3. *Larry King Live*, CNN, Los Angeles, June 1, 2010.
4. *MTV Video Music Awards* (New York, MTV, September 13, 2009), http://www
.mtv.com/videos/misc/436018/lady-gaga-wins-best-new-artist.jhtml#id=
1620604 (accessed January 20, 2011).
5. *Madonna: Truth or Dare*, DVD, directed by Alek Keshishian and Mark Aldo
Miceli (Santa Monica, CA: Live Entertainment, 1997).
6. Jean Baudrillard, *Simulacres et Simulation*, trans. Sheila Faria Glaser (Ann
Arbor: University of Michigan Press, 1994), 1.
7. Jean Baudrillard, "The Evil Demon of Images and the Precession of Simulacra,"
in *Postmodernism: A Reader*, ed. Thomas Docherty (New York: Columbia University Press, 1993), 194.
8. Baudrillard, *Simulacres et Simulation*, 2.
9. Baudrillard, "Evil Demon," 196.
10. Ibid.
11. Ibid.
12. Ibid.
13. Baudrillard, *Simulacres et Simulation*, 2.
14. A major Christian pop culture site that sells these products is http://www.C28
.com.
15. Baudrillard, *Simulacres et Simulation*, 196, 197.
16. David H. Nikkel, *Panentheism in Hartshorne and Tillich: A Creative Synthesis*
(New York: Peter Lang, 1995), 2.
17. Ibid.
18. Charles Hartshorne, *The Divine Relativity: A Social Conception of God*, 2nd ed.
(New Haven, CT: Yale University Press, 1964), ix.
19. Ibid., x.
20. Ibid., ix.
21. Ibid., xvii.
22. Ibid., 6.
23. Marcella Althaus-Reid and Lisa Isherwood, eds., *The Sexual Theologian: Essays
on Sex, God, and Politics* (London: T&T Clark International, 2004), 7.
24. Don Romesberg, "She's a Gay Old Flag," *The Advocate* (July 7, 1998), 20.

Chapter 13

Queer Theory and the Study of Religion[1]

Melissa M. Wilcox

In 1991, in a special issue of the journal *differences*, Teresa de Lauretis introduced a new term into academic discourse: "queer theory."[2] "The term 'queer,'" she explained, "juxtaposed to . . . 'lesbian and gay' . . . is intended to mark a certain critical distance from the latter, by now established and often convenient, formula."[3] Drawing on the newly visible, resistant political use of the once-derogatory term "queer," de Lauretis suggested moving into a more deconstructive, critical mode of theorizing in lesbian and gay studies, as it was then known. Her proposed theoretical orientation was to have two foci: "the conceptual and speculative work involved in discourse production, and . . . the necessary critical work of deconstructing our own discourses and their constructed silences."[4] Queer theory was to address the elisions in mainstream gay studies—the experiences of those not white and male—and in so doing, would have consequences for activism as well as academics. "Racial and gender differences," de Lauretis asserted, "are a crucial area of concern for queer theory, and one where critical dialogue alone can provide a better understanding of the specificity and partiality of our respective histories as well as the stakes of some common struggles."[5]

Subsequent to de Lauretis's writing, the term "queer theory" has had a varied fate. It has developed a genealogy, beginning with works predating the *differences* issue such as Michel Foucault's *History of Sexuality*, volume 1, Eve Kosofsky Sedgwick's *Epistemology of the Closet*, Cherríe Moraga and Gloria Anzaldúa's *This Bridge Called My Back*, and Judith Butler's *Gender Trouble*.[6] It has been rejected by its own creator.[7] It has been maligned as too academic, too inaccessible, too white, too male, too mainstream. And it has been used in books and essays by lesbians and gay men of color, challenged and developed by authors interested in globalization and democracy, joined with disability theory, developed and altered.[8] It has even, in small amounts, entered the hallowed halls of religious studies—though not without resistance and not in a very widespread way. This essay provides an introduction to queer theory, reviews works in religious studies that make use of queer theory, and suggests future directions for this promising but under-studied intersection of fields.

A Brief Introduction to Queer Theory

To encapsulate two decades of queer theoretical work into a mere handful of pages is a daunting task on its own, made more difficult by the fact that queer theory itself defies definition. De Lauretis never defined the term explicitly, and later authors have refused definition, claiming with David Halperin that "queer is by definition *whatever* is at odds with the normal, the legitimate, the dominant. *There is nothing in particular to which it necessarily refers.* It is an identity without an essence."[9] Queer theory, thus, is a theoretical approach that positions itself outside of and against dominant discourses, critically examining the normative from a standpoint beyond it. Moreover, queer theory is especially concerned with queer gender and sexuality; therefore, central to the normativity against which it most often positions itself are heteronormativity and gender normativity.

Heteronormativity, discussed at length by Michael Warner in his introduction to *Fear of a Queer Planet*, refers to the social normalization of monogamous, reproductive, heterosexual, binary coupling, or, as Warner defines it, "the culture's assurance (read: insistence) that humanity and heterosexuality are synonymous."[10] It is not the normalization of all heterosexuality; some forms of heterosexuality can be non-heteronormative, or queer, as well. Some theorists argue that even non-reproductive heterosexual coupling can function as queer in a heteronormative culture; others retain the term for more explicitly non-normative heterosexualities such as polyamory or BDSM (neither of which is, of course, exclusively heterosexual). Likewise, some homosexualities can be heteronormative: for instance, the married, monogamous, gender-normative couple with children who believe in living quietly among their neighbors, whom they feel they resemble in all ways except the biological sex of their spouse. In a 2002 article, Lisa Duggan labeled this trend, and especially its political perspective, "the new homonormativity."[11]

Duggan argues that, during the 1990s, a "new neoliberal sexual politics"[12] developed in which privatization was valued in both sexual and economic terms. Whereas queer politics, as Warner and others have defined it, carries with it an awareness of the interconnectedness of different forms of oppression, values a broad vision of social and economic justice, and supports the development of public sexual cultures, homonormativity values the privacy of the conjugal home and has little, if anything, to say about connections to social justice movements. In fact, Duggan notes of gay conservative Andrew Sullivan that "he ultimately critiques the Civil Rights movement's legacy of antidiscrimination law, particularly affirmative action, as veering too far away from the proper goals of state neutrality and private freedom of contract."[13] Homonormativity stresses free market capitalism and privatization, and critiques government involvement even in the arena of social justice. This is a far cry from the hopes held out for queer politics, and yet Duggan fears it is drawing in followers by claiming to be the moderate middle, thus casting queer politics as unreasonably radical, literally out in left field.

Yet David Halperin, who so succinctly defined "queer" in 1995, by 2003 had declared queer theory "a more trendy version of 'liberal.'"[14] Indeed, many activists have complained that the term "queer" has lost its radical implications, becoming instead simply a way of saying "LGBT" or even "gay and lesbian" while using fewer syllables. Halperin argues that queer theory has suffered from its own popularity: "as queer theory becomes more widely diffused throughout the disciplines, it becomes harder to figure out what's so very queer about it."[15] Has queer theory lost its edge, or is it redeemable? Before considering that question, I want to go back to the beginning.

Queer theory has its roots in the work of Michel Foucault, who famously made a case for the social construction of sexuality.[16] Though same-sex eroticism has existed throughout Western history, Foucault argued that it came to take a particular form in the nineteenth century West, when the term "homosexual" was first coined. In this era of categorization and the rise of what Foucault calls "bio-power"—that is, power controlling forms of life—sexologists distinguished a particular type of human as the "sexual invert"—one whose gender identity and consequently sexual attraction were "inverted" from those considered "normal" for that sex. Thus, the female "invert" was masculine and attracted to women, while the male "invert" was feminine and attracted to men.[17] Sexual inversion was generally considered to be a permanent trait, and one that fundamentally defined the life and personhood of the invert. For many centuries prior to the nineteenth, Western cultures regarded same-sex eroticism as deviant, but not as indicative of a fundamental difference in the practitioner. The development of the concept of the invert marks the invention of the contemporary Western concept of sexual orientation. Foucault's history has since been critiqued—among others, by scholars working in countries outside the West, who argue that Western cultures do not have sole claim to the concept of sexual orientation as an innate and fundamental difference.[18] However, the concept of the social construction of sexuality remains a powerful one, especially for queer theorists.

Published in 1990, shortly before de Lauretis's *differences* article, Judith Butler's *Gender Trouble* drew on Foucault's social constructionist perspectives to argue that not only is gender socially constructed (an idea already well developed in some branches of feminist thought), but sex itself is as well, through the performative subjectification of the self. The self as subject—meaning both that which acts and that which is subjected to power—is brought into being, Butler argues, through actions that simultaneously perform gender and inscribe genderedness on the body. Thus, even a simple act such as walking can inscribe gender: one walks "like a woman" or "like a man" (note that there are no other choices here—the system is binary), and in that act enforces not only others' perceptions of oneself but also one's own sense of inhabiting a gendered body and a gendered reality. Our gendered actions, Butler argues, are learned and are powerfully and sometimes violently enforced by those around us. In an argument that has influenced performance activists such as Queer Nation, Butler suggests that resistant performances are one key to subverting the gender system.

Such ideas formed the base upon which de Lauretis built when she coined the term "queer theory" in 1991.[19] Fundamental to the growing body of theory were a concept of both gender and sexual orientation as social constructs, a Foucauldian understanding of power as something mobilized by various groups and individuals rather than something held by one group or individual over another, and a concern with the practical, political implications of theoretical work, especially for lesbian, gay, and eventually bisexual and transgender communities.

Yet, bisexuals and transgender people have had little voice in queer theory. In queer theoretical works, bisexuality appears most often in the form of historic individuals from the nineteenth or early twentieth century who were known to sleep with both men and women. All too quickly, these figures fade as the text in question focuses in on same-sex attraction and allows different-sex attraction to fade into the background. Transgender people, who were coining the concept of transgender as queer theory was developing, produced a number of important works in the 1990s. In queer theory, however, they appeared until 1998 only as examples in books that otherwise addressed those who were cisgender (non-transgender). In 1998, Judith Halberstam published her much-lauded work *Female Masculinity*. In it, she argued that masculinity among those assigned female at birth has a great deal to tell us about masculinity in general, because "widespread indifference to female masculinity . . . has clearly ideological motivations and has sustained the complex social structures that wed masculinity to maleness and to power and domination."[20] Exploring Western female masculinities from the nineteenth-century "invert" through the twentieth-century "stone butch" lesbian, the "border wars" between butch lesbians and FTMs (female-to-male transgender people), and drag kings, Halberstam suggests that in order to understand female masculinities we need to conceive of identity as a process rather than a status. Furthermore, "to understand such a process . . . we would need . . . to think in fractal terms and about gender geometries."[21]

In her more recent work, Halberstam continues her attention on non-normative genders by developing the concepts of "queer time" and "queer place."[22] Perhaps the opposite of Duggan's "homonormativity," Halberstam's "queer time" refers to a concept of time developed in the contexts of queer lives: the fleeting temporality associated with living with HIV during the height of the epidemic, and the organization of life courses when there are no expectations of a timely marriage, childbearing, child rearing, and so on. Likewise, the production of queer time necessitates thinking as well about queer place—the ways in which queer subjects construct a sense of place, and in fact construct places themselves, differ from the ways in which place is constructed in the heteronormative world, and this has consequences not only for queer communities and individuals but potentially for activism as well.

Unlike much of queer theory, Halberstam goes beyond literary and film criticism to engage what she calls a "queer methodology." Employing the tools of a number of different disciplines and "refus[ing] the academic compulsion toward disciplinary coherence," Halberstam defines a queer methodology as that which "collect[s] and produce[s] information on subjects who have been deliberately or accidentally excluded from traditional studies of human behavior."[23] Such collection and production, though carried out in a much more (ethnographically) disciplinary manner, is also the goal of David Valentine's recent study, *Imagining Transgender*.[24]

Having begun his work as an ethnographic study of transgender communities in New York City, Valentine was struck almost immediately by the discrepancies in the ways his study participants identified. While transgender activists—often white and from middle-class backgrounds—proudly claimed their identity as transgender, others—often working class or working poor and people of color—had other names for themselves and refused the transgender designation. Valentine's study became an ethnography of the term "transgender." With a strong commitment to the importance ethnography can hold for activists, Valentine suggests that, rather than assume the automatic separability of sexuality and gender, we should instead "ask other kinds of questions, such as: 'For whom is this the case? Where? When? With what effects? From whose perspective?'" and so on.[25] Answers to such questions, he argues, will help activists to determine how best to serve gender-variant populations.

Despite Halperin's challenge that queer theory has become "a more trendy version of 'liberal,'" in studies of gender variance, at least, it has maintained or even further developed its activist orientation. Yet queer theory has also been charged with being predominantly male and predominantly white. While several of the currently prominent names in queer theory—Judith Butler, Lisa Duggan, Gayatri Gopinath—are female, it is true that queer theory has been dominated by men, and a number of works in queer theory focus specifically on (cisgender) men. Likewise, although queer theory has always had a thread of concern with race, interrogating whiteness has not been on the queer theoretical radar. There, has, however, been an upswing in queer writings by people of color. Especially since the 1999 publication of José Esteban Muñoz's oft-cited book *Disidentifications*, a number of queer theoretical works have appeared dealing with the experiences of people of color, those of people from non-Western countries, and queer theoretical approaches to globalization.

Pointing out that "the field of queer theory . . . is . . . a place where a scholar of color can easily be lost in an immersion of vanilla while her or his critical faculties can be frozen by an avalanche of snow," Muñoz seeks "to contribute to an understanding of the ways in which queers of color identify with ethnos or queerness despite the phobic charges in both fields."[26] Drawing on the work of Michel Pêcheux, Muñoz develops the concept of "disidentification" as "a strategy that works on and against dominant ideology" and "tries to transform a cultural logic from within."[27] Contrary to identification with a cultural norm—going along with it—or counteridentification—directly opposing it—disidentification makes use of parody, play, and performativity to subvert that norm. Offering examples from art, film, and performance art, Muñoz explores the ways in which queer people of color disidentify with whiteness and heteronormativity.

As Siobhan Somerville demonstrated in 2000, the invention of sexual orientation and the increasingly insistent cultural efforts to police it—to distinguish clearly between the heterosexual and the homosexual—paralleled and intertwined with the nineteenth-century social construction of race as it is known today in the United States, and the often violent efforts to divide black clearly from white.[28] Thus, attempts to theorize queerness can never be complete without simultaneous attention to race, something Robert Reid-Pharr demonstrates elegantly in his collection of essays, *Black Gay Man*.[29] This is not to say that Reid-Pharr focuses on identity politics; where he does, it is in order to critically question such politics even as he sometimes acknowledges a need for them. His explorations of race, gender, and sexuality serve a larger goal of developing an effective coalition on the political left, while at the same time remaining deeply personal.

Likewise, Roderick Ferguson explicitly offers a "queer of color critique" in his *Aberrations in Black*, in part as "another step in the move beyond identity politics" and toward coalitional politics.[30] Drawing on Karl Marx's historical materialism yet finding it silent on issues of gender, race, and sexuality, Ferguson proposes disidentifying with this theoretical perspective, inhabiting it in order simultaneously to make use of and alter it. Further, he uses this approach to critique the traditional discipline of sociology, reading African American culture through the form of the novel and through an intersectional analysis that takes into account race, sexuality, class, and gender.

In addition to the increasing attention paid to U.S. racial dynamics in queer theory, since 2000 there has been a steady increase in the number of works offering global queer perspectives. These works rightly take existing queer theory to task for its focus on the West and especially the United States, arguing that valuable theoretical perspectives can come from other areas of the globe as well. Perhaps the earliest of these works to be influential among queer theorists was José Quiroga's *Tropics of Desire*, which utilizes literary, film, and cultural analysis to critique the monolithic representations of Latin American queer cultures in queer theory and LGBT studies. Also of interest are several collections, two of which fruitfully explore the intersections of postcolonial and queer theory and one of which focuses more broadly on the intersections of globalization, queer theory, and postcolonial/neo-colonial international relations.[31]

Two more recent works helpfully bring in the concept of diaspora, addressing globalization directly through the lives of those who live in transit, either literally through trips between a sending country and a receiving one, or figuratively through telephone, computer, and commercial connections between the two. Martin Manalansan describes the "new queer studies," of which he considers himself a part, by quoting fellow "new queer" scholar Gayatri Gopinath: "a more nuanced understanding of the traffic and travel of competing systems of desire in a transnational frame . . . and of how colonial structures of knowing and seeing remain in place within a discourse of an 'international' lesbian and gay movement."[32] Both Manalansan and Gopinath grapple with these overlapping dimensions of travel, desire, and transnationalism, the former in the context of Filipino gay men and the latter in her study of what she terms "queer female diasporic subjectivity" in the context of South Asia and South Asian diasporas.[33] While the former study is primarily anthropological and the latter leans more in the direction of cultural studies, both works stress the importance of diaspora studies for queer studies as well as the impact that queer studies can have on diaspora studies. Gopinath explains: "queerness is to heterosexuality as diaspora is to nation. . . . If 'diaspora' needs 'queerness' in order to rescue it from its genealogical implications, 'queerness' also needs 'diaspora' in order to make it more supple in relation to questions of race, colonialism, migration and globalization."[34]

Another point of agreement in works that bring queer theory together with the study of globalization is the fact that queer cultures are deeply affected by global politics and the spread of global capitalism. Jasbir Puar's recent *Terrorist Assemblages* makes this connection especially clear in her exploration of the relationships between homonormativity and the state-sponsored terrorism known as the War on Terror.[35] Puar posits a new form of homonormativity in the United States, "homonationalism," that casts certain homonormative gay men and lesbians as "proper" national (and capitalist) subjects; she offers as an example an advertisement for Gay.com that pictures two apparently naked white men wrapped together in an American flag. In turn, just as a small group of gay men and lesbians are coming to be defined as proper citizens, their sexuality acceptably normative, sexuality continues to be used, along with race, class, gender, and nationality, to construct national Others as fundamentalist—and fundamentally—sexual perverts. The concept of "assemblages," Puar argues, can help us to see these connections in all their fluidity, as it moves beyond the static nature of intersectional analysis. Understanding assemblages as events implies that as

> opposed to an intersectional model of identity, which presumes that components—race class, gender, sexuality, nation, age, religion—are separable analytics and can thus be disassembled, an assemblage is more attuned to interwoven forces that merge and dissipate time, space, and body against linearity, coherency, and permanency.[36]

The terrorist, like the queer, is an assemblage that carries with it a particular ontology and affect, and thus has particular effects on global politics and economics.

Another relatively new development in queer theory, and one that is still in the developing stages, is the intersection of queer theory with disability theory. The leader in this arena to date is Robert McRuer, whose book *Crip Theory* appeared in 2006. As McRuer and Abby Wilkerson point out in the introduction to a 2003 special issue of the journal *GLQ*, queer and disabled populations have in common that they are defined by and read through their bodies.[37] Both types of bodies are seen as monstrous, perverted, and in some way sexually deviant: either over-sexed (queer bodies) or sexless (disabled bodies). And both have developed their own movements that claim difference as a virtue, a position from which to critique larger structures of power, especially neo-liberalism and global capitalism. Pairing a theory of "compulsory able-bodiedness" with Adrienne Rich's "compulsory heterosexuality,"[38] McRuer argues, like Puar, that neo-liberalism is built, in part, upon the tolerance of a limited range of queer and disabled bodies, thus creating an able-bodied heterosexuality that is "more 'flexible' ... than either queer theory or disability studies has fully acknowledged."[39] Exploring the ways in which able-bodiedness relies on the existence of disability, as heterosexuality relies on the existence of queerness, crip theory offers yet more new directions for queer interventions, both theoretical and activist.

Queer Theory and Religious Studies

Notably absent in this admittedly brief survey of queer theoretical writing is the topic of religion. Some coverage appears in Manalansan's work on Filipino gay men, as a chapter of the book describes a cross-dressed version of a traditional Filipino ritual that has Catholic roots. Yet, aside from discussing how seriously (or not) people participated in the ritual aspects of the performance, Manalansan pays little attention to its religious roots in his analysis, preferring to focus on identity, performance, and the queer diasporic significance of the event. Though queer theorists have been reluctant so far to engage religion, within the field of religious studies, there have been some very productive appropriations of queer theory, especially in the fields of Jewish studies, Christian theology, biblical studies, and Christian history.

Defining "queer religious studies" for the purposes of this essay is challenging, because many works in the field term themselves "queer." Often, however, this terminology reflects the use of "queer" as an umbrella term for "LGBT," and the works so named have little if anything to do with queer theory. Yet some works that cite little queer theory remain close kin to those discussed in the preceding section. If "queer" is, as Halperin says, "an identity without an essence,"[40] then what criteria do we have by which to distinguish queer theoretical approaches to religion from others? Perhaps Halperin's word "essence" is the key. Much of what is written about religion in LGBT communities takes identity *as* essence, and even uses that essence as a basis from which to rethink and re-enact religion. Queer work in religion, on the other hand, to return to de Lauretis's original vision, might concern "the conceptual and speculative work involved in [religious] discourse production, and . . . the necessary critical work of deconstructing our own [religious] discourses and their constructed silences."[41] It would be, as I wrote above, "a theoretical approach that positions itself outside of and against dominant [religious/religious studies] discourses, critically examining the normative [in religion and religious studies] from a standpoint beyond it." Though much of the work in queer religious studies draws explicitly on queer theory, some comes to fit this definition through reliance on forerunners of queer theory such as Foucault and psychoanalytic theory.

Perhaps the earliest queer theoretical work in religious studies is Howard Eilberg-Schwartz's innovative book *God's Phallus*.[42] Beginning by asking why Judaism prohibits representations of God, Eilberg-Schwartz suggests that "it is 'male-morphism,' rather than anthropomorphism, about which [ancient] Jews felt ambivalent."[43] He offers several reasons for this ambivalence, the most striking being the implicit homoeroticism in an arrangement where a people (Israel) is seen as the bride of a male deity, and the male representatives of that people (priests) interact most closely with the deity. How to avoid thinking about a homoerotic encounter with the divine? Studiously ignore the body of the divine, and especially his loins. Eilberg-Schwartz offers a number of intriguing biblical examples wherein parts of the divine body become visible but the viewer's gaze never reaches the genital area.[44] Furthermore, he suggests, the marital imagery used to describe the relationship between God and Israel raised the specter of feminization for Jewish men, possibly contributing to the misogyny pointed out by many feminist scholars of the Bible and the Talmud.

The feminization of Jewish men, at least in the eyes of Western European, Christian cultures, has been the topic of much work by Talmud scholar Daniel Boyarin. In *Unheroic Conduct*, Boyarin traces what he calls the "femminization" (from "femme") of the Jewish man in Ashkenazi (northern European) Jewish culture.[45] Beginning with Talmudic texts, Boyarin analyzes the development of this masculine ideal through stories of the early rabbis that explicitly and favorably compare the femminized rabbis (one even has a lance that wilts in his hand) to the boorish and hyper-masculine *goyim*. Like Eilberg-Schwartz, Boyarin sees connections between the femminization and homosociality of the rabbis, on the one hand, and rabbinic misogyny, on the other. Yet, as he notes in the introduction, Boyarin wishes to reclaim this model of masculinity, shorn of its misogyny, for the late twentieth-century feminist man.[46] In the second half of *Unheroic Conduct*, Boyarin traces the effects on Ashkenazi masculinity of the nineteenth-century partial integration of Jews into mainstream, Northern European cultures. Focusing his attention on

Sigmund Freud, Zionism, and feminist Bertha Pappenheim (the "Anna O." of psychoanalytic fame), he argues that traditional Ashkenazi gender roles directly conflicted with mainstream European gender roles in the late nineteenth and early twentieth centuries, and that one can trace the effects of these conflicts in Freud's ambivalence toward Judaism, in the hyper-masculinity of Zionism ("Jews in colonial drag"[47]), and in the "hysterical" reactions of an activist to confinement within middle-class Victorian femininity.

Following these two striking works was a collection of queer studies in Judaism, edited by Daniel Boyarin, Daniel Iskovitz, and Ann Pellegrini.[48] Excerpts from the work of Marjorie Garber and Eve Kosofsky Sedgwick open the volume, and are followed by Janet Jakobsen's characteristically intricate musings on the connections and disconnections between Judaism and queerness. Other articles range from an examination of antisemitism and homophobia in an early twentieth-century murder trial, through an exploration of the links between queer theory and postcolonial theory in the context of Jewish cultural studies, to literary and cultural analyses of Geoffrey Chaucer, Charles Dickens, Yiddish theater, filmmaker Jean Cocteau, and others. Finally, this stellar collection closes with Judith Butler's thought-provoking reflections on feminism, homophobia, racism, and the legacy of National Socialism in contemporary Germany. After this collection and the important contributions by Eilberg-Schwartz and Boyarin, the field is left to await the next exciting work in queer Jewish studies.

In the meantime, the related field of biblical studies has also made important strides in the application of queer theory. A key figure here has been Ken Stone, who in 2001 edited a collection of queer commentaries on the Hebrew Bible.[49] Stone notes that

> "queer commentary on the Bible" might be … understood … as a range of approaches to biblical interpretation that take as their point of departure a critical interrogation and active contestation of the many ways in which the Bible is and has been read to support heteronormative and normalizing configurations of sexual practices and sexual identities.[50]

There is, indeed, a range of hermeneutical approaches here, from those that mine the biblical text for resources for LGBT communities to those that truly queer the text and offer new perspectives on the roles of sexuality in the Hebrew Bible. Mona West, for example, suggests reading the book of Lamentations as a resource for responding to AIDS. A thoughtful and important contribution, this chapter does not engage in the kind of "critical interrogation" that Stone and other queer theorists indicate is central to the practice of queer theory. At the other end of the spectrum, however, is Roland Boer's vision of a queer gathering atop Mount Sinai that includes such figures as the Marquis de Sade, Sigmund Freud, and Moses, and that casts Yahweh as a fussy interior decorator, obsessing over the finest details of his tabernacle.

Ken Stone's contribution to this collection is drawn from what was at the time a work in progress, later published as *Practicing Safer Texts*.[51] Stone argues that advocates of safer sex practices walk a middle road between throwing caution to the wind and abstaining from all sexual practices out of concern for safety. So, too, he suggests, should queer biblical commentators walk a middle road. Acknowledging that biblical texts have proved dangerous for LGBTIQ people, and that one must handle them cautiously, at the same time he does not advocate removing oneself entirely from engagement with the Bible; thus, queer readers of the Bible should practice "safer text." Stone puts his own recommendations into practice by examining the roles of food and sex in a number of biblical settings, ranging from the obvious—the Garden of Eden and the Song of Songs—to the less evident, such as the wisdom literature.

Less exciting than Stone's collection, though nonetheless an impressive and groundbreaking work, is *The Queer Bible Commentary*, a systematic collection of reflections from LGBT authors on every book of the Hebrew Bible and the Christian New Testament.[52] The commentaries range in style, from formal structures that outline and then explain the book in question to more loosely structured essays that focus only on particular sections of a book. Much of this collection falls closer to LGBT studies than to queer theory: authors explore the relevance of each book for same-sex attracted readers (and occasionally for gender-variant readers as well), noting places where the books speak to LGBT experiences but not deeply interrogating the text. A few truly queer contributions spice up this collection, however. Elizabeth Stuart, for example, draws on Butler's exploration of the melancholy subject in *Undoing Gender* in order to explore the irruption of the feminine and the consequent queering of the divine through the figure of Wisdom in the book of Proverbs. And the late Marcella Althaus-Reid, known like Stuart for producing deeply queer readings of Christian tradition, provocatively compares the crucifixion of Jesus to the murder of a transvestite prostitute on a street in Buenos Aires.

Stuart and Althaus-Reid are both best known not for biblical commentary but for queer theology, and it is here that the intersection of queer theory and religion has been the most fruitful. In her helpful introduction to gay, lesbian, and queer theologies, Stuart draws a clear distinction between "gay and lesbian theology" and "queer theology": "In gay and lesbian theology sexuality interrogated theology; in queer theology, theology interrogates sexuality but from a different place than modern theology has traditionally done."[53] Stuart argues that not only are Christian theology and queer theory compatible, but the former can enhance the latter as well. "Queer theory," she argues, "needs disruption from the transcendent to save it from hopeless idealism and nihilism. For there is only one community charged with being queer and that is the Church and it is so charged for a purpose: the preparation of the kingdom of heaven."[54] Here, in this relatively early articulation of queer theology, Christian triumphalism seems to grate against the social radicalism of queer theory. Other queer theologians, however, manage to avoid this problem.

Queer theology burst into the theological scene with Althaus-Reid's *Indecent Theology*, published in 2000.[55] Combining Latin American liberation theology and feminist theology with a concern for taking sexuality seriously, Althaus-Reid defines indecent theology as "a theology which problematizes and undresses the mythical layers of multiple oppression in Latin America, a theology which, finding its point of departure at the crossroads of Liberation Theology and Queer Thinking, will reflect on economic and theological oppression with passion and imprudence."[56] Insisting that a theology with a "preferential option for the poor" should include the voices of all of the poor, including the sexually and gender-diverse poor and those whose religious festivals play with gender, Althaus-Reid critiques both liberation theology and feminist theology for their inattentiveness to the sexual body. To demonstrate the alternatives to these desexualized meditations on theology, she suggests "per/verting" Mary ("allowing [her] fixed identities to be ... more imprecise and mutable"[57]); imaging Christ as bisexual (the "Bi/Christ"[58]); and rethinking soteriology through the lens of sexual fetishism. She concludes with reflections on the Christian role in neo-colonialism and economic globalization.

Working in conversation with Althaus-Reid is Robert Goss, whose *Queering Christ* marked his transition from gay and lesbian theology to queer theology.[59] As Althaus-Reid conceives of Christ as the Bi/Christ in order to stress the sexual fluidity of the Christ figure, so Goss pushes the concept further by suggesting a "Transvestite/Christ"[60] or simply a "Queer Christ" to encompass gender as well as sexual diversity in the divine figure. Althaus-Reid followed this in 2003 with an argument for queering God.[61] Her aim in this densely written and often convoluted book is first to describe and then to practice queer theology as she envisions it: as a radical rethinking, or perhaps re-embodying, of God, hermeneutics, and the theologian herself. Moreover, for Althaus-Reid, theology cannot be truly queer unless it attends to more than just sexual margins: following in the tradition of liberation theology, which is, in fact, the taproot of queer theology, Althaus-Reid insists that queer theologians look as well to the experiences of those marginalized by class and by colonization. Drawing on people, locations, history, and literature from her native Argentina as well as from other parts of South and Central America, Althaus-Reid unrelentingly pulls together feminist, queer, and postcolonial perspectives in order to present such provocative concepts as God the Sodomite; Rahab the co-opted, colonized subject; and Lot's wife the protester against (divine) fascism, the biblical parallel to the mothers of the Plaza de Mayo.

The denial of tenure to Goss in 2003 and the passing of Althaus-Reid in 2009 left a significant gap in the development of queer theology; however, one of those who has kept the field alive and on the cutting edge is Gerard Loughlin. His engrossing 2004 work, *Alien Sex*, uses film analysis as a lens through which to construct theology. Loughlin suggests a "theology of the cinema," which is "a discerning of lights, of screen-visions," adding that such a theology is closely connected with a theology of the body and of sexuality: "for it is from desire that we learn of divine eros, the love that comes to us in the flesh so that we might enter into the triune mystery, the embrace of God, and with our bodies see the beatific vision."[62] Exploring images of the sacred and of sexuality in film, Loughlin uses these images as a tool for unpacking the connections between the sacred and sexuality in theology itself.

The newest indication of developments in queer theology is an excellent collection recently edited by Loughlin, who argues insightfully in the introduction that "gay sexuality is not marginal to Christian thought and culture, but oddly central. It [is] the disavowed but necessary condition for the Christian symbolic."[63] Such challenging observations abound in this group of essays written by a range of prominent queer scholars, some of whom are theologians but many of whom work in other areas relevant to theology. As with other collections, this one too is somewhat uneven in its relationship to queer theory; a few of the chapters are better termed gay and lesbian theology than queer theology. Overall, however, *Queer Theology* offers a thought-provoking introduction to queer work in Judaism and (mostly) Christianity.

Readers familiar with the literature will notice that I have neglected to mention Mark Jordan's work in the above discussion. This is because Jordan's unique work deserves treatment on its own. By far the most prolific writer in queer studies in religion, Jordan produces essays that offer a brilliant interweaving of theology, history, Foucauldian analysis, and queer theory. Among his works published in the past decade, perhaps the best known is the earliest: *The Silence of Sodom*.[64] Written like Jordan's other works in a conversational style, this book is especially indebted to Walter Benjamin's Arcades Project, which Benjamin envisioned as a "literary montage." Jordan explains:

> I am convinced that the homosexuality of modern Catholicism can't be written about except by "constellating" moral theology, church history, queer theory, the novel of manners, and utopian reveries. By gathering scraps from these

kinds of texts, I hope to demonstrate both the inadequacy of official Catholic speeches about homosexuality and how challenging it will be to create more adequate ones.[65]

The Silence of Sodom applies this "montage" approach to the study of official Roman Catholic speech about homosexuality, to the lives of gay men in the Church (his chapter "Clerical Camp" is especially delightful), and to rethinking the place of homosexuality, and especially gay men, in the Church.

Although in *The Ethics of Sex* Jordan's signature method is more muted, it is fruitfully present in *Telling Truths in Church* and in *Blessing Same-Sex Unions*.[66] The former of these two is a lecture series first given in Boston in 2002, just as the pedophilia scandals were beginning in the U.S. Catholic churches. Picking up on themes raised in *The Silence of Sodom*, Jordan explores the power of the Church to silence what he calls "truth-telling" through "broadcasting the kind of scandal that sounds so harshly around us right now." The Church broadcasts scandal "by pretending to make claims: that the truth-telling is *angry*, that it is *anti-Catholic prejudice*, and that it has *no proof*."[67] The book goes on to explore efforts at truth-telling and churchly efforts at silencing in the context of same-sex marriage, God, and Jesus.

The theme of same-sex marriage returns in full in Jordan's most recent book, *Blessing Same-Sex Unions*. True to his inimitable style, Jordan notes at the outset that "the reader who likes to tally disciplines will find pages that look like cultural criticism, qualitative sociology, narrative history, literary criticism, and amateur satire."[68] Interweaving these diverse approaches, Jordan comments upon both male same-sex bonding (in its many different forms) and Christian marriage, and he explores the possible outcomes of an intersection of the two. Some of the tenor of the book can be found in Jordan's closing line: "In the end, will queers get married in a real church with a real minister? Just like everyone else—unless they are very careful."[69]

Like Jordan, Virginia Burrus has become a leading queer theorist on the topic of Christianity; unlike Jordan, she works in the context of early Christian history. In *The Sex Lives of Saints*, Burrus explores representations and intimations of the erotic in early Christian hagiography. She offers a queer reading of the saints' lives of Jerome; explores sexualized masochism in the lives of virgin martyrs ("A 'woman,' it seems," she quips, "must die in order to get a Life"[70]); enacts a queer, postcolonial reading of Sulpicius's *Life of Martin*; and discusses the role of seduction in the hagiographies of prostitutes-turned-saints. A historian rather than a theologian, Burrus nevertheless concludes her work with the significance of these undercurrents of eroticism for the lives of Christians today.

Likewise, Burrus's recent study of shame in early Christianity concludes with reflections on the role of shame in contemporary U.S. society.[71] The book as a whole, though, concentrates on the various ways in which shame appears in a variety of early Christian texts. Martyrs, for instance, experienced in their enforced shaming a route to the glory of God. Ascetics sought out shame as part of their self-abasement before God, and Jesus—God in the flesh, or perhaps flesh itself—was shamed on the cross. Burrus's final chapter focuses on the roles of shame and shamelessness in confession, especially in the work of Augustine. Like *The Sex Lives of Saints*, *Saving Shame* is clever and insightful, offering queerly new perspectives on the early history of Christianity. Worth noting, as well, is that Burrus has begun to have some company in her work on queer readings of early Christianity: a recently published article in the *Journal of the American Academy of Religion* explores homoeroticism and restrictions placed on the bodies of boys in the writings of early Egyptian monks.[72]

Other queer innovations in the study of religion range from a comparison of queer and Catholic passing (and attendant anxieties among heterosexual Protestants) in the nineteenth-century United States,[73] to an intriguing edited collection on the intersections of Jewish, Christian, and/or queer identities.[74] In the latter work, a few of the contributors focus on Jewish/Christian intersections, but most offer queer readings of some aspect of Judaism, Christianity, or both. Notably, this book was published as part of the new series, "Queer Interventions," edited by well-known queer scholars Noreen Giffney and Michael O'Rourke. This is only the second text to perform such a publishing crossover: a queer study of religion being published as part of a larger queer studies publishing project. The first was Janet Jakobsen and Ann Pellegrini's well-known book, *Love the Sin*, which appeared as part of the "Sexual Cultures" series that has included a number of prominent works in queer theory.[75]

Love the Sin is also one of the few books in queer religious studies to reach out beyond the study of religion itself and engage topics of concern to queer theory more broadly. Arguing that tolerance and equal rights are inadequate goals for the gay and lesbian movement, Jakobsen and Pellegrini suggest instead turning to the First Amendment for guidance. Tolerance, they suggest, is inadequate because one can claim to be tolerant of a group while still considering the members of that group to be inferior. Furthermore, the rhetoric of tolerance casts all political activists as "extremists" and thus "has important [negative] implications for participatory democracy."[76] Advocating what they call "the free exercise of sex,"[77] Jakobsen and Pellegrini suggest that sexual practices should be treated like religious practices—that, in fact, the choice of sexual practices *is* in part a freedom-of-religion issue because laws controlling how and with whom people have sex in the United States impose the ethics of a particular branch of Christianity on everyone in the country. Ultimately, Jakobsen and Pellegrini argue for "a public that allows for robust contestation and radical pluralism, rather than one split by divisions between those who are the same and those who are different."[78]

Taking Stock: The Future of Queer Theory in Religious Studies

Queer theoretical work in the field of religious studies has expanded significantly over the past decade, but it is really still in its infancy. In Christian theology and in biblical studies, it is developing steadily, although the passing of Marcella Althaus-Reid marks a tremendous loss to the field and Bob Goss's departure from academia likewise struck a blow. Queer Jewish studies holds a great deal of promise, although it too has been hurt by the disdain that tenure committees apparently hold for queer theory in religion: its earliest proponent, Howard Eilberg-Schwartz, was denied tenure and subsequently left the academic world. Further developments from those scholars who are able to continue doing queer work in Jewish studies would be most welcome. In the areas of queer Christian commentary and queer studies of Christian history, Mark Jordan and Virginia Burrus stand somewhat alone, and more work like theirs is greatly needed.

In all of these areas there is a great deal of space for further inquiry; many opportunities exist for new scholars to gain a foothold while relying on the work of those who have gone before them for inspiration and support. Both in Christian theology and in biblical studies, there is also a need to continue working to distinguish between lesbian and gay work, on the one hand, and queer work, on the other. This is not to say that lesbian and gay theology and biblical studies are not useful; there is a real need for such work in communities of faith. However, at the more theoretical level, lesbian and gay theology and biblical studies tend toward the homonormative and can fail to be as radically inclusive in their thinking as queer theory strives to be.

It is also critical for queer theory in religion to branch out beyond the study of Judaism and Christianity. But is queer theory relevant beyond these areas? The study of religion has been critiqued as a colonial enterprise based on a Western construct; given the vulnerability of queer theory to the same claim, should queer theorists really want to associate with the study of religion, especially outside of Western cultures? These are questions that deserve serious thought, and that have been addressed by some of the recent work in queer theory as well as in religion. Certainly one must be aware of neocolonial dynamics in extending either queer theory or the study of religion to cultures outside of their own origins; but as both fields have made such extensions with appropriate caution, it seems logical for them to work together in some of these areas.

Why, for instance, does Manalansan's study of Filipino gay men not consider religion in any depth, despite the fact that he covers a drag enactment of a popular Filipino religious ritual? Parody constructs an interesting relationship to religion that could be plumbed in more depth. Relatedly, why does Gopinath not discuss religion in her work on South Asian diasporas? Surely it is not because no queer South Asians are involved in religions. Is it because religion is less relevant to sexuality in the context of South Asia, or is this neglect of religion part of a larger resistance on the part of queer theorists to considering religion as a valid topic of inquiry?

Furthermore, it would be interesting to see queer theory applied to the field of religious studies itself. What would it mean to queer the field? It might mean, for starters, unearthing and questioning the hetero- and gender-normativity of classical studies of religion. It might mean asking what studies of queer phenomena in religion can tell us about the field as a whole—what does the ritual in Manalansan's work tell us about ritual itself, and how often does ritual studies consider drag? What does the ritual tell us about Catholicism and Catholic practice, or about the religious practices of the excluded? And it might mean asking queer questions of any new research—where is sexuality, where gender, in studies appearing today? Are they only in the form of dominant narratives? What lies beneath the surface of these narratives? Who is silenced in order to produce the picture painted by scholars?

Queer theory in religion, even in those areas where it is developing well, also needs to push beyond the isolated study of sexuality to take on the broader concern for justice articulated by de Lauretis and carried out especially in the work of queer theorists of color. How do sexuality and gender, or gender variance, intersect in religion? What about race, class, or global capitalism—areas sorely under-studied by religionists in general, and certainly by those interested in queer theory?[79] In some ways, queer theory in religion stands now where queer theory as a whole stood in the mid-1990s: surrounded by a great deal of enthusiasm but lacking in the radicalism hoped for by de Lauretis when she coined the term. It is dominated by white, gay, middle-class, cisgendered men who write from, and often solely about, their own experiences and the experiences of people like them. Althaus-Reid has blazed the trail to another approach to queerly studying religion; hopefully the field will follow her and develop in the ways that queer theory has developed in the first decade of the new millennium.

In a response to Ken Stone's collection, *Queer Commentary and the Hebrew Bible*, Tat-siong Benny Liew wrote that "as biblical scholars, we must not only read the Bible with the help of queer theory, but we must also use our reading of the Bible to interrogate, or even transform queer theory."[80] As he notes, until now religious studies has made use of queer theory, has applied it, without reciprocal attention from queer theorists. But *can* there be a useful, bi- or even multi-directional conversation between religious studies and queer theory? Is Liew right that religious studies can even transform queer theory? Further, has the current failure of religious studies to gain the attention of queer theorists resulted from a weakness in queer studies in religion or a cynicism on the part of queer theorists about religion as a whole? The answer may be some of both.

Roden's *Jewish/Christian/Queer* and Jakobsen and Pellegrini's *Love the Sin* both attracted enough attention to be published as part of a series on queer theory. Interestingly, although these scholars are interested in religion, none of the three and very few of Roden's contributors are actually employed in religious studies departments. Is this because of the discomfort that religious studies has shown toward queer studies in general, or because religious studies scholars are ill-equipped to study queer theory? Again, the answer may be both. We have a queer studies that is largely cynical about religion, though willing to consider it in studies countering fundamentalism or studies of identity undertaken by literature scholars; a religious studies wary enough of things queer to occasionally deny tenure to and sometimes refuse to hire scholars who work in the area; queer studies scholars untrained in the study of religion; and religious studies scholars untrained in queer studies—the latter two as a result of the former. This, at least, must change. Religious studies scholars must show how our work can contribute to the development of queer theory—in its fullest, most justice-oriented sense, and not in the guise of Christian supremacism—and queer theorists must consider whether a serious look at religion might not be in the interest of their ultimate goals.

What would a study look like that contributed equally to the development of queer theory and to the study of religion? It could be a study of religious parody, as seen in Manalansan's work or in the infamous Sisters of Perpetual Indulgence. The Sisters, who take their name from the medieval practice of selling indulgences that would exonerate one of one's sins, offer a "perpetual indulgence" to those whose identities or practices have been declared sinful by traditional religions—especially LGBT communities. They are a charity organization that raises money for a wide variety of causes and promotes safer sex practices, and they consider themselves to be nuns who serve their community much in the way that Catholic nuns do. They are best known, however, for their parody of Catholic nuns through the use of whiteface and drag. Most (though certainly not all) of the Sisters are gay men; when in their formal dress, they wear full nuns' habits, but most of the time the U.S. Sisters can be found in wimples, veils, and outrageous drag.

Cathy Glenn, one of the very few scholars to have written on the Sisters, argues that the Sisters "set into motion a mimetic identification with their own adaptation of 'nun'"; in being nuns, they re-signify the concept of "nun," thus contributing to a changing perception of nuns in the twenty-first century.[81] Glenn takes seriously the concept of the sacred in evaluating the symbolic significance of the Sisters and the vituperative reactions of some Catholics to the presence of the Sisters. For some Catholics, she explains, "the move to bring the mundane into the temple, to sanctify the queer bodies and politics of SPI, constitutes profanity."[82] Without these key concepts from the study of religion—sacred and profane—Glenn would have been unable to adequately evaluate the relationship between the Sisters and the Roman Catholic Church. And yet, there is much more to be said about this relationship. Certainly the Sisters' efforts to sacralize queer bodies are part of their "profanity," and certainly an even more significant aspect is their representation of queer bodies as Catholic nuns. Yet others dress as nuns without such violent responses; is it the organized aspect of the Sisters that sparks outrage, or is it something about the queerness of the bodies they sacralize? I would argue the latter.

But this is about more than queerness. Queer bodies are fundamentally sexual in the rhetoric of the Roman Catholic Church: homosexuality (under which are subsumed bisexuality and transgender identities) is "intrinsically disordered." To bring queer bodies into sacred roles is to bring sexuality into the Church. To bring predominantly *male* queer bodies into the Church is to draw attention to the rampant presence of homoeroticism within the culture of the Church, to boisterously shatter the glass closet the Church has been trying so hard to paint over in the past decade, especially in its ban on admitting gay men to seminary. In extending Glenn's analysis, religious studies offers queer theory concerted attention to the interconnections and tensions between the sacred and sexuality.

Religious studies also offers the perspective that religion is a fundamental part of culture; yet cultural studies, in which queer theory plays a major part, attends only rarely to religion, and then often only in passing. What would it mean to consider religion through a cultural studies lens, and what would this add to queer theory? Certainly religion is a source of both heteronormativity and homonormativity, but as the Sisters demonstrate, it can also be a force of subversion. Queer theory is currently missing religion's role on both sides of this dynamic, and therefore, its grasp of heteronormativity, homonormativity, and subversion is incomplete.

Finally, religious studies offers a unique approach to religion as a *sui generis* phenomenon. Although we disagree vociferously on the definition of religion, religious studies scholars generally agree in refusing to reduce the phenomenon of religion to other causes, such as psychological functions or the effects of narcotics (real or metaphorical). Taking religion seriously in this way allows us to comprehend more fully the influence of religion on people's lives and on their understanding of themselves and of the world around them. Religion is a powerful force in subjectification, and it can also be a powerful form of resistance. To deny this power through ignoring religion or approaching it from a reductionist perspective is to miss an important social and cultural dynamic.

So religious studies can contribute to queer theory, just as queer theory has contributed to religious studies. As the field expands and grows, this is an important direction to develop in order for queer theory in religion to reach maturity. Still in its first decade of real growth, queer theory in religion has developed rapidly in some areas and more slowly in others. It offers sophisticated analyses in some areas, while others are sorely in need of scholarly attention. The field is wide open for new and established scholars alike to join in the conversation and add new perspectives that will benefit the larger fields of both religious studies and queer theory.

Notes

1. Thanks to Beth Currans for recommending works in queer theory, and to Janet Mallen for thought-provoking discussions on the contributions of religious studies to queer theory. A sabbatical leave from Whitman College enabled the production of this essay.
2. Teresa de Lauretis, "Queer Theory: Lesbian and Gay Sexualities: An Introduction," *differences* 3:2 (1991): iii–xviii.
3. Ibid., iv.
4. Ibid.
5. Ibid., xi.
6. Michel Foucault, *The History of Sexuality, Vol. 1: An Introduction*, trans. Robert Hurley (New York: Vintage Books, [1978] 1990); Eve Kosofsky Sedgwick, *Epistemology of the Closet* (Berkeley: University of California Press, 1990); Cherríe Moraga and Gloria Anzaldúa, eds., *This Bridge Called My Back: Writings by Radical Women of Color* (New York: Kitchen Table Press, 1983); Judith Butler, *Gender Trouble: Feminism and the Subversion of Identity* (New York: Routledge, 1990).
7. "As for 'queer theory,' ... [it] has quickly become a conceptually vacuous creature of the publishing industry" (Teresa de Lauretis, "Habit Changes," *differences* 6:2–3 [1994]: 297).

8. For a good overview of more recent developments in queer theory, see David L. Eng, Judith Halberstam, and José Esteban Muñoz, eds., "What's Queer about Queer Studies Now?" *Social Text* 23:3–4 (2005).

9. David M. Halperin, *Saint Foucault: Towards a Gay Hagiography* (New York: Oxford University Press, 1995), 62, emphasis in original.

10. Michael Warner, ed., *Fear of a Queer Planet: Queer Politics and Social Theory* (Minneapolis: University of Minnesota Press, 1993), xxii.

11. Lisa Duggan, "The New Homonormativity: The Sexual Politics of Neoliberalism," in *Materializing Democracy: Toward a Revitalized Cultural Politics*, ed. Russ Castronovo and Dana D. Nelson (Durham, NC: Duke University Press, 2002), 175–94.

12. Ibid., 179.

13. Ibid., 186.

14. David Halperin, "The Normalization of Queer Theory," *Journal of Homosexuality* 45:2–4 (2003): 341.

15. Ibid., 342.

16. See Foucault, *History of Sexuality*.

17. As Lisa Duggan points out, this theory created an odd paradox, for inverts were believed to be attracted to "normal" members of their own sex. What, then, did that make the "normal" partner of an invert? In the case of a woman, she was simply considered wild or loose. See Lisa Duggan, *Sapphic Slashers: Sex, Violence, and American Modernity* (Durham, NC: Duke University Press, 2000).

18. Cf. Ruth Vanita, "Introduction," in *Queering India: Same-Sex Love and Eroticism in Indian Culture and Society*, ed. Ruth Vanita (New York: Routledge, 2002), 1–11.

19. Among other influential precursors were de Lauretis's *Technologies of Gender: Essays on Theory, Film, and Fiction* (Bloomington: Indiana University Press, 1987); and Diana Fuss, ed., *Inside/Out: Lesbian Theories, Gay Theories* (New York: Routledge, 1991).

20. Judith Halberstam, *Female Masculinity* (Durham, NC: Duke University Press, 1998), 2.

21. Ibid., 21.

22. Judith Halberstam, *In a Queer Time and Place: Transgender Bodies, Subcultural Lives* (New York: New York University Press, 2005).

23. Ibid., 13.

24. David Valentine, *Imagining Transgender: An Ethnography of a Category* (Durham, NC: Duke University Press, 2007).

25. Ibid., 250.

26. José Esteban Muñoz, *Disidentifications: Queers of Color and the Performance of Politics* (Minneapolis: University of Minnesota Press, 1999), 11.

27. Ibid.

28. Siobhan B. Somerville, *Queering the Color Line: Race and the Invention of Homosexuality in American Culture* (Durham, NC: Duke University Press, 2000).

29. Robert F. Reid-Pharr, *Black Gay Man: Essays* (New York: New York University Press, 2001).

30. Roderick A. Ferguson, *Aberrations in Black: Toward a Queer of Color Critique* (Minneapolis: University of Minnesota Press, 2004), 29. See p. 149 for a definition of "queer of color analysis."

31. Jose Quiroga, *Tropics of Desire: Interventions from Queer Latino America* (New York: New York University Press, 2000). John C. Hawley, ed., *Postcolonial and Queer Theories: Intersections and Essays* (Westport, CT: Greenwood Press, 2001); John C. Hawley, ed., *Postcolonial, Queer: Theoretical Intersections* (Albany: State University of New York Press, 2001); Arnaldo Cruz-Malavé and Martin F. Manalansan IV, eds., *Queer Globalizations: Citizenship and the Afterlife of Colonialism* (New York: New York University Press, 2002).

32. Gayatri Gopinath, "Homo Economics: Queer Sexualities in a Transnational Frame," in *Burning Down the House: Recycling Domesticity*, ed. Rosemary Marangoly George (Boulder, CO: Westview Press, 1998), 117, quoted in Martin F. Manalansan IV, *Global Divas: Filipino Gay Men in the Diaspora* (Durham, NC: Duke University Press, 2003), 6.

33. Gayatri Gopinath, *Impossible Desires: Queer Diasporas and South Asian Public Cultures* (Durham, NC: Duke University Press, 2005), 15.

34. Ibid., 11.

35. Jasbir K. Puar, *Terrorist Assemblages: Homonationalism in Queer Times* (Durham, NC: Duke University Press, 2007).

36. Ibid., 212.

37. Robert McRuer and Abby L. Wilkerson, "Introduction," *GLQ* 9:1–2 (2003): 1–23.

38. Adrienne Rich, "Compulsory Heterosexuality and Lesbian Existence," in *Blood, Bread, and Poetry: Selected Prose 1978–1985* (New York: Norton, 1986).

39. Robert McRuer, *Crip Theory: Cultural Signs of Queerness and Disability* (New York: New York University Press, 2006), 3.

40. Halperin, *Saint Foucault*, 62.

41. de Lauretis, "Queer Theory," iv.

42. Howard Eilberg-Schwartz, *God's Phallus and Other Problems for Men and Monotheism* (Boston: Beacon Press, 1994).

43. Ibid., 9.

44. See ibid., Part 2.

45. Daniel Boyarin, *Unheroic Conduct: The Rise of Heterosexuality and the Invention of the Jewish Man* (Berkeley: University of California Press, 1997).

46. See ibid., xvii.

47. Ibid., 309.

48. Daniel Boyarin, Daniel Iskovitz, and Ann Pellegrini, eds., *Queer Theory and the Jewish Question* (New York: Columbia University Press, 2003).

49. Ken Stone, ed., *Queer Commentary and the Hebrew Bible* (Cleveland: The Pilgrim Press, 2001). In recent years, The Pilgrim Press has played an important role in publishing LGBT and queer work in Christian theology.

50. Ibid., 33.

51. Ken Stone, *Practicing Safer Texts: Food, Sex, and the Bible in Queer Perspective* (New York: T&T Clark, 2004).

52. Deryn Guest, Robert E. Goss, Mona West, and Thomas Bohache, eds., *The Queer Bible Commentary* (London: SCM Press, 2006).

53. Elizabeth Stuart, *Gay and Lesbian Theologies: Repetitions with Critical Difference* (Burlington, VT: Ashgate, 2003), 102.

54. Ibid., 106.

55. Marcella Althaus-Reid, *Indecent Theology: Theological Perversions in Sex, Gender, and Politics* (New York: Routledge, 2000).

56. Ibid., 2.

57. Ibid., 69–70.

58. Ibid., 112–20.

59. Robert E. Goss, *Queering Christ: Beyond Jesus Acted Up* (Cleveland: The Pilgrim Press, 2002).

60. Ibid., 182.

61. Marcella Althaus-Reid, *The Queer God* (New York: Routledge, 2003).

62. Gerard Loughlin, *Alien Sex: The Body and Desire in Cinema and Theology* (Malden, MA: Blackwell, 2004), 95.

63. Gerard Loughlin, ed., *Queer Theology: Rethinking the Western Body* (Malden, MA: Blackwell, 2007), 9.

64. Mark D. Jordan, *The Silence of Sodom: Homosexuality in Modern Catholicism* (Chicago: University of Chicago Press, 2000).

65. Ibid., 15.

66. Mark D. Jordan, *The Ethics of Sex* (Malden, MA: Blackwell, 2002); idem, *Telling Truths in Church: Scandal, Flesh, and Christian Speech* (Boston: Beacon Press, 2003); idem, *Blessing Same-Sex Unions: The Perils of Queer Romance and the Confusions of Christian Marriage* (Chicago: University of Chicago Press, 2005).

67. Jordan, *Telling Truths*, 19, emphasis in original.

68. Jordan, *Blessing*, 19.

69. Ibid., 207.

70. Virginia Burrus, *The Sex Lives of Saints: An Erotics of Ancient Hagiography* (Philadelphia: University of Pennsylvania Press, 2004), 12.

71. Virginia Burrus, *Saving Shame: Martyrs, Saints, and Other Abject Subjects* (Philadelphia: University of Pennsylvania Press, 2008).

72. Caroline T. Schroeder, "Queer Eye for the Ascetic Guy? Homoeroticism, Children, and the Making of Monks in Late Antique Egypt," *Journal of the American Academy of Religion* 77:2 (2009): 333–47.

73. Patrick R. O'Malley, "'The Church's Closet': Confessionals, Victorian Catholicism, and the Crisis of Identification," in *Passing: Identity and Interpretation in Sexuality, Race, and Religion*, ed. María Carla Sánchez and Linda Schlossberg (New York: New York University Press, 2001), 228–59.

74. Frederick Roden, ed., *Jewish/Christian/Queer: Crossroads and Identities* (Burlington, VT: Ashgate, 2009).

75. Janet R. Jakobsen and Ann Pellegrini, eds., *Love the Sin: Sexual Regulation and the Limits of Religious Tolerance* (New York: New York University Press, 2003).

76. Ibid., 58.

77. Ibid., chap. 4.

78. Ibid., 149.

79. An important development in this area took place at the 2009 annual meeting of the American Academy of Religion, which hosted a panel session on the topic "Hidden and Invisible in Plain Sight: Queer and Lesbian in the Black Church and Community." Well attended and very well received, this panel demonstrated the promise inherent in combining Womanist and queer work in religion.

80. Tat-siong Benny Liew, "(Cor)Responding: A Letter to the Editor," in *Queer Commentary and the Hebrew Bible*, 185.

81. Cathy B. Glenn, "Queering the (Sacred) Body Politic: Considering the Performative Cultural Politics of the Sisters of Perpetual Indulgence," *Theory & Event* 7:1 (2003): par. 37.

82. Ibid., par. 54.

Index

About the Editors and Contributors

Editors

Jay Emerson Johnson is a priest in the Episcopal Church (USA) and a member of the core doctoral faculty at the Graduate Theological Union in Berkeley, California. He is also the Director of Academic Research and Resources at the Center for Lesbian and Gay Studies in Religion and Ministry at Pacific School of Religion. His first book, *Dancing with God: Anglican Christianity and the Practice of Hope*, was published in 2005.

Donald L. Boisvert teaches in the Department of Religion at Concordia University in Montreal, Quebec, where he is also a member of the sexuality studies program. He is the author of two books: *Out on Holy Ground: Meditations on Gay Men's Spirituality* (2000) and *Sanctity and Male Desire: A Gay Reading of Saints* (2004). He is currently studying for ordination in the Anglican Church of Canada.

Contributors

David Dunn Bauer served as the rabbi of the Jewish Community of Amherst in Amherst, Massachusetts, from 2003 to 2010. Before his rabbinical studies, he directed theater and opera productions around the United States, Israel, and Europe and in 2010 was the first rabbinical fellow to the Liz Lerman Dance Exchange in Washington, D.C. He teaches about religion, theater, queer Judaism, and erotic spirituality at colleges, synagogues, and retreat centers nationwide and has led Torah study at the LGBT community center in Jerusalem. He is an alumnus of Yale University, the Reconstructionist Rabbinical College, the Institute for Jewish Spirituality rabbinic leadership program, and the certificate program in Sexuality and Religion at Pacific School of Religion in Berkeley, California.

John Blevins is an associate research professor in the Interfaith Health Program of the Rollins School of Public Health at Emory University. His doctoral studies focused on practical theology and human sexuality, and his current work focuses on the ways that religion functions as a sociopolitical force in both national and international contexts, particularly in relation to health and illness. Much of that work is centered in eastern and southern Africa, with an emphasis on sexual health and on the social factors that contribute to HIV risk.

Patrick Califia is a grassroots organizer of the American leather community and a veteran of the "feminist sex wars," circa 1979–1989. His fiction and non-fiction work frequently questions state control of diverse sex/gender identities and explores the connection between radical sex and spirituality. His most influential works include *Macho Sluts*, *Public Sex*, and *Speaking Sex to Power*. The Spiral Path, a nonprofit pagan umbrella group and school, provided him with the training and consecration to become a member of the Wiccan clergy. He also has a private practice as a therapist in San Francisco. He does public speaking on the history of the BDSM community and safe S/M technique, anti-censorship work, and challenging the psychiatric profession's pathologization of sex and gender minorities.

Michael Sepidoza Campos is a doctoral candidate in Interdisciplinary Studies at the Graduate Theological Union, Berkeley, California. His research interests include Filipino-American diaspora, postcolonial theory, queer theory, and critical pedagogy. Campos's work in Catholic education both constitutes his ministerial context and provides the theoretical space in which he investigates the intersection of pedagogy, theology, ethnicity, and gender. He is a member of the working group Emerging Queer API Religions Scholars based out of the Center for Lesbian and Gay Studies in Religion and Ministry at Pacific School of Religion.

Paul J. Gorrell is an ethicist and leadership development professional who consults with organizations, facilitates teams, and coaches executives in business and nonprofit settings. His academic writing has appeared in *Gay Religion* (2005), Religion Dispatches, and *Theology and Sexuality*. He has published an op-ed in the *Washington Post* on President Barack Obama's leadership style, as well as business articles in multiple publications. Since 2007, he has served with Peter Savastano as the co-chair of the Gay Men and Religion Group of the American Academy of Religion.

Jakob Hero holds a master of divinity degree from Pacific School of Religion and a master of arts in Ethics and Social Theory from the Graduate Theological Union in Berkeley, California. He is a transgender activist and has worked extensively throughout the United States and Europe. In 2005, while living in Zagreb, Croatia, he co-directed the first international conference on transgender concerns ever held in the former Yugoslavia region. He is currently a clergy candidate for ordination in the Universal Fellowship of Metropolitan Community Churches.

Mary E. Hunt is a feminist theologian who is co-founder and co-director of the Women's Alliance for Theology, Ethics and Ritual (WATER) in Silver Spring, Maryland. A Catholic active in the women-church movement, she lectures and writes on theology and ethics with particular attention to liberation issues. She is the editor of *A Guide for Women in Religion: Making Your Way from A to Z* (2004) and co-editor with Diann L. Neu of *New Feminist Christianity: Many Voices, Many Views* (2010).

Richard Lindsay is a doctoral candidate at Graduate Theological Union in Berkeley, California, where his work focuses on the intersections between religion, sexuality, and popular culture. He is a graduate of the University of Louisville and Yale Divinity School. He has published articles in Religion Dispatches and on Patheos.com and regularly contributes reviews on film, television, and music to PopTheology.com.

Heike Peckruhn is a doctoral candidate at Iliff School of Theology and the University of Denver. She holds a theology degree from Bienenberg Theological Seminary (Switzerland) and is also a Licensed Professional Counselor. She was raised in Germany in a family of German and Thai descent. With her religious roots shaped by being part of a Mennonite church community, her theological commitments are to postcolonial inquiry, liberationist ethics, and feminist theological epistemologies. She is particularly interested in studying the intersections of body epistemologies and their relation to constructive theologies.

Laurel C. Schneider is Professor of Theology, Ethics, and Culture at Chicago Theological Seminary. She is the editor of *Polydoxy: Theologies of Multiplicity and Relation* (2010) and author of *Beyond Monotheism: A Theology of Multiplicity* (2008), along with numerous articles and anthology chapters that variously work at the intersections of theology with queer, postcolonial, feminist, and race theories.

Melissa M. Wilcox is Associate Professor and Chair of Religion and Director of Gender Studies at Whitman College. She is author or co-editor of several books and numerous articles on gender, sexuality, and religion, including *Coming Out in Christianity: Religion, Identity, and Community*; *Queer Women and Religious Individualism*; and (with David W. Machacek) *Sexuality and the World's Religions*.

Lai-shan Yip is a Ph.D. student in interdisciplinary studies at the Graduate Theological Union in Berkeley, California. Her research interests include postcolonial theory, Catholic moral theology, Chinese philosophy, and Asian feminist theology. She also holds master's degrees in pastoral ministry and in social work from Boston College. She participates in an Asian and Pacific Islander LGBTQ religious roundtable at Pacific School of Religion in Berkeley and is a founding member of EQARS (Emerging Queer API Religions Scholars). She has been involved in social justice ministry as well as feminist and social movements in Hong Kong.

Kuukua Dzigbordi Yomekpe was born and raised in Ghana and immigrated to the United States at age nineteen. Her essays "All Because of a Name" and "Immigrants in a Foreign Land" were published in *African Women Writing Resistance* (2010). The project on which her essay in this volume was based, "The Audacity to Remain Single: The Single Black Woman and the Black Church," won the Marcella Althaus-Reid Award at Pacific School of Religion in 2010. Her coming out essay, "Becoming Bi: The First Time," was published in the second edition of *Getting Bi: Voices of Bisexuals Around the World* (2009). She is proud to be an African woman and a politically queer woman of color who believes in equality for all peoples. She blogs at ewurabasempe .wordpress.com.